The Prose Life of Alexander.
(THORNTON MS.)

EARLY ENGLISH TEXT SOCIETY.

Original Series, 143.

Original Series
No. 143.

The Prose Life of Alexander.

FROM THE THORNTON MS.

EDITED BY

J. S. WESTLAKE, M.A.

THE TEXT.
*

LONDON:
PUBLISHED FOR THE EARLY ENGLISH TEXT SOCIETY
BY KEGAN PAUL, TRENCH, TRÜBNER & CO., Ltd.,
68–74 CARTER LANE, E.C.
AND BY HUMPHREY MILFORD, OXFORD UNIVERSITY PRESS,
AMEN CORNER, E.C.

OXFORD
UNIVERSITY PRESS

Great Clarendon Street, Oxford OX2 6DP
United Kingdom

Oxford University Press is a department of the University of Oxford.
It furthers the University's objective of excellence in research, scholarship,
and education by publishing worldwide. Oxford is a registered trade mark of
Oxford University Press in the UK and in certain other countries

© The Early English Text Society 1913

The moral rights of the authors have been asserted

Database right Oxford University Press (maker)

First Edition published in 1913

All rights reserved. No part of this publication may be reproduced,
stored in a retrieval system, or transmitted, in any form or by any means,
without the prior permission in writing of Oxford University Press,
or as expressly permitted by law, or under terms agreed with the appropriate
reprographics rights organization. Enquiries concerning reproduction
outside the scope of the above should be sent to the Rights Department,
Oxford University Press, at the address above

You must not circulate this book in any other form
and you must impose this same condition on any acquirer

Published in the United States of America by Oxford University Press
198 Madison Avenue, New York, NY 10016, United States of America

British Library Cataloguing in Publication Data
Data available

Library of Congress Cataloging in Publication Data
Data available

Original Series, 143

ISBN 978-0-85-991887-9

PREFATORY NOTE

THE delay in issuing this important prose romance has been due to the prolonged illness of its editor, Mr. J. S. Westlake. Even now Mr. Westlake has not been able to attend to the revision and publication of the book. The collation with the manuscript has been made for the Society by Miss E. M. Thompson, the proofs have been read over by Mr. John Munro, and a few changes have been made in the side-notes, foot-notes and head-lines, which otherwise remain as Mr. Westlake left them. The translations from the Latin text which make good the lacunae in the manuscript have also been inserted by Mr. Westlake.

The Introduction, together with the Notes and Glossary, are reserved for a future volume. Mr. Westlake's elaborate side-notes provide, meanwhile, a useful epitome of the story.

The Society is greatly indebted to the Dean and Chapter of Lincoln for depositing the manuscript in the British Museum, and to the Keeper of the Manuscripts, Mr. J. P. Gilson, for receiving it there.

I. G.

THE PROSE LIFE OF ALEXANDER.

LIFE OF ALEXANDER

THE most learned Egyptians who know of the size of the earth, the waves of the sea, and the order of the heavens (betokening the way of the stars and the turning of the skies), have bequeathed these things to the whole world through the highness and the wisdom of magic knowledge. And they tell of a king of that land, by name Anectanabus, great in understanding, and full of love in astrology and mathematics. Now, upon a day it happened that a messenger came, and said unto him that Artaxerxes, king of the Persians, was drawing nigh towards him with a very great force of foes. Yet he did not call out his army, nor get ready his advance. Instead of this, he hurried into his bed-chambers in his palace, and, taking down a brazen shell, which was full of rain-water, and holding in his hand a brazen rod, sought by magic spells to summon the devils. By which wizardry he felt, in the shell itself, the fleets sailing over him amid fearful affray.

_{Of the Wisdom of the Egyptians and of their king Anectanabus.}

_{How Anectanabus saw by wizardry the oncoming of the Persian hosts.}

Now there were lords of Anectanabus set in sway over his armies to guard the Persian border.

And one hapless man coming to him, besought him : ' O most mighty King Anectanabus, there ariseth against thee Artaxerxes, the king of the Persians, with an untold horde of foes and strange races. For they are Parthians, Medes, Persians, Syrians, Mesopotamians, Brapes, Phares, Argiri, Chaldaeans, Bachiri, Confires, Hircanians, and Agiophii, and many other folks coming from Eastern lands.' On hearing this, Anectanabus said, sighing : ' The trust that I gave to thee, heed thou right well ; yet thy prowess hath not been the prowess of a doughty man, but the doings of a cowardly fellow. For worth showeth itself, not in the greatness of the folk, but in the steadfastness of their souls. Dost thou not know one lion putteth many

_{A lord of the Marshes tells him of the advancing myriads of foes and is chidden for his cowardice.}

1

2 Anectanabus's flight from the Persians. He greets Olympias.

The king sees his further ill-luck by wizardry.

does to flight?' And having said these words, he went into his chamber alone, and made brazen shells, and filled them with rain-water, and held in his hand a palm rod, and gazing into this, began, as hard as he could, to utter spells, and beheld how 4 the Egyptians were being smitten down at the onslaught of the Barbarians' ships.

Forthwith he changed his dress, and shaved his head and beard, and took gold as much as he might bear, and which might 8 be needful to him to busy himself with wizardry. And thus

He fleeth unto Ethiopia and from Ethiopia to Macedonia and is there a soothsayer.

he fled from Egypt, near by Pelusium. And at length, coming into Ethiopia, he put on linen apparel, [and] in the guise of an Egyptian seer went into Macedonia. And there he sate 12 himself, and before all the Greeks, and in their sight was soothsaying. But the Egyptians, when they saw how Anectanabus was not at Court, went to Serapis, who was their greatest god, and besought him that he might give them answer as to 16 Anectanabus their king. And Serapis replied: 'Anectanabus, your king, is gone from Egypt because of Artaxerxes, the king of the Persians, who will subdue you unto his lordship. Never-

The Egyptians learning his absence get an oracle why he is gone and when he shall come back again victorious. They make of him a black stone image.

theless, when a short time hath flown by, he will come back 20 to shake off his thraldom, and will be avenged on your foes, and yoke them under you.' And as soon as they had got this answer, they made a kingly statue out of a black stone, in honour of Anectanabus. And they wrote on it, at his feet, this 24 saying, that it might be handed down for their offspring to think of. But Anectanabus remained in Macedonia, nor was he known.

How Anectanabus went up to the Palace to Olympia the Queen.

Philip, king of Macedon, being gone to battle, Anectanabus meeting Olympia greets her and is answered.

In the meantime, Philip, king of Macedonia, went out to 28 battle. But Anectanabus went forward to the palace, that he might behold Olympia the queen, and see how fair she was. And when he saw her, his heart was smitten with love of her, and stretching forth his hand, he greeted her, saying, 32 'Hail, Queen of Macedonia,' disdaining to call her 'lady'. And she, Olympia, answered him, speaking thus: 'Hail, master, come thou and sit near.' And when he sate thus, Olympia

He would lie as a god with the young Queen.

asked many things of him. 'Art thou not an Egyptian?' And Anectanabus answered: 'The word thou saidst was kingly, when thou didst name the Egyptians. For the Egyptians are wise, and read dreams, understand the birds of the air in their flight, open up the hidden places, and tell the fate of those new-born babes. Of all these things, as a seer, I, too, have knowledge.' And Olympia saw how he gazed upon her, and spoke, 'Master, of what dost thou bethink thee, who thus lookest on me?' And Anectanabus answered, 'I call to my mind many answers of the gods. One answer had been that I was to look upon a queen.' And saying this, he drew forth from his breast a cleansing tablet of bronze and ivory, inwrought with gold and silver, and on its face were three whirls. The first contained in itself the Twelve Minds, and in the third, sun and moon were fashioned. Next to them, was seen a chain of ivory, and from it he pulled forth seven wonder-bright stars, that told the hours and birth-dooms of men, and seven carven stones, and two stones for the saving men whole.

[margin: And the queen hearing that he is an Egyptian asks him of many things. He looks on her, and telling her of an oracle, shows the instruments of his sorcery.]

And Olympia beheld these things, and said: 'Master, if thou wouldst I should believe thee, tell me the year, the day and hour of the king's birth.' And upon this, he said to the queen, 'Wishest thou to hear nothing else from me?' Quoth the queen, 'Tell me what shall fall out betwixt Philip and me, for men say that, when Philip shall come from the war, he will thrust me forth, and take another mate.' And Anectanabus answered: 'They prate of many things untruly; but ere a long time pass, it shall be as they say.' And the queen answered: 'I beg thee, master, unveil me all the truth.' Thereupon Anectanabus:—'One of the mightiest gods shall share thy bed and uphold thee through all thy thrivings and downfalls, even if they be overstrong.' Olympia replied: 'I beseech thee, say what shape this god shall put on?' Anectanabus replied: 'Neither young, nor old; his beard besprinkled with white hairs. Wherefore, if this please thee, be ready for him, for at night shalt thou see him, and in thy sleep shall he lie by thee.' The queen said: 'If I behold this, neither as a seer, nor as godly, but, as the god himself, will I worship' [thee]. And at once Anectanabus said, 'Fare thee well, O queen.' After this Anectanabus, leaving the palace, and walking straight forth

[margin: Olympia asks as to the king's birth; and as to what shall befall her, for men foretell evil. Anectanabus gainsays them and foretells that she shall be beloved and have the embraces of a god in man's shape.]

4   As a god he knows her, begets Alexander, beshields her.

<small>Leaving her he digs up herbs that he may so delude her.</small> to the city's camp in a desert spot, tore up herbs, and ground them, and took their juice, and wrought spells and other like things of the fiend, that in that same night Olympia might behold the god Hamon lying beside her, and saying to her 4 thereafter, 'Woman, thou hast conceived him who shall beshield thee.' And, on the morrow, Olympia awoke from her slumbers,

<small>And having dreamt Olympia calls him to her, he tells her how to enable the ... to her ... seeming as a snake.</small> and called Anectanabus to her, and told him of the dream she had beheld. Then Anectanabus said: 'If thou wilt give me 8 room in the palace, thou shalt see the god himself, face to face. For that god shall come to thee in the shape of a great snake, and soon after, taking on a manlike body, he shall seem to be in my likeness.' And to this Olympia said: 'As thou hast spoken, 12 master, do. Take to thyself a bed in the palace, and canst thou

<small>She gives him a chamber in the palace.</small> make good the truth thereof, I will deem thee to be the father of the boy.' And, about the first watch of the night, Anectanabus took on him, through spells and wizardry to be changed into 16

<small>He lieth by the queen seemingly as a god and sealeth her womb, saying the child shall not be up-braided for his birth.</small> the shape of a great snake, and whistling on to the bedchamber of Olympia, to fly through. And he entered her room, and rose on to her bed, and with great love began to kiss her, and the kisses betokened to her who he was. And when he rose up 20 from the bed, he smote her on the womb, and spake: 'This begetting be thy avenging, and in no wise may it be upbraided of men.'

<small>Thus was she cheated; and was with child.</small> On such a fashion was Olympia cheated, who had lain with 24 a man as though he had been a god. And in the morning, Anectanabus went down from the palace, and the queen was with child.

<small>But she, in fear, asks him how to escape Philip's wrath.</small> And when she began to be big, she called unto her Anec- 28 tanabus, saying: 'Master, tell me, what doom will Philip wreak on me, when he shall come back?' And Anectanabus

<small>He comforts her and through wizardry makes King Philip dream a god is lying with his wife who, after, seals her womb.</small> said to her, 'Be not afraid: god Hamon will champion thee.' And with these words he left the palace, and went outside the 32 town, to a barren spot. And, uprooting grasses, rubbed them, and grated them, and took their sap. And he caught a sea-bird, and began to sing over the herbs, and anoint the herbs with the sap. This he did in fellowship with the fiends, that he might 36 betray King Philip through a dream. And this was brought about. That same night the god Hamon appeared to Philip, in a dream, lying with his wife Olympia, and, the night ended, he

He makes Philip dream that she by a god conceives her saviour. 5

saw him touch her womb, and seal it with a golden ring. And on this ring there was a stone, and graven on this a lion's head, and the chariot of the sun, and a very sharp sword. And he 4 said to her: 'Woman, thou hast conceived thy saviour.' And Philip awoke from his sleep, and calling Arideus, made known to him the dream, and what he had seen. And Arideus said: 'Philip, not from man, but from a god, hath thy wife conceived. 8 In truth, the lion's head and the chariot of the sun and the sharp sword, foretoken that he, who shall be born of her, shall journey to the East whence riseth the sun! And with the sharp sword shall he underyoke to himself the nations of the 12 whole world.'

telling her she has conceived her saviour.

And awaking from the dream his seer reads him its meaning, and that the child shall be glorious.

How Anectanabus in the Shape of a Mighty Dragon went to the fore in front of Philip and overcame his Enemies in the Fray.

In the meanwhile, King Philip fought and won. For there appeared in the battle a dragon, who went before him and laid low his foes. And when he came back to Macedonia, he met 16 and kissed Olympia. And King Philip gazed on her, and said, 'To whom, O Olympia, hast thou given thyself up. For sinned thou hast, yet not sinned, for as much as thou hast brooked frowardness from a god. But I have seen all that has 20 been done by a god on thee, in a dream: therefore be blameless in my eyes, and the eyes of all men!'

With the dragon's aid King Philip wins the fight, and coming back he speaks as in joke to his wife as to what has befallen her.

How Anectanabus in the Shape of a Dragon came before Philip at a Festival and kissed Olympia.

On a certain day Philip was feasting with his lords and chieftains of Macedonia and with Olympia his wife. And 24 Anectanabus through wizardry took on himself the shape of a dragon, and, passing through the midst of the couch whereon they lay apart, whistled so loudly that all the revellers were stricken with fear, and the greatest dread, and coming near 28 Olympia, he put his head on her breast and kissed her. Philip, seeing this, spoke to Olympia, 'Woman, thee and all I tell; beheld this dragon, what time I laid my enemies low.'

At a feast Anectanabus comes to Olympia as a dragon and Philip tells the guests what has happened.

Amid wonders the child is born.

How a Bird laid an Egg in Philip's Bosom at whose breaking there came forth a Serpent, which forthwith died.

A bird lays an egg in King Philip's lap, which breaking gives forth a snake, which before it can go back dies. His sorcerer reads him its meaning.

And a few days after this Philip the king was sitting in his palace, and there appeared unto him a little and most gentle bird, which flew into his bosom and laid an egg. And the egg, falling to the ground, was broken. And at once there crept forth from it a very little snake. And it turned around, wishful to go into the egg, but, before it might put in its head, it was quenched. And Philip, seeing this, was heavily distressed, and called to him Arideus, and showed him the monstrous thing he had seen. And Arideus said to him, 'King Philip, a son shall be born to thee, who shall reign after thy death, and shall fare forth over the whole world and sway all peoples, and ere he come back to the land of his birth, shall die by a most swift death.'

The queen is comforted by wizardry till the child is born.

And as the time of child-birth was drawing nigh, Olympia began to feel pain, and her womb was tormented, and she bade Arideus be called to her, and spoke with him: 'Master, my womb is wrenched with very heavy labours.' Anectanabus [*sic in both editions* 1489 and 1494] then spake: 'Raise thyself awhile from thy throne, for in this hour the elements are troubled by the sun.' This was done, and the pain went from her. And soon after, Anectanabus said to her, 'Sit down, O Queen!' and she sate herself and bore a child. And as soon as the boy was fallen on to the earth, a mighty thunderclap and thunderbolts, with tokens and lightnings came about throughout the whole world. Then night was spread forth and lasted, it reaching unto the last hour of day. Then parts of the clouds fell down in Italy. And seeing these signs, Philip the king was afrighted, and went in to Olympia, and said: 'I deemed that this little babe should in no wise be fostered. For he is not conceived of me, but of some god, for at his birth I beheld the heavens changed. Yet let him be fostered in my memory, as though he were my son, and follow in the stead of a son I begot through another wife.' And when he said this, she handled the babe with great care. And the boy's face had the likeness neither of father nor mother. The hair on his head

Mighty wonders happen, and Philip is persuaded to let the child be fostered as though he were his own son.

The child is named Alexander; his wondrousness.

was shaggy as a lion's. His eyes glistened like the stars, but each beamed with its own hue, one black, the other yellow. And his teeth were sharp, and his eager rush as a lion's. His
4 shape foreshadowed his energy and forethought. By his parents he was called Alexander. In the schools, and wheresoever he sate, he strove with them in letters and disputations, and by his keen swiftness won the mastership. And when he was twelve
8 years old, he was beweaponed for battle, and excelled in arms. And Philip, seeing how quick he was, praised him, and said: 'Son Alexander, I love thy speed, and wit of mind for its work. But I am sore and feel foolish that thy form is so unlike mine.'
12 And Olympia heard this, and was greatly afraid. And she called hither Anectanabus, and said: 'Master, learn from me what Philip misdeemeth. For he said to Alexander, "Son, I love thy speed and wit of mind. But, that thy shape is
16 unlike mine, I am saddened."' And Anectanabus began to think, and said: 'His thought is nowise harmful.' And gazing aloft as he was wont, he looked on a certain star, and riddled out his wish. And when Alexander heard this, he spake:
20 'The star thou seest is seen in the heavens?' And Anectanabus replied: 'My son, it is.' Alexander said: 'Canst thou show it unto me?' Anectanabus answered: 'Follow me in the hour of night, and I will show it unto thee.' Alexander said: 'Thy
24 fate is not known to thee, or uncertain?' Anectanabus replied: 'Enough of this.' Alexander said: 'I would fain know it.' Anectanabus answered: 'In truth know that from my son shall come my death.' This said, as he went down from the palace,
28 Alexander followed him in the hour of the evening without the city. And when they arrived up on to the ditch of the city, Anectanabus spake: 'Son Alexander, gaze thou on the stars; look how the star of Hercules is perplexed, and how Mercury's
32 star is blithe. If I see Jove sparkling, my doom telleth me of my coming death at the hands of my son.' At this sight Alexander came up nigh to him, and made an onslaught on him, making him fall

[The early Text begins.]

36 dowñ in to þe dyke, and thare he felle, & was all to-frusched; and þañ Alex*ander* said vñ-to hy*m* one this wyse. 'Fals

The child is like neither father nor mother; his eyes are starlike, one black one yellow, his teeth sharp. He is called Alexander. In the schools and at arms he excels all. Philip tells him how he loved him yet was grieved at his birth. Olympia fearing tells this to Anectanabus, who says it is not harmful. Anectanabus, being with Alexander, sees a star which when shown again, he announces to foretell his death at his son's hands. Alexander holding this a lie rushes against him.

Leaf 1. Anectanabus falls

wreche,' quoþ he, 'that presumeȝ to tell thyngeȝ þat ere to com, reȝte als þou were a prophete, and knewe þe preuateȝ of heuen. Now may þou see that þou lyeȝ, And þare-fore þou arte worthy to hafe swilke a dede.' And than Anectanabus ansuerd, & said: 'I wyste wele ynoghe,' quoþ he, 'þat I scholde die swylke a dede. Talde I noȝte lange are to þe, that myn awenn son schulde slae me?' 'Whi, ame I thi son?' þan quoþ Alexandire: 'ȝaa, for sothe,' quoþ Anectanabus, 'I gat the.' And wit þat word, he ȝalde þe gaste. And than Alexander hert tendird on his Fader, And he tuke hym vp on his bakke, and bare hym to þe palace. And when his moder Olympias saw hym, Scho said vn-till hym. 'Son,' quoþ scho, 'what es that?' 'Als thi foly hase made it,' quoþ he, 'so it es.' And than he gert berye hym wirchipfully.

[1] In the mene tyme, a prynce of Macedoyne broghte þe [2] kyng a horse vn-temed, a grete and a faire; & he was tyed on ilke side wit chynes of Iren, for he walde wery men and ete þam. This ilke horse was called Buktiphalas [3], bi-cause of his vgly lukynge, For he hade a heued lyke a bulle, & knottills in his frount, as þay had bene þe bygynnyng of hournes. And when þe kyng saw þe bewtee of this horse, he said till his seruandis, 'Takeȝ this horse and putteȝ hym in a stable, and makes barreȝ of yren be-fore hym, that thefeȝ and oþer mysdoers, þat sall be done to dede, may be putt in-till hym, to be slaen of hym. And þay didd soo. In þe mene tyme þe kynge Philippe had ane answere of his goddes, that hee schulde regne nexte after hym, the whilke myghte ryde that wylde horse wit-owtten harme. So it felle þat Alexander þe whilke was þan twelue ȝere alde, wexe strange & reȝte hardy, & was wysse and discrete; for he was wele lered & connand in all þe seuen sciences, þe whilke twa philosophirs had teched hym: þat es to say, Arestotle & Calistene. And one a day, as Alexander passed for-by þe place þare als þe foresaide stode, he luked in be-twene þe barreȝ of yrnne and saw, bifore þe horse, mens hend and fete, & oþer of þaire membris, liggand scatered here & thare, and he had grete wonder þare-off. And he putt in his

---

[1] Space for miniature blank, ten lines.
[2] *a* changed by scribe into þe.
[3] Buktiphalas. In MS. a blot has smudged out all the *i* except a dot, and obscured the *p*, making it look like *Buktsphalas*, but it reads really as above.

The winning of Bucephalus, and the encounter with the king.

hande bitwene þe barreȝ, And þe horse * strekede oute his nekke,   *Leaf 1 bk.
als ferre als he myghte, and likkedʼ Alexander handʼ; and he   Alexander
knelidʼ douñ oñ his kneesse, and bi-helde Alexander in þe vesage   sees Bucephalus.
4 langly. And Alexander vnderstode wele þe wiłł of þe horse,   Bucephalus
and opyndʼ the barreȝ, and went into þe horse, and strakedʼ him   bows and submits to
softely on þe bakke w*i*t his riȝte handʼ; And belyfe þe horse   him.
wexe wonderly meke tiłł Alexander; and riȝte as a honde wiłł
8 couche wheñ his maist*er* biddes hy*m*, so dide he tiłł Alexander;
aud Alex*ander* lukede besides hy*m*, & sawe a sadiłł & a brydełł
hyng thare ; and he tuke & dydʼ þa*m̃* oñ hy*m̃*, & leppe one his
bakke ; & rade furthe oñ hy*m*. And wheñ the kynge Philippe
12 sawe hy*m* do so, he saidʼ vn-tiłł hy*m* 'Mi soñ Alexander' quoþ   Philip sees
he : 'Ałł þe ansuers of our goddeȝ are fulfillede in the! For   Alexander riding
wheñ I ame dede, þou moñ regne aft*er* me' And Alexander   Bucephalus and says
ansuerdʼ, & saidʼ 'I p*r*ay the, Fader,' quoþ he, 'ordeyne me horse   the oracles
16 & meñ, for I gaa seke dedeȝ of armeȝ.' 'For sothe' quoþ þe   are fulfilled.
kynge w*i*t a glade chere, 'Take þe a hundreth horse, and
xl thosandeȝ pou*n*de of golde ; and take w*i*t the of þe worthieste
knyghteȝ þat langeȝ to me, and wendis furthe.' And he diddʼ so.
20 And he tuke w*i*t hy*m* also a philosop̃re þat highte Eu-   Philip at
festi*us*, whilke he traystedʼ mekiłł in, And twelue childre þat   Alexander's asking
he chese to be his playfers, and went hy*m* furthe, and come   gives him arms and
in-tiłł a contreth þat es called Polipone. And wheñ the   men to invade
24 kynge of þe landʼ herdʼ tełł, þat swilke meñ ware entredʼ i*n*-to   foreign territory.
his rewme in swilke araye, he raysedʼ a gret Oste, and come
agaynes Alexander for to feghte w*i*t hy*m̃*. And wheñ he
come nerehandʼ hym, he saidʼ vn-tiłł hy*m*. 'Tełł me' quoþ he
28 'whatt þou ert ?' And Alexander ansuerdʼ 'I am Alexander'   Alexander's
qu*o*þ he 'þe soñ of Philippe, þe kynge of Macedoyne.' 'And   encounter with the
what hopeȝ þou þat I be ?' quoþ þe kynge tiłł hy*m*. And   King of the Arridons.
Alexander ansuerdʼ. 'Þou ert kynge of Arridouns' quoþ he.
32 'Neu*er*-þe-lesse, if ałł I do þe þat wirchippe þat I calle þe
kynge, emp*r*ide þe nathynge þ*are*-of. For meñ seeȝ ofte tymes
meñ þat ere in heghe astate co*m̃* to lawe degree, & meñ þat
ere in lawe degree, come tiłł heghe astate.' 'Þou sais riȝte
36 wele' quoþ þe kynge. 'Take hede to thyñ aweñ selfe!' And
Alexander ansuerdʼ & said 'Ga hetheñ away fra me' quoþ he   They quarrel fiercely.
'for þou cañ say noghte to mee, ne I hafe noghte at do w*i*t þe.'
And þañ þe kyng was worder wrathe, And said tiłł Alexander

10   Alexander's first encounter, and victory.

Leaf. 2

The king challenges Alexander.

Alexander accepts, and they both go home to gather forces.

'Luke on me'* quoþ he 'þat spekes to the: Fore I swere the be my Fader hele, & I anes spitte in thi face, þou schale dye.' And wit þat he spitte at Alexander, & said: 'Take þe þare, þou biche whelpe, þat þe semez till hafe.' And Alexander 4 stepped furthe, & said vn-till hym. 'For þou' quoþ he 'hase dispised me, by-cause I ame littill; I swere þe, bi þe pete of my Fader, & by my moders wambe, in þe whilke I was consayued of godd Amon, þat þou schall see mee, are oughte lange, in 8 þi rewme, redi to feghte wit þe; and owþer I schall wyn thi rewme wit dynte of swerd, & brynge it vnder my subieccionn, or þou schall make me subiecte vn-to þe.' And þare þay assignede day of Batelle; and ayther of þam went hame fra 12 oþer.

Alexander gathers his army, meets King Nicholas and slays him after the fight.

¹And agaynes þe day of Batelle, Alexander, bi ascent & ordynance of kynge Philippe, gadird a grete Oste, & went to the place þare þe Batelle was assigned, and fand all redy þare, 16 kyng Nicoll and his oste. And þay trumpped vp appon bathe þe parties, and bigan to feghte, & many men ware slaen on bathe þe sydez. Bot at þe laste, Alexander hade þe felde, & tuke kyng Nicholl, & gart smytte of his heued, & went in-till 20 his land, and conquered it; and his knyghtes went and corounð hym kynge þare-off. And sythen he went hame till his fader,

On his home-coming, he finds his father at bridal with a new wife, and begs him to take Olympia back again,

kyng Philippe, and fand hym sittand at the mete at a bridale: For he had put awaye fra hym his wyfe Olympias, Alexander 24 moder, and taken hym an-oþer þat highte Cleopatra; And Alexander went in-to þe haulle, and said vn-to þe kynge Philipp: 'Fader,' quoþ he, 'I pray zow, þat for a rewarde of my firste iournee þat I hafe now made, ze graunte me to take 28 my Moder Olympias agayne vn-to zow, & do to hir as awe

lest Alexander, giving her to another king, be his foe.

to be done to a qwenne², rathere þan I gyffe hir to anoþer kynge; so þat I be nozte zoure enemy for euer. For this weddyng, þat ze hafe now made here, es vnlefull!' When 32

One Lesias jeeringly foretelling that Cleopatra shall bear Philip an heir,

he hadd said thir wordes, ane of þe þat satt at þe kynges burde, whase name was Lesias, ansuerd & said to þe kyng: 'lord' quoþ he 'þou schall hafe a son of Cleopatra, and he schall regne after þe!' Alexander, than, was gretly greuede at his 36 wordes, and wit a wardrere þat he hade in his hande, he went

¹ Place for miniature blank, twelve half-lines.   ² MS. *qwnne* with *e* inserted above text.

Alexander's quarrel with Philip, and the reconciliation. 11

tiłł hym and kellede¹ hym. Wheñ kyng Philippe sawe this, he was gretly stirred, and rase vp, & gatt a swerde * & ranne to-warde3 Alexander, for to hafe smytteñ hym͞. Bot onane
4 he fełłe dowñ; and ay þe nerre Alex*ander* þat he drewe, þe mare he fełłe to the erthe ri3te as he bene ferd. And þañ Alexander said vn-tiłł hy*m*: 'Philippe' qu*o*þ he 'how es it soo, that þou, þat hase wonñ w*i*t dynt of swerde ałłe Grece,
8 ne hase now na strenghe to stande on thi fete.' And þañ ałł þe haułłe was troubbled, and the brydale letted. And Alexander went abowte þe haułłe, and keste douñ þe bourde3 w*i*t þe mete, & þe drynke þat ware appoñ þam͞, and tuke
12 Cleopatra, and schotte² hir oute at þe haułłe dore. And the kynge Philippe, for sorowe þat he tuke tiłł, fełłe grefe seke. And a littiłł aft*e*rwarde3, Alexander went tiłł hym for to vesett hy*m* & comforthe hy*m*, and said vn-tiłł hy*m* 'Philippe,'
16 qu*o*þ he, 'if ałł it be no3te semely, þat I calle þe be þi *p*ropre name; neuere-þe-lesse, no3te as þi soñ, bot as þi gud frend, I sałł tełłe the myñ avice. It es fully my c*o*nsaile þat þou reco*nn*selle agayne vn-to the my lady,
20 my Moder Olympias, and at þou grefe þe na-thynge at þe dede of Lesias, ne take na heuynes to the þ*are-*fore. For vn-kyndely me thynke þat þou didd, and vngudely, þat þou drewe þi swerde for to smytte me þ*are-*w*i*t.' And wheñ Philippe
24 herd þir wordes, his hert tendird, & he bigane to wepe. And þañ Alexander went tiłł his Moder Olympyas, and said vn-tiłł hir: 'Be no3te ferde' qu*o*þ he 'ne be no3te heuy to my fader, for if ałłe thi trespas be *p*reuee, & no3te knaweñ, neu*er*-þe-lesse
28 þou erte in *p*arty to blame.' And wheñ he hade sayde thus, he ledd hir furthe to þe kyng Philippe. And he tuk & kyssid hir, and thus was scho reco*nn*selde vn-tiłł hym agayne.

³After þis, þ*are* come messeng*ers* Fra Dari*us*, þe emp*er*our
32 of P*er*se, to kyng Philippe, and asked hy*m* tribute And Alexander answerd to thir messeng*ers*, & saide, 'Saise to Dari*us*, 3o*ur* lorde,' qu*o*þ he, 'þat señ þe tyme þat Philippe soñ was waxeñ of age þe hen þat ay es waxeñ barayne & consumed

Alexander slays him.
* Leaf 2 bk.

King Philip having in vain sought to kill Alexander, Alexander upsets the feast and casts out Cleopatra.

King Philip having fallen sick, Alexander goes to be reconciled with him.

Philip weeps and Alexander brings him and Olympia together again.

Messengers come from Darius the Emperor of Persia, to whom Alexander refuses the

---

¹ The first vowel is either a *y* changed into *e*, or an *e* changed into *y*. Hence it is uncertain if *kyllede* or *kellede* was written first. I think *kyllede* was first written and changed to *kellede* from the link with next letter.
² MS. seems certainly when magnified to write *o*, *schotte*, although it is blotted.
³ Space left for miniature, eleven half lines.

12 The First Eastern wars; murder of Philip.

[sidenote: wonted tribute.] awaye, and so es Darius pryuede of his trybute.' And [when] thir messengers herd' thir wordes; þay hade grete wounder of þam & of þe witt & þe wisedome of Alexander.

*[sidenote: Armenia rises, Alexander subjugates it. *Leaf 3.]* In þe mene tyme tythyngeȝ come to kyng Philippe, þat Ermonye, þe whilke bi-fore was suget vn-till hym, was rebelle & raysse agaynes hym. And he garte *semble a grete Oste, and sent Alexander thedir þare wit to feghte wit þam, and to putt þam agayne vnder his subieccionn. Alexander þan went wit this Oste till Ermony & broghte it agayne in subieccion, as it was bi-fore.

[sidenote: Pansamy, a lord, covets Philip's wife and kingdom; he revolts and wounds king Philip to the death.] An in þe mene tyme, whils he was þare, a lorde of Macedoyne þe whilke highte Pansamy, a strange man & a balde, suget vn-to Philippe, and hade of lange tyme couette for to hafe þe quene Olympias, conspirede agaynes þe kynge, and come with a grete multytude of folke appon þe kynge, to for-do hym. And when tythyngeȝ here of come to kyng Philippe, he went to mete hym in þe felde wit a fewe menȝee. And when he sawe þe grete multitude þat Pansamy hade wit hym, he turned' & fledd, and Pansamy persued' after hym, and ouerhied' hym, and strake hym thurghe wit a spere, and ȝitt ife all he were greuosely wonded, he dyed' noȝte alsone, bot he laye halfe dede in the waye. And than þe Macedoynes, þat wenede he hade bene dede, made mekill sorowe. And when þis iournee was done Pansamy was gretly empridede þare offe, & went in to þe kynges palace for to take þe qwene Olympias oute of it and hafe hir with hym.

[sidenote: Alexander comes back in the midst of the troubles and his mother goes to meet him.] And euen þe same tyme, Alexander come fra Hermony, & sawe[1] swylke trouble & styrrynge in the rewme, and hyed' hym faste towarde þe kynges palace, and when Olympias herd' telle þat Alexander hir son had þe victorye of his enemys, & was comande nere, Scho went furthe of þe palace at a preuee posterne to mete hir son, and to welcome hym hame. And alsone als scho come nere hym, scho criede appon hym & said:

'A A, my son Alexander, whare es þe grace & þe fortune þat oure goddes highte the, þat es to say, þat þou scholde alwaye ouercome thynn enemys & noȝte be ouercomen, þat Pansamy hase one þis wyse slaen thi Fader.' And alsone the worde come to Pansamy þat Alexander was comen, and he went furthe of palace for to mete hym. And also faste als Alexander sawe hym, he oute wit a swerd' and clafe his heued'

[sidenote: Pansamy goes forth to meet Alexander, but Alexander slays him.]

---
[1] MS. blotted at sawe.

King Philip's death and burial. Alexander's harangue. 13

in to þe tethe, & slewe hym. And ane of þe Oste said tiłł *Alexander is told of his father's dying state. He goes to him and hears his last words.*
Alexander: 'Philippe þi fader' quoþ he, 'lyes dede in þe
felde.' And þan Alexander went thedir thare he laye, and
4 saw hym eueñ at þe dyinge. And þañ he begañ faste for to
wepe. And Philippe luked apoñ hym̄, & said. ' A A, my dere
son Alexander,' quoþ he, 'wit a glade hert [I] may now dye,
for þat þou so soune hase venged my dede,' & eueñ wit * þat *Philip dies.*
8 worde he ȝalde þe gaste. And Alexander wirchipfully gert *Leaf 3 bk.*
hym be entered.

¹ When kyng Philippe was entered, Alexander went and sett *After Philip's burial, Alexander calls his folk together and harangues them.*
hym in his trone, and gerte calle by-fore hym alle þe folke þat
12 was gaderd thedir, lordes & oþer, and said vn-to þam̄ on þis
wyse. 'Meñ,' quoþ he, 'of Macedoyne of Tracy, and of Grece
byhaldeȝ þe fegure of Alexander and putteȝ oute of ȝour
hertes drede of ałłe ȝour enemys. For sekerly, and ȝe wiłł take
16 gude hertis to ȝow, thurghe þe helpe of oure goddis he schałł hafe
þe ouerhande of ałł ȝoure neghtebours, and ȝour name schałł
spred ouer alle the werlde. And þare-fore ilkane of ȝow þat *He foretells to them their rule over the world, and bids them get ready their weapons for war.*
hase Armour, makes it redy, and he þat hase nane come to my
20 palace & I sałł gerre delyuer hym̄ ałł þat hym nedis, and ilk
a mañ make hym redy to þe werre.' And wheñ þe lordes and
knyghtis þat ware of grete age, herd thir wordes þay ansuerd
Alexander, & said vn-tiłł hym̄: 'lorde,' quoþ thaye, 'we hafe
24 seruede ȝoure fader a longe tyme & traueld wit hym in his *But those of great age beg leave that they should not be made to go on new wars, but rather the younger men.*
werres, & þare-fore we ere now so bryssed in armes þat þare
[es] no myghte lefte in vs for to suffre disesse þat ofteñ tymes
falles to meñ of werre. For we ere strekeñ in grete age. And
28 þare-fore, if it be plesynge vn-to ȝow, we consaile ȝow & we
beseken ȝowe, that ȝe chese ȝow ȝong lordes & ȝong knyghtes,
þat ere listy meñ & able for to suffre disesse for to be wit ȝow.
For here we giffe vp att armes if it be ȝour wiłł & forsakes
32 þam̄ for euer.' And þañ Alexander answerd & said: 'I wiłł
rathere,' quoþ he, 'chese þe sadnesse of an alde wyse mañ þañ *Old men work with wisdom, young men with boldness and rashness.*
þe vnavesy lightenesse of ȝonge meñ. For ȝong meñ often
tymes traystand to mekiłł in thaire aweñ doghtynes thurgh
36 þaire aweñ foly ere mescheued. Bot alde meñ wirkes ałł by
consaile & by witte.' Wheñ he had said thir wordes ałł meñ

---

¹ Twelve half lines space for miniature in MS.

14 Alexander wars with the Romans and Africans.

They allow and consent to his words.

alowed his hie witte and hally þay assentede to hym for to do his lyste.

¹ Sone after Alexander assemblede a grete Oste, & went bi Schippe to-wardeȝ Ytaly, and als he come by Calcedoyne, he 4

* Leaf 4.
Gathering an army, Alexander ships to Italy, first taking Chalcedonia.

assaylled it reȝte strangly, and þe folke of Calcedoyne *went to þe walles of þe Citee and defendid manly. Bot at the laste Alexander wan the Citee, and fra thethyn he Schippede in-till Italy. And alsone als þe Romaynes herd of his comynge 8 þay were wonder ferde for hym, and the grete lordes of þe lande tuke fourty thowsandeȝ of besandeȝ and 1ᶜ corounes of

He takes tribute of the Romans and of all Europe as far as the West Ocean.

golde, and went vn-till hym, and presant hym wit þam & bysoughte hym þat he scholde noȝte werrey appon þam, ne 12 do þam na harme. And than Alexander tuke trybute of þe Romaynes, and of alle the folkes þat duelt bitwixe that & þe weste Occeane, þe whilke regione es callede Europe, & lefte þam in gude pesse. 16

Thence sailing to Africa he subjugates it.

² Fra thethyn he Schippede in-till Affrice, in thee whilke he fande bot fewe þat rebelled agaynes hym and þare-fore als [men] swa saye, euen sodeynly he conquerid it & broghte it vnder his subieccion. And fra Affric he went by Schippe till ane 20 Ile, þat es called Frontides, for to consaile wit a godd þat þay called Amon. And as Alexander & his men went to-wardeȝ

The adventure with the hart.

þe temple of þis for-said godd, þay mett in þe waye a grete hert þe whilke Alexander bad his men sla wit arowes. And 24 þay schott at hym; bot nane of þam myghte hitt hym. And þan Alexander tuke a bowe & schotte at hym & hitt

He sacrifices to Amon, praying the oracle.

hym & slewe hym. And þan Alexander went in-to þe temple, & made sacrafyce of þis hert vn-to godd Amon, and by-soughte 28 hym þat he schulde gyffe hym ansuares. When Alexander hade made his prayers þare to godd Amon, he went wit his Oste

He goes to Taphoresey and sacrifices to his gods.

in-till a place þat highte Taphoresey, In þe whilke were feftene ³ gude townnes, & þay hade twelue grete reuers þat rane in-to 32 þe see, and at þe entree of þam in-to þe see þare was drawen ouer grete chynes of yryne, and thare Alexandir made Sacrafice

The Vision of Serapis.

till his goddeȝ. And on þe same nyghte, a godd þat [hight] Serapis apperid vn-till hym in his slepe, cledd in riche 36 clothynge in ane horrible forme & a dredefull, and said vn-till

---

¹ Three lines miniature S.
² Five lines miniature F.

³ MS. has xv crossed through before *feftene.*

The Vision of Serapis; Anectanabus's image. 15

hym. 'Alexander,' quoþ he, 'may þou take þis montayne on þi schulder & bere it a-way?' Quoþ Alexander, 'how myghte any man do þat?' And Serapis ansuerd & said, 'righte as þis
4 montayne salł neuer wit-owten *end be remowed hethen, so thi name & thi dedes schalł be made mynde of to the worldes end.' And than Alexander prayed hym þat he walde prophycye hym what kyns dede he scholde die. Serapis ansuerd and said, 'It
8 es noghte spedfulł tilł a man to knawe his paynefulł endynge. For if he knewe it, perauenture, he scholde neuer hafe loye in his hert. Neuer þe lesse bi-cause þou hase prayede me to telle þe, I salł say the. After a drynke þou schalł take thi dede.
12 For in thi ʒouthe þou salł make thyn endynge. Bot spirre me noþer þe tyme ne þe houre when it schal be, For I wilł on na wyse telłe it to the. For-whi goddeʒ of þe este partieʒ of þe werlde salł telłe the alłe thi werdeʒ.' When Alexander
16 wakkened of his dreme, he was reghte heuy, and sent þe maste substance of his Oste to þe Cite of Askalon and bad þam habide hym thare, and hym selfe & a certane of menʒe wit hym habade & thare he garte make a Citee & called it Alexander
20 after his awenn name.
    [1] In the mene tyme þe Egipcyens herd of þe comyngeʃ of Alexander, & þay went agaynes hym & submytt þam vn-tilł hym & resayffed hym wirchipfully. And when Alexander come
24 in-tilł Egipte, he fand ane ymage of a kyng made of blake stane curiousely coruen, and he askede þe Egipciens whase ymage it was, and þay ansuerd & said, 'It es þe ymage,' quoþ þay, 'of Anectanabus that was kynge of Egipte noʒte lange sythen
28 gane, þe wyseste & þe worthiest þat euer was þare-in.' For sothe quoþ [2] Alexander, 'Anectanabus was my Fader.' And þan he knelid doun with grete reuerence & kyssed þe ymage. Fra thethyn he went wit his Oste to Surry. But þe
32 Surriens agayne-stude [3] hym and faghte wit hym and slewe many of his knyghtes. Neuer þe lesse Alexander had þe victorye. And þan he went to Damaske, & Ensegged it & wanne it, and fra thethyn he went to Sydon & wan it.
36 And þan he went vnto þe Citee of Tyre and layde Ensegge abowte it, and [in] þis Ensegge he laye many a day. And thare

*Leaf 4 bk.

Serapis foretells him his lasting fame, his deeds, his death. But of some things Serapis may not speak.

Alexander awakens saddened. He sends his main strength on to Askal. Where he was he founded the city of Alexandria.

The Egyptians hearing of his coming submit. He sees the image of Anectanabus.

He acknowledges Anectanabus as his father.

He invades Syria, takes Damascus, Sidon, and sets about the siege of Tyre.

---
[1] Five half lines space for miniature I.
[2] quoþ Alexander in margin.
[3] Scribe wrote agaynesande and altered it to agaynestude.

16   *The conquest of Syria; the battle of Josaphat.*

Tyre resists stoutly, and he has to set a boom across the haven.
* Leaf 5.

his Oste suffred̛ many dysesse3. For þat Cite was so strange in it-selfe by-cause of þe ground̛, þat it was sett apon̄, and by-cause of grete towres & many þat ware abowte it, and also bicause it was so enclosed̛ wit the see þat it myghte noghte 4 lightly * be wonnen̄ by nane assawte. Alexander þan̄ vmbithoghte hym, one what wyse he myghte best com̄ to for to destruy þis citee, and he gerte make a grete bastelt of tree, and sett it apon̄ schippes in þe see euen̄ forgaynes þe cete, so þat 8 þare myghte no shippe3 come nere the hauen̄ for to vetaille þe Citee or suppoelt it wit men̄ by-cause of þe bastelte. In

Alexander sends for help to Jadus, Bishop of the Jews, and also demands tribute.

þe mene tyme Alexander Oste hade grete defawte of vetaylts, and þan̄ he sent lettres vnto Iadus, þat at that tyme was 12 bischoppe & gouernoure of þe Iewes, and prayede hym for to suppoelt hym wit som̄ men̄, and also þat he walde send̛ sum̄ vetails for hym & his Oste, and he scholde pay for þam̄ wit a glade chere, and þat he scholde also send̛ hym the tribute 16 þat he scholde gyffe Darius þe emperour of Perse. For hym ware better, he said̛, hafe his frenchippe þan̄ þe frenchipe of

The Bishop pleads the oath of fealty sworn to Darius.

Darius. The Bischope þan̄ of þe Iewes ansuerd̛ þe messangers þat broghte hym þe lettres & said̛, 'I hafe,' quoþ he, 'made 20 athe to Darius, þat, whils he leffe3, I schalt neuer bere armes agaynes hym̄, and þarefore I ne may no3te do agaynes myn̄ Athe.' The Messagers þan̄ went till Alexander & talde hym

Alexander swears to wreak vengeance on the Jews.

þe bischopes ansuere, and he was greued̛ & said̛, ' I make myn̄ 24 avowe,' quoþ he, 'vntilt oure goddes, þat I schalt take swilke vengeance on þe Iewes þat I salt make þam̄ to knawe, whethir it es better to þam̄ to be obeisant vn-to [my?] commandement,

He sends Meleager with 500 men to Josaphat to forage. They defeat the Lord of the country and slay him.

or vn-to þe kynges of Perse.' And he callede a duke, þat highte 28 Melagere, and wit vᶜ men̄ of armes, and badd̛ þam̄ gaa in to þe vale of Iosaphat, þe whilke was fult of beste3 & brynge of thase beste3 to þe Oste for to vetailte þam̄ wit. And ane Sampson, þat knewe þe cuntre wele was þaire gyde. Þay went in to þe 32 vale, and gadird̛ to gedir catell wit-owte nombir & be-gan̄ for to dryfe on̄ þam̄. And he þat was lorde of þe cuntre, Theosellas bi name, raysed̛ a grete multitude of folke and mett þam̄ & faughte wit þam̄ & slewe many of þam̄. Bot Melagere & his 36

But the Lord of the city sends help and

felaws at þat tym̄ had þe better. And ane þat highte Caulus went baldly to Theosellas, & smate of his heued̛. Alt this was done bot a littilt fra þe citee of Gadir. And þan̄ Bertyne,

The siege of Tyre. 17

lorde of þe citee, seand' this, was gretely stirrede and ischewede
owte of þe citee & wit xxx feghtyng men and sett vp a schowte
apon the * Macedoynes alle at anes, that alle þe erthe trembled'
4 wit-alle. And' when þe Macedoyns saw that grete multytude
of folke com appon þam, þay were reȝte ferde. And þan
Melagere walde hafe sent a Messangere to þaire lorde Alexander,
for to come & socoure þam, bot he mygte fynd' na man þat
8 walde vndertake þe Message. Than thir twa batalles met
Samen & faughte to-gedir, and thare was Sampson slaen,
and Bertyne. And þe Macedoyns wit þe grete multitude of
þaire enemys ware dreuen abakke, and lyke for to be dreuen
12 abakke & discomfites. And ane of þe grekkes, þat highte
Arttes, seynge þe meschefe þay stode In, wann hym owte of the
Bataile & went in alle þe haste, þat he myghte, till Alexander
& talde hym þat þe Grekkes & þe Macedoynes ware in poynte
16 to be mescheuede, bot if he suppoellde þam þe tittere. And
than Alexander lefte þe segge of Tyre, and went wit his
Oste to þe vale of Iosaphat, and fand' his men riȝte harde
by-stadde wit þaire enemys. And he and his Oste vmbylapped'
20 alle þaire enemys, and daunge þam doun & slewe þam ilke
a moder son. And when he had so done he turned' agayne
vn-to Tyre, and fande the Bastelle, þat he hade made in þe See,
dongen doune to þe grounde. For alson als Alexandere was
24 gane fra Tire to þe vale of Iosaphat, Balan þat was lorde of
Tyre ischewid' oute of þe citee wit thee folke þare-of, & assailled'
the bastell manfully, and tuk it & dange it doune. And when
Alexander sawe that, he was gretly angerde, and his hert
28 wonder heuy, and so ware alle þe Macedoynes and the Grekes.
In so mekill thay ware nerehand' in dispeire for to wyn þe
citee, and ware in poynte to hafe riffen[1] up þe segge. And
one þe nyghte nexte suande, Alexander, als he laye & slept,
32 dremyd' þat he hadd' in his hand' a grape, þe whilke hym
thoghte he keste downe vnder his fete, and trade þare-one,
& alsone þare ran oute of it a grete dele of wyne. And when
Alexander wakned', he called' till hym a Philosophre & talde
36 hym his dreme. And þe Philosophre ansuerde, 'be balde,'
quoþ he, ' & lefe noȝte to ensegge Tyre, for þe grape þat þou

the Macedonians are driven back.
* Leaf 5 bk.

One of the Greeks sends for help to Alexander, who, leaving the siege of Tyre, outflanks the enemy of Josaphat and slays them all.

Alexander, returning to Tyre, finds his boom thrown down, for Balan had sortied with all his people. So despairing are the Greeks that they almost give up the siege.

The next night Alexander dreams a dream and, when his

---

[1] MS. riffen, perhaps for ȝiffen, but the same idiom is found elsewhere.

2

18 Alexander dreams a dream and conquers Tyre.

Philosopher interprets it, he is cheered.

helde in thi hand, and keste vnder thi fete, and trade þare-one, es þe Citee of Tyre, þe whilk þou salt wynn thurgh strenth and trede it with thi fote, and þare-fore be na-thynge abaiste.' When Alexander herd' thire wordes, he was gretly comforthed, 4 and vmbithoghte hym one whate wyse he myghte gette this Citee.

*Leaf 6.

He makes another boom on ships higher than the highest city tower. He directs his men how to attack.

And than he *garte make anoþer bastelle in þe see, grettere, & hyere, and strangere þan þe toþer was. For it was hiere 8 þan þe hegheste towre of þe citee. And þis bastelle was tyede wit a hundrethe ankers. Þan Alexander gert armede hyn[1] suerely & wele, & wente by hym ane vp apon this bastelle, and badd' alt his men þat þay schulde make þam redy for to feghte 12 & to giffe assawte to þe citee. And alsone als þay sawe hym entire in to þe citee, þay scholde alt at anes presse to þe walles, and scale þam, and clymbe ouer þe walles baldely & wyn þe

Cutting the cables he lets the towers over the boom float in upon the city. He, climbing the walls, slays Balan, and his followers rush all at once into the city. Tyre is destroyed.

citee. And when alt men weren redy, hee gerte smyte 16 sounderé þe cabilts þat þe bastelle was tyed wit, & þe wawes of þe see bare it to þe walles of þe Citee. And Alexander delyuerlye stert apon [þe] walles, whare Balan stode, and ran apon hym & slew hym and keste hym ouer þe walles in-to 20 þe dyke of þe citee. And when þe Macedoyns & þe Grekes sawe Alexander entir in-to þe citee, þay schouffed' to þe walles alt at anes, and clambe ouer, sum wit leddirs sum on oþer wyse wit-owtten any resistence. For þe Tyreyenes was so ferde by- 24 cause of þe dedde of Balan þaire duc þat þay ne durste noghte turne agayne ne defende þe walle3. And on this wyse was þe citee taken and doungen doune to þe erthe.

Alexander takes Gaza and marches on Jerusalem.

Fra þe segge of Tyre Alexander & his men went to þe citee 28 of Ga3a and assailed' it, & wit schorte while þay wan it. And Fra thethyn hyed' hym towarde3 Ierusalem for to ensegge it.

The Bishop of the Jews, hearing this, calls the Jews before him, and orders fasting, prayer, and sacrifice. An Angel

[2] Qwhen þe Bischoppe of þe Iewes herde telle þat Alexander was commaund toward' Ierusalem, he gert call bifore hym alt 32 þe iewes þat ware in þe citee, and talde þam þe tythynge3 þat ware talde hym. And sythen he commandid' þam þat þay schuld' com to þe temple, and be þare in praynge Fastynge3 and wakynge & in sacrafice makyng vn-to godd, bisekand hym 36 of helpe & socoure. And þay did' soo. And on þe nyghte nexte

---

[1] The y of hyn for hym is written over another letter scratched out.   [2] Twelve half lines space with miniature of a Q.

The Bishop of the Jews' dream. 19

after, when þe Bischoppe hadd' made his sacrafice, and was *of the Lord appears by*
lyand' in prayers, he felt on slomeryng and ane Angelle appered' *night to*
vn-till hym, and sayd', 'Be noȝte ferd',' quoþ he, 'bot swythe *the High Priest and*
4 gere araye honestly all þe stretis of (þe) citee, and caste open *shows him how the*
the ȝates, and warne all þe folke þat þay aray þam̄ in whitte *city may*
clethynge, and thi-selfe & alle þe prestis reuesteȝ ȝow solempnely, *be freed— and utters*
and to-morne arely wendeȝ furthe of þe citee agaynes Alexander *a prophecy.*
8 in processioun̄. For hym by-houeȝ *regne & be lorde of alle *Leaf 6 bk.
þe werlde. Bot at þe laste þe wrethe of godd' sall falle apon̄
hym.' When̄ þe bischoppe wakened' of his slepe, he called' till *The Bishop awakens,*
hym þe iewes and talde þam̄ his reuelacion̄, and bad þam̄ do *and, doing*
12 all als þe Angelle hade schewed' hym̄. And þay did' so. For *as the Angel bids,*
þay arayed' þe streteȝ of þe cetee and cledde þam̄ in whitte *he and his people go*
clethynge, and the bischope & þe prestis reueste þam̄, and *forth to meet Alex-*
bathe thay and alle þe folke went furthe of þe citee till a place *ander, the*
16 whare þe temple & all þe citee may be seen̄. And þare þay *folk in white, the*
habade þe comynge of Alexander. And when̄ Alexander come *Bishop in*
nere þis foresaid place, and sawe be-for hym̄ swilke a multitude *full Ponti- ficals.*
of folke, cledd' alle in whitte, and þe presteȝ arayed' solempnely
20 in riche vestymentis, and þe byschope also in his pontyfycales
and a mytir one his heued', and þare-apon̄ a plate of golde,
whare-one was wretyn þe name of grete godd' Tetragramaton, he
commaunded all his men̄ þat þay schulde halde þam̄ by-hynd'
24 hym, and habyde till he com̄ to þam̄. And he lighte off his *Alexander, seeing*
horse, and went bi hym ane to þe iewes, And knelid' down̄ to *them, dis- mounting,*
þe erthe and wirchippede þe hye name of godd, þat he saw *kneels and*
þare wretyn̄ apon̄ þe bischopes heued'. And þan̄ alle þe iewes *worships the Name*
28 knelid' doun̄ & saluste Alexander and cried all wit a voyce: *of God.*
'lyff lyffe,' quoþ þay, 'grete Alexander, lyffe, lyffe the gretteste
Emperour of þe werlde, lyffe he þat sall ouer-com̄ all men̄ and
noȝte be ouercomen̄. Prynce maste gloryous and maste worthy
32 of all þe princeȝ þat regneȝ apon̄ erthe.' When̄ þe kyngeȝ of
Surry saw þis, þay hadd' grete wonder þare-off. And a prynce
of Alexanders, þat highte Parmenon̄, said' vn-till Alexander:
'Mi lorde þe Emperour,' quoþ he, 'we mervelle vs gretely þat
36 þou, wham̄ all men̄ wirchippeȝ and lowteȝ, wirchippeȝ here þe
bischope of þe Iewes.' And Alexander ansuered', 'I wirchipe *Alexander, being*
noȝte hym,' þis quoþ he, 'Bot Godd', whase state he presenteȝ. *asked, tells them that*
For when̄ I was in Macedoyne, and vmbithoghte me, on̄ what *he wor-*

2—2

Alexander worships Jehovah.

[ships not the High Priest but God, and this because of a vision promising him the conquest of Darius.]

wyse I my3te conquere Assye, I saw hym slepand, in swilk habite & in swylke araye; and he lete as he sett no3te by me, bot went baldely furthe bi me. And for I see nane¹ in swilke arraye bot hym, I suppose it be he þat I saw in my slepe. And þare-fore I trowe þat thurgh þe helpe of Godd I saƚƚ ouercoɯ Daryus, þe kyng of Perse, and his grete pryde fordo. And aƚƚ thynge3 þat I caste in my hert fo[r] to do, it es my fuƚƚ triste þat thurgh his helpe I saƚƚ fulfiƚƚ it, and wele bryng it to end. And þis es þe cause I wirchipped hym.' And

[He goes into Solomon's Temple and sacrifices. The Bishop shows him the prophecy of Daniel.]
[* Leaf 7.]

wheɯ he hadd said thies wordes, he went in-to þe citee wit the bischope & þe preste3, and went in-to þe temple þat Salamoɯ made. And as þe bischope teched hyɯ he offred sacrafice vn-to Godd. And þe bischope tuke Alexander in hande a buke of þe prophicye of Daniel*, in þe whilke he fande wretyɯ, þat a maɯ of Grece sulde distruy þe powere of Perse². And Alexander was reghte gladde, supposynge þat it was hym-selfe. And þaɯ he gaffe þe bischoppe & þe oþer preste3 grete gyfte3 & riche & precyous, And badd þe bischope

[The Bishop of the Jews asks that the laws of their fathers might be granted.]

ashe of hym what so he walde. And the bischope askede þat he walde giffe þaɯ leue to vse þe same lawes þat þaire faderes vsed bifore þaɯ, and he graunted it. And þaɯ þe bischoppe askede þat³ walde giffe þe Iewes þat ware in Medee & in Babyloyne, leue for to vse þaire lawes, & he graunted hym þat & aƚƚ oþer thynge3 þat he walde aske.

[Alexander conquers the rest of Judaea.]

⁴ Alexander thaɯ went fra Ierusalem, & lefte thare Andromac his Messagere, and hym selfe & his Oste went to þe oþer cite3 þat ware in þe lande of Iudee, and at ilke a citee þat he come

[Darius asks the fugitive Syrians as to what kind of man Alexander was.]

to. he was wirchipfully ressayued. In þe mene tyme þe Surryens þat fledd fra Alexander, went to Perse, and talde þe emperour Darius how Alexander hadd done to þaɯ. And Darius spirred thayɯ of his stature & of his schappe, and þay

[They show him a parchment]

schewed hym purtrayed in a parchemyɯ skynɯ þe ymage of Alexander. And alsone als Darius sawe it, he dispysed Alexander bycause of his littiƚƚ stature, and be-lyfe he gerte

---

¹ MS. *see nane* twice over : ' see nane, see nane.'
² A more open handwriting begins most clearly after *Perse.*
³ Supply *he* between *þat* and *walde.*
⁴ Eleven half lines space for a miniature which is lacking. A square is roughly drawn out, and in the square the words ' *hic incipit* ' scribbled. Beside the miniature in the margin is written ' *rex equitans.*'

Darius's letter to Alexander.

write a lett*r*e and sent it till Alexander. And þa*r*e-wit he sent hy*m* a handbaƚƚ & oþer certane Iapeȝ in scorne. And þis is þe tenou*r* of þe l*e*ttre þat he sent tiƚƚ hy*m*. <small>portrait and he despises him for his short stature.</small>

4 [1]'Dari*u*s, kyng of kynges, and lord' of aƚƚ e*r*thely lordes eueñ like vnto son*n*e schynande, w*i*t þe goddeȝ of Perse, vntiƚƚ Alexander oure s*er*uand' we send'. We hafe vnderstandeñ now on late, whare-of we m*er*uelle vs gretely, þat þou ert so raysed' 8 in pride and vayne glorye, þat þou hase semblede togedir a company of robbo*ur*s and thefeȝ oute of þe weste p*ar*ties, and casteȝ þe for to coñ in-tiƚƚ oure p*ar*tieȝ, supposynge thurgh þañ for to ou*er*-sett and constreyne þe grete myghte & þe 12 v*er*tue of þe p*er*cyens, whase st*r*enghte þou may neu*er* slokeñ ne ou*er*come, suppose þou gadirde & sembled' togedir aƚƚ þe werlde. <small>Darius writes to Alexander, telling him how he has heard of his band of thieves and robbers, and that they could never overcome the power of Persia.</small>

For I do þe wele to wiete þou myghte nerehand' alson*n*e nommer þe st*er*nes of heueñ, as þe folke of þe empire of Pe*r*se. Oure 16 goddeȝ also[2], *by whayñ aƚƚ þis werlde es gouerned' & sus- tened', prayssȝ & co*m*mendeȝ oure name passyng aƚƚ oþer nacyons. 'Bot noȝte w*i*t-standynge þis; þou as a littiƚƚ bisne & a dwerghe, a halfe mañ & orteȝ of aƚƚe meñ, desyrand' to ou*er*- 20 passe þi littiƚƚnesse, riȝte as a mouse crepeȝ oute of hir hole, so þou ert cropeñ out of þe lande of Sethyñ, wenynge w*i*t a few rebawdeȝ to co*n*quere & optene þe landeȝ of Perse brade & lange, & to ryotte & playe the in thayñ as my*e*sse douse in þe house 24 whare na cattes ere. Bot I þat p*ri*ualy hase aspied' thi gateȝ, wheñ þou weneȝ moste seurely for to stertle abowte, I saƚƚ sterte apoñ þe & take þe; & so in wrechidnes saƚƚ thi dayes fouly hafe añ ende. 'A grete Foly þou dide for to take apoñ the 28 swylke a p*re*sumpcyon. It ware fuƚƚ faire to þe, if þou myghte bi oure lefe, w*i*t oure beneuolence, ocupie aƚƚ anely þe rewme of Macedoyne, ȝeldynge þa*re*fore tiƚƚ vs ȝerely a certane tribute, if aƚƚ þou couetid' noȝte oure empire. Þare-fore it es gude þat 32 þou lefe thi fonned' p*ur*posse, and wende hame agayne, and sett the in thi moder knee. And lo, I sende the here a littiƚƚ baƚƚe, w*i*t þe whilke als a childe þou may play the. For þou ert bot a childe. It es mare semely þat þou vse childeȝ ga*m*meȝ þan 36 dedeȝ of armes. 'We knawe wele thi pouert and thi nede, and <small>* Leaf 7 bk. He tells Alexander of his meanness and wretchedness who wishes, like some mouse crept out of her hole when the cat is gone, to dispart him in the broad lands of Persia. But Darius shall pounce upon him when least awaited. It were a great gift to leave him Macedonia alone, under tribute. He had better go home to his mother's knee. He sends him a play ball as more beseeming him.</small>

---

[1] Four half lines and miniature D with a king's head within. written in large characters indistinctly ... kychyn ys att a Rio ...
[2] At bottom of leaf 7, first side, are

22   Alexander and the ambassadors of Darius.

Side notes (left margin):
- Does Alexander dream of subduing the rich Empire of Persia. He advises him to return home again or he will send a force to hang him as a thief on a gibbet.
- The messengers deliver Alexander the ball and the letters. His knights, hearing it read, are astounded and cast down.
- * Leaf 8.
- Alexander consoles his men with the hope that what Darius says of the wealth of Persia may be true, and he exhorts them to fight for it manfully.
- He bids his knights bind the messengers and lead them forth to be hanged. They lead them forth thus, but the messengers beg for mercy. Alexander tells them why he

---

þat þou hase vnnethes whare wit þou may sustene thi caytyfde
corse. Wene3 þou, than, to brynge vnder thi subieccion the
empyre of Darius. I say the by my Fader saule, þat in the
rewme of Perse þare es so grete plente of golde, þat, & it were 4
gadirde to gedir on a hepe, It schulde passe þe clerenes of þe
son. Whare-fore we commande the, and straitely enioyne3 the,
þat þou leue thi fole pride and thi vayne glory, & tourne hame
agayne to Macedoyne. And if þou will no3te soo, we sall sende 8
to þe a multitude of men of arme3 swilke ane saw þou neuer, þe
whilke sall take þe, and hynge þe hye on a gebett as a traytour
and a mayster of theefe3: and no3te as þe son of Philippe.'

¹ When þe messangers þat were sent fra Darius come to 12
king Alexander, þay gaffe hym the lettres, and þe balle & oþer
certane Iapes, þat þe emperour sent hym in scorne. And
Alexander tuke þe lettres, and gert rede it openly by-fore alle
men, and Alexander knyghtes when þay herde þe tenour of þe 16
lettres ware gretly astonayde and wonder heuy. And when
Alexander sawe þam so heuy by cause of þe lettre, he saide vn-
to þam: 'a a, my worthy knyghtis,' quoþ he, 'are 3e ferecf for þe
prowde worde3 þat are contened in Darius lettres, wate 3e 20
noghte wele þat hunde3, þat berkes * mekill, byte3 men noghte
so sone, als doe3 hundes þat comme3 one men wit-outten
berkynge. We trewe wele þe lettre says sothe of some thynge3,
þat es to ² saye, of þe grete plentee of golde, þat Darius sais he 24
hase. And þarefore late vs manly feghte wit hym and we sall
hafe þat golde. For þe grete multitude of his golde, als me
thynke, schulde gare vs be balde and hardy for to fighte wit
hym manly.'   28

When Alexander had saide thir worde3 he bade his knyghtis
take the messangers of Darius and bynd' þaire hande3 bi-hynde
þam, & lede þam furthe to the galowes, & hynge þam. And
þay tuke þe messangers & bande þam, and began for to lede 32
þam furthe to þe galowes-warde, and þan þe messengers bigan
for to crye rewfully vntill Alexander & sayd': 'A, A wirchipfull
lorde & kynge', quoþ þay, 'whate hafe we trespaste, þat we
schall be haungede for oure kynges dedis'. And þan kyng 36
Alexander ansuerd': 'þe worde3 of 3our Emperour', quoþ he,
'gers me do þis, þat sent 3ow vn-to me, as vnto a theeffe, as þe

---

¹ Five half lines space with a miniature W.   ² *to* in margin of MS.

Letter of Alexander to Darius.

-ettre whilke ȝe broghte witnesseȝ': 'A, A lorde', quoþ þay, 'oure emperour sent[1] thus to ȝou: for ȝour powere & ȝour myghte was unknawwen vn-tiłł hym. Bot we be-seke ȝow lateȝ
4 vs gaa, and we schałł mak aknaweñ vntiłł hym ȝour grete glory, ȝour ryaltee, & ȝour noblaye.'
Þañ kyng Alexander badd' his knyghtis lowse þam͞, and bryng þam͞ in-tiłł his haułłe, to þe mete. And thare he made
8 þam͞ a grete feste & a ryałł. And as þay satt at the mete, þir messangers saide vn tiłł Alexander, 'lorde,' quoþ þay, 'if it be plesynge to ȝour hye maiestee sendeȝ with vs a thowsand of doghty meñ of armes, and we sałł delyuer þam͞ þe
12 Emperour Darius,' and Alexander ansuerde agayne & said[2] 'Sittes stiłłe', quoþ he, '& makes ȝow mery. For I tełł ȝow in certayne, for þe betrayinge of ȝour kynge, I wiłł noghte graunt ȝow a knyghte wit ȝow'. Apon þe morne,
16 Alexander gart write a lettre vn-to Darius, whareoffe þe tenour was this.

will hang them.
They promise to make known to Darius Alexander's real character.
King Alexander, loosing them, bids them come to meat.
They propose to Alexander that they should deliver Darius into his hands.
He scornfully rejects it.

Þe letter of Alexandere[3]

[4] 'Alexander, the soñ of Philippe & of qwene Olympias, vn-to Darius, kyng of þe land' þat schynes[5] wit þe goddeȝ of Perse,
20 we sende. If we graythely & sothefastly be-halde oure selfe þare es na thynge þat we here hafe þat we may bi righte całłe ours, bot ałł it es lent vs for a tyme. For ałłe we þat ere whirlede aboute wit þe whele of fortune, now ere we broghte
24 fra reches in-to pouerte: now fra myrthe & ioy in-to Sorowe & heuynesse; and agaynwardeȝ: and now fra heghte, we are plungede in-to lawnesse. Þare-fore þare schulde na mañ þat es sett in hye degre triste to mekiłł in his hyenesse, that, thurgh
28 pride & vayne glorye, he schulde despyse þe dedis of oþer meñ lesse * þan he. For he wate neuer how sone þe whele of fortune may turne abowte, and caste hym doune to lawe degree, þat sitteȝ hye oñ-lofte: and rayse hym to hye wirchipe and
32 grete noblaye þat bifore was pore and in lawe degree. And þarefore the aughte to thynke grete schame, þat swilke a worthy emperour as meñ haldeȝ the, schulde sende swylke

Alexander, writing, reminds Darius of the unsteadfastness of earthly wealth.
No man of high degree should scorn those lower, for he never knows when the wheel of Fortune may turn about.
* Leaf 8 bk.
Therefore Darius should be ashamed that he, a great

---
[1] *sent* in margin of MS.
[2] *& said* in margin.
[3] The rubric is wrongly placed in the MS. after *dignyteȝ*, p. 24, i.e. at the end of the letter.
[4] Five half lines with miniature A.
[5] *schynes* in margin of MS.

Marginal notes (left):

man, behaves so to Alexander, a little man.

The Undying Gods do not associate with men that die.

Alexander comes as a mortal man to fight Darius. Even if Darius overcome Alexander he shall win nothing by it, for he is but a little man and a thief.

Darius's boasts of the Persians of old have heartened them to attack the Empire. The play ball that was sent was also a forecast of his rule over the world. The other toys likewise foretell his rule over all men. By the same, Darius has sent tribute to Alexander.

The letter is taken to Darius. He then marches on Persia.

* Leaf 9. Darius, receiving

Main text:

a message vnto me so littill a man and so pore. For þou ert
euen lyke to þe sonne, as thi selfe says, sittande in þe trone of
Nitas wit þe goddeʒ of Perse. Bot goddeʒ þat euermare are
liffaunde & neuermare dyeʒ, deyneʒ noʒte for to hafe þe fela- 4
chipe of dedely men. Sekerly I am a dedely man; and to þe
I come as to a dedely man, for to feghte wit the. Bot þou þat
arte so grete & so gloryous & calleʒ thi selfe vndedely, þou sall
wynne na thynge of me, if alle þou hafe þe ouerhande of me. 8
For þou hase ouercommen bot a littill man, and a theeffe[3] als
þou sayse. And if I hafe þe ouerhande ouer the, It sall be to me
þe grettteste wirchipe þat euere byfell me, for als mekill als I sall
hafe þe victorye of þe worthieste emperour of þe werlde. Bot 12
þare þou saide, þat, in þe rewme of Perse, es so grete plentee
of golde, þou hase scharpede oure hertiʒ, and made mare
balde for to feghte with the, & for to wynne þat golde; for
to relefe oure pouerte wit-all, & putte awaye our nede whilke 16
þou says we hafe. In þat also, þat þou sent vs a hande-balle
and oþer barne-laykaynes, þou prophicyed riʒte, and betakend
bi-fore, thynges þat we trewe, thurgh goddeʒ helpe, sall falle
vn-till vs. By þe rowndenes of þe balle, we vnderstande 20
all the werld aboute vs, þe whilke sall falle vnder oure subieccion. Bi þe tane of þe laykanes þat þou sent vs, þe whilke es
made of wandeʒ and crukeʒ donwardeʒ at þe ouerend, we vnderstand þat all þe kynges of þe werlde, and all þe grete lordeʒ, 24
sall lowte till vs. Bi þe toþer laykan, þat es of golde, and
hase apon it, as it ware, a manneʒ hede, we vnderstande þat
we sall hafe þe victorye of all men and neuer be ouercommen.
And þou þat ert so grete & so myghty hase now onwardeʒ sent 28
vs trybute, in als mekell als þou sent vs a handballe, and þir
oþer thynges þat I rehersed by-fore, the whilke conteneʒ in
þam so grete dignyteʒ.'

[1] When þis lettre was wreten, Alexander called till þe mes- 32
sangers of þe Emperour of Perse, and gaffe þam riche gyftes
and betuke þam þe lettre, and badd þam bere it to þaire lorde.
And þan Alexander sembled his Oste, and by-gan for to wende
towarde Perse. When the messangers of Perse come to þe 36
emperour þay talde hym of þe grete ryaltee of kyng Alexander * and tuke hym the letters þat Alexander sent hym. And

---

[1] Four half lines space with miniature W.

Darius writes to his Satraps. 25

þe emp*er*o*ur* garte rede þa͞m. And when he herd' þa͞m redde
he was wonder wrathe, and sent a *lett*re belyue vn-tiłł twa
grete lordeȝ that hadd' þe goue*r*nance of þe empire vnder hy*m*
4 sayand' to þam on this wiese. *Alexander's letter, writes to his two great lords,*

[1] 'Dari*us* kyng of kynges and lorde of lordes vntiłł oure trewe
legeȝ Prim*us* & Antyochus, gretynge and ioy. We here tełł þat
Alexander, Philippe son*n*e of Macedoyne, es so heghe raysede in
8 pryde, þat he es rebełłe agaynes vs, & es comme͞n in-tiłł Asye,
and hase distroyed' it vtterly. And ȝitt hy*m* thynke noȝte this
ynoghe, bot he p*ur*poseȝ hy*m* for to come nere vs, and do þe
same tiłł oþerre cuntreȝ of oure empire as he hase done tyłł
12 Asye. Whare-fore we comande ȝowe o payne of ȝo*ur* legeance,
þat ȝe semble þe grete me͞n & þe worthy of oure empyre, w*it*
oþ*er* of our trewe legeȝ : and, i*n* ałł þe haste þ*a*t ȝe may, gase
& counters ȝone childe, takand' hy*m*, and bryngand' hy*m* bi-fore
16 oure p*re*sence, þat we may lasche hy*m* wele, als a wanto͞n
childe schulde be : and clethe hy*m* in p*ur*poure ; & so send'
hy*m* tiłł his moder Oly*m*pias wele chastyede. For it semeȝ
noȝte to be a feghter : but for to vse childe gammeȝ.
telling them of Alexander's boldness and bidding them take him prisoner so that Darius may whip him as a naughty child and send him home to his mother.

20 [2] Thire twa lordes Prim*us* and Antyochus, when þay hadde
redde this *lett*re of þe emp*er*o*ur*, þay wrate agayne vntiłł him
on this wyse. 'Vn-to Dari*us*, kyng of kyngeȝ, grete godd',
Prim*us* & Antiochus, seruyce þat þay ka͞n do. To ȝo*ur* heghe
24 maieste we make it aknawe͞n, þat þe childe Alexandere, whilke
ȝe speke off, hase ałł vtterly distroyed' ȝo*ur* cuntree. And we
sembled' a grete multytude of folke, and faughte w*it* hy*m* ; bot
he hase discomfit vs, and we were fayne for to flee. For un-
28 nethe myghte any of vs wynne awaye w*it* þe lyfe. Þare-fore
we þat ȝe say ere helpers vnto ȝowe, besekeȝ ȝo*ur* hye maiestee
that ȝe send' su͞m socoure tiłł vs ȝo*ur* trewe leges.' Whe͞n
Dari*us* hadde redde þis *lett*re, þare come anoþer messang*er*
32 tiłł hy*m* and talde hy*m* þat Alexander and his Oste hade lugede
þam appon the water of Strume. And whe͞n Dari*us* herd'
þat he wrate anoþ*er* *lett*re vntiłł Alexander, of whilke þis was þe
teno*ur*.
Primus and Antiochus reply, telling of their utter defeat at the hands of Alexander and begging for help.

Darius is told of the camping of Alexander on the river Strume.

36 [3] 'Dari*us*, kyng of kynges, and lorde of lordeȝ, vn-tiłł oure
*ser*uande Alexander. Thorowte ałł þe werlde þe name of
Darius writes again to

---
[1] Space for four lines.   [3] Four half lines and space with a minia-
[2] Miniature and M space for four lines.   ture D, with king's head within.

26 Darius writes again to Alexander.

Alexander telling him to retire before his vengeance fall upon him.
* Leaf 9 bk.

Darius es praysed & commended. Oure goddez also hase it wreten in thaire bukes. How than durste þou be so balde, for to passe so many waters, and seez, Mountaynes & craggez, for to werraye agaynes oure royalle maiestee. A grete wirchip me thynke it* ware to þe, if þou myghte mawgre oures, hafe in possessioun þe kyngdome of Macedoyne all anely, wit-owtten mare. Thare-fore the es better amend þe of thi mysededis, þan we take swilke wreke appon the, þat oþer men take bisne þare- by, sen alle þe erthe wit-owtten oure lordchipe, may be callede wedowe. Torne agayne þare-fore, we consaile þe, in-to thyn awenn cuntree, are oure wrethe and oure wreke falle apon

He sends him also a token of the number of his own people.

þe. Neuer-þe-lesse, þat oure wirchippe & oure grete noblaye be sumwhate knawen to þe, we sende the a malefull of chesebolle sede, in takennyng þare-of. Luke if þou may nombir & telle all þir chessebolle sedez, & if þou do þatt þan may þe folke of oure oste be nowmerd. And if þou may nozte do þat oure folke may nozte be nowmerd. Þarefor turnee hame agayne in-to þi cuntree and lefe þi foly þat þou hase bygun, and take na mare apon þe swilke a presumpcion, for I tell þe we haffe men of armes wit-oute nowmmere '.

They bring Alexander the letter. But he finds another meaning for the tokens. He hears of the heavy sickness of his mother. Altho' cast down by the news he writes a letter to Darius. He tells him that for other reasons he is forced unwillingly to return, but bids him not put it

[1] When þe Messangers of Darius come till Alexander, þay tuk hym þe lettre and þe malefull of chessebolle sedez. Alexander þan gerte rede þe letter. And sythen he putt his hand in þe male, and tuke of þe chessebolle sedez & putt in his mouthe, & chewed it, & said, 'I see wele', quoþ he, 'þat he hase many men, bot þay are rizte softe as this sedez are'. In þe mene tyme þare come a Messanger till Alexander fra Macedoyne: and talde hym þat his Moder Olympias was grefe seke. And [when] Alexander herd þis, he was wonder heuy. Neuer þe lesse, he wrate vn to Darius a lettre, þat spakke on this wyse.

'[2] Alexander þe son of Philippe & of qwene Olympias vn-to Darius kynge of Perse, we sende. We do þe wele to wiete þat we hafe herde certane tythyngez, whilke gers vs agaynez oure will do þat we now sall saye. Bot trow þou nozte þat we for fere or dowte of thi pride and þi vayne glorye turne hame agayne now till oure awenn cuntre, Bot all anely for to vesett

4

8

12

16

20

24

28

32

36

---
[1] Four lines space with miniature W.   [2] Three lines space.

The Persians defeated in three days' battle. 27

oure Moder Olympias, whilke lygges grefe seke. Bot wete þou
wele, wit in schorte tym̄, we schall haste vs agayne, wit a grete
nowmere of fresche knyghtis. And riȝte als þou sent vs a
4 malefull of chessebolle sedeȝ; so we sende þe here a littill peper.
For þou schulde witte þat riȝte as þe scharpenes of þis littill
peper passeȝ þe multitude of þe chessebolle sedeȝ, riȝte so þe
grete multitude of þe Persyenes sall be ouer-comen̄ wit a fewe
8 knyghtis of Macedoyne.'

¹ This lettre be-kende Alexander to þe knyghtis of Darius,
þe peper also, & bad' þam̄ bere þam̄ to þe emperour. And
he gaffe þam̄ grete gyftes and riche, and sent þam̄ furthe.
12 And þan̄ he turnede * agayne wit his Oste towarde Macedoyne.

Thare was þe same tyme a wonder wyse man̄ of werre þe
whilke highte Amorca. and he was prynce-werres in Araby,
and lay þare wit a grete multitude of men̄ in awayte of
16 Alexander & his Oste. And when̄ he herde tell of þe commyng
of Alexander, he redied' hym for to kepe hym. And when̄ þay
mett, þay faught to-geder all þe daye fra þe morne till þe euen̄.
And so þay dide all þase thre deyes. And þare was so mekill
20 folke dede in þat bataile, þat þe sone wexe eclipte & wit-drewe
his lighte, vggande for to see so mekill scheddynge of blude.
Bot at laste þe Percyenes ware so thikke-falde felled' to þe
grounde, þat þaire prynce Amorca turned' þe bakke & fledd,̄
24 and vnnetheȝ myghte wynn̄ awaye, and a fewe wit hym.
So hastyly fledd' Amorca, þat he come nerehand' alsone to
Darius, as his messagers did' þat come fra Alexander, and fand'
Darius haldand' þe lettre in his hande, þat Alexander sent hym̄,
28 and spirrande what Alexander did' wit þe chessbolle sedeȝ.
And þe messangers ansuerd' & said': 'He tuke of þe chessbolle
sedeȝ', quoþ þay, 'and chewed' of þam̄, & said'. I see wele,' quoþ
he, 'þat Darius hase many men̄, bot þay are wonder softe';
32 And than Darius tuk of þe peper, þat Alexander sent, and
putt in his mouthe and chewed' it. And when he felide þe
strenghe of it, and þe grete hete, he syghede sare, and saide:
'Alexander knyghtis', quoþ he, 'are bot fewe, bot and þay be
36 als strange in þam̄ selfe, as þis peper es in it selfe, þay sall
fynde nane in þis werlde þat may agaynestande þam̄.' And
þan ansuerde Amorca & saide, 'Forsothe, lorde', quoþ he, 'ȝe

¹ Five lines space with miniature A.

*down to his own vainglory or pride. He shall come again with a fresh host. And he sends him in return a little pepper. He dispatches messengers back with the letter. * Leaf 10, Amorca tries to ambuscade Alexander.*

They fought three whole days till the sun grew dark with dread, seeing the number of the slain. So many of the Persians were slain that at last Amorca had to flee. He fled so quickly to Darius that he found him reading Alexander's letter. Darius sighs at the sharpness of the pepper.

The return; second campaign against Persia.

Alexander's humility and courtesy to his fallen foes.

say sothe, Alexander hase few knyghtis, bot þay ere strange, þat hase slaeñ my knyghtis þat ware so many, so þat¹ vnnetheȝ myghte I eschappe owte of þaire handeȝ.' Alexander, if alle² he hade þe victorye of his enemys, he bare hym neuer þe hiere þare-fore, ne empridede hym noȝte þare-of. Bot bathe Percyeneȝ & the Macedoyns þat ware slaeñ, he gert brynge to beryell. And þañ he come wit his Oste in-to Cecill, whare many Citeȝ submyt þamֿ₊vñ-till hym, and of that rewme, þare went wit hym̄: xvij. M. feghtynge meñ. And fra thethyñ he come till Ysaury, þe whilke, wit-owtteñ any agayne

His further march.

standynge, was ȝolden vntill hym. And Alexander went vp apoñ þe Mounte Taurus, and fande þare a citee þat meñ callede Persypolis, and thare he tuk wit hym a certane of meñ of

Alexander sacrifices to the Sun in Phrygia.

Armes, and went so thurgh Asye, and wañ many Citeȝ. And so he come in-to Frigy, and went in-to þe temple of þe soñ, and thare he made sacrafyce to þe soñ. Fra thethyñ, he come to a reuere, þat es calleď Stamandra, and þare he saiď till his

* Leaf 10 bk.

men. 'Blyste mote ȝe be',* quoþ he, 'þat hase getyñ þe comendacions & þe praysyngeȝ of þe gude doctour Homerus', and ane of his meñ ansuerde & saiď, 'Mi lorde kyng', quoþ he, 'Me thynke I may sauely writte ma praysyngeȝ, & lonyngeȝ of the, þañ Homerus diď of þam̄ þat distruyede þe Citee of Trayane. For þou hase done in þi tyme ma wirchipfull

Alexander answers a flatterer, he had rather be a wise man's disciple than have the praises of Achilles.

thyngeȝ, þañ euer diď þay.' And Alexander [ansuerd,] & saiď, 'Me ware leuer,' quoþ he, 'be a wyse manes disciple þan for to hafe þe lonyngeȝ of Achilleȝ.' After this he remouede wit his Oste into Macedoyne, & fande his Modir Olympias wele couerď of hir sekenes, and suggournede þare wit her a while. And thañ he ordeyned hym̄ for to wende agayne into Persy,

Alexander marches again towards Persia.

And keste hym for to logge at a Citee, þat meñ calleȝ Abandryañ. The meñ of þe Citee, wheñ þay herde telle of his commynge, þay sperede þe ȝates of þe Citee, and wachede þe citee one ilke a syde. And wheñ Alexander saw þat, he went &

The citizens of Abandria shut their gates against him. But

assaillede þe Citee. And þe burgeȝ of þe Citee, wheñ þay sawe þat þe citee was noȝte strange ynoghe of þe selfe, for to agaynstande þe assawte of þaire enemys, þay criede till Alexander & saide: 'Kyng Alexander,' quoþ þay, 'we spereď

---

¹ 'þat' almost blotted out by stain in MS.
² 'alle' almost blotted out by same stain as above.

Alexander denounces the oracle of Apollo. 29

noȝte þe ȝates of [the] citee to þat entent for to agaynestande   fearing
the, Bot allanly for þe drede of Darius, kyng of Perse, þe   him they
                                                                     tell him
whilke as it was tolde tiłł vs, es purpossede for to send' his   that they
                                                                     had done
4 men̅ hedir, for to destruye vs & oure citee.' And þan̅ Alexander   so to with-
                                                                     stand Da-
said' vnto þam̅ agayn̅. 'Iffe ȝe wiłł,' quoþ he, 'þat we distruy   rius. And
ȝow noghte, openeȝ ȝour ȝates, and when̅ I hafe made an ende   they open
                                                                     their gates.
wit Darius, þan̅ słł I come agayne, & speke wit ȝowe.' And
8 þan̅ þe Citaȝenes opened' þe ȝates. Fra thethen̅ þay went to
Comnoliche. And fra thethyn̅ to Bihoy, and so to Caldiple.
Syne þay come[1] tiłł a grete reuere, whare Alexander Oste hadd'   Alexan-
                                                                     der's
grete defaute of vetałłs, and þan̅ his knyghtis murnede gretely   knights
12 and said', 'Oure horses,' quoþ þay, 'fayleȝ vs ay mare & mare.'   complain
                                                                     that their
Alexander ansuerd', & said', 'A A, my doghty knyghtis,' quoþ   horses are
he, 'þat ȝitt heder-towardeȝ hase in werreȝ suffred' many   failing
                                                                     them.
periłłs & mekiłł disesse, ere ȝe nowe in despeyre of ȝour hele   Alexander
                                                                     exhorts
16 for þe failynge of ȝour horseȝ, Słł we noȝte gete horseȝ ynowe,   them to
and we lyffe & hafe qwert, and if we dye we słł hafe na nede   endure to
                                                                     the end.
of horse, na þay may do us na prophete. Haste we vs þare-fore
in ałł þat we maye to þe place whare[2] we słł gete horseȝ wit-
20 owtten̅ nowmer, and vetaiłłs also, bathe for oure selfe & for oure
horseȝ.' When̅ he hadd' ałł saide, þay went furthe and come tiłł
a place þat es called Luctus, þat es to saye wepynge,*[3] whar þay   * Leaf 11.
fande vetails ynoghe, and mete ynoghe for þaire horse. Fra
24 thethyn̅ þay remoued' & come tiłł a place þat hatt Trigagantes,
and þare þay luged' þam̅. And Alexander went in-to a temple
of Apollo; whare als he aghteled' to hafe made Sacrafice, and
hafe hadd ansuere of that godd' of certane thynges þat he walde   Alexander
                                                                     gets a lying
28 hafe aschede. Bot a woman þat hiȝte ȝacora, whilke was preste   answer of
of þat temple, talde Alexander þat þan̅ was noȝte þe tyme of   Apollo,
                                                                     who calls
ansuere. On þe Morne Alexander come to þe temple & made   him Her-
his sacrafice. And Apollo said' tiłł Alexander, 'Hercules,'   cules.
32 quoþ he. And Alexander ansuered', & said', 'Now þat þou
calleȝ me Hercules,' quoþ he : ' I see wele þat ałł thyn̅ ansuers
ere false.' Fra thethyn Alexander went till a citee þat es called' Alexander
Thebea, and said vn-to þe folke of þe citee : 'Sendeȝ me furthe,'   calls on
                                                                     the The-
36 quoþ he, 'foure hundreth knyghtis, wele armed', for to wend wit   beans to

---

[1] MS. *went* crossed through by the scribe, and replaced by *come* in MS. itself.
[2] *whare* corrected from *þare* in MS.
[3] On leaf 11 a more regular, orderly, and distinctive handwriting begins in the MS.

send him help. But they, refusing, shut their gates.

Alexander jeers at them.

He sends four thousand archers to shoot down the watches on the wall, two hundred miners to mine the walls, a hundred to burn down the gates, and four hundred engineers to batter the walls in. Himself with the rest lay by to help them when necessary.

The story of Cicesterus and Hismon.

* Leaf 11 bk.

Alexander refuses mercy to the city, and rases it to the earth. Clitomarus, one of the citizens, fares away with the conquerors. The Thebeans ask

vs in suppoellyng of vs.' And wheñ þe Thebeans herd' thir wordeȝ, þay spered' þe ȝates of þe citee, for to agayne-stande Alexander, and went to þe walleȝ, and cried' lowde þat Alexander myghte here: 'Alexander,' quoþ þay, ' bot if [þou] gaa hethyñ fra vs, we 4 saƚƚ do the a velany, & thi knyghtis also.' When Alexander herde this, he smyled' & saide: ' ȝe Thebeens,' quoþ he, ' þat ere so mekiƚƚ praysed' & commended' of strenghe, Spere ȝe ȝour ȝates & saise ȝe wiƚƚ feghte wit me; þare es na doghety mañ of armeȝ 8 þat coueteȝ for to haue wirchip̃ and loos; þat wiƚƚ close hym̃ witin walles, bot fightes wit his enemys manly in þe felde.' Wheñ he hadd' saide thir wordeȝ, he bad þat foure thowsandeȝ archers sulde gaa abowte þe citee wit þaire bowes, & lay apoñ 12 þam̃ wit arowes þat stode apoñ þe walleȝ. And he bad two hundreth meñ of armes ga to þe walles, and myne þam̃ doune, and a hundrethe he bad take fyrebrandeȝ, & gaa to þe ȝates & brynne þam̃. And he ordeynde oþer foure hundreth meñ, 16 for to bett douñ þe walles wit Sewes of werre, Engynes and Gonnes & oþer maner of Instrumenteȝ of werre. And hym selfe, and þe remenant of þe oste lay nere þam̃ to socour þam̃ wheñ þay hadd' nede. And belyfe fra þay hadd' gyffeñ assawte to þe 20 citee, þe ȝates ware brynt, & mekiƚƚ folke was slayne witin þe citee, Sum̃ wit arowes, sum̃ wit stanes of Engynes; þe Fire also by-gañ for to sett in houseȝ wit-in þe citee, & rayse a grete lowe. In þe Oste of Alexander was, þe same tyme, a mañ þe 24 whilke highte Cicesterus, a grete enemy to þe citee. He, wheñ he sawe þe citee bryne, made righte mery.* Bot a mañ of the citee þat highte Hismoñ, wheñ he saw his cuntree þusgates be distruyed, come and feƚƚe one knees be-fore Alexander, and 28 bigañ for to synge a sange of Musyke & of murnyge wit an Instrument of Musike, Supposyng þare-by for to drawe Alexanders herte to Mercy, & styrre hym to hafe rewthe on þe citee. Alexander be-helde hym, & sayde: 'Maister,' quoþ he, 'whare- 32 to syngeȝ þou me þis sange?' 'A A lorde,' quoþ Hismon, 'to luke ȝife I myȝte styrre þi herte to hafe mercy oñ þe citee.' And þañ Alexander was wonder wrathe, and bad dynge þe walles of þe cetee douñ to þe harde erthe. And wheñ þay had so done 36 þay remoued' & went þaire way, and ane of þe worthieste meñ of þe citee, þe whilke hyghte Clitomarus, went wit þam̃ in company. Bot þe Thebeens þat ware lefte aftire þe birnynge

of þe citee went to þe temple of Apollo, and askede weþer euer
mare þaire citee sulde be repaireld agayne. Apollo ansuerde,
& said, 'he þat schall bygge þis citee agayne sall hafe thre
4 victories. And when he hase geten thre victories, he sall
onane come & parell this citee, and bigge it agayne, also
wele, als euer it was.'

[1] Alexander fra þe citee of Thebe, went to Corynthe, and þare
8 come till hym certane lordes, prayand hym þat he walde come
& see a wrestillynge. And he graunted þam. And to þis Ilke
wrestillynge þare come folke witowtten nowmer. And when
all men were gadirde, Alexander saide: 'whilk of ȝowe,' quoþ
12 he, 'sall gaa & be-gynn þis playe'. Clitomarus þan, of whaym
I spake bifore, knelid bi-fore þe kyng, & saide: 'lorde,' quoþ
he, '& ȝe wolle vouche-saffe to giffe me leue, I will be-gyn.'
And Alexander bad hym ga to. And Clitomarus went in-to þe
16 place, and þe firste man þat come in his hande, at the first
tourne he threwe hym wide open. And Alexander said vntill
hym: 'Caste thre men,' quoþ he, '& þou sall be corownd'.
Þan þare come anoþer man to Clitomarus and vnnetheȝ he come
20 in his handeȝ, when he was casten wyde open. And one þe
same wyse he seruede þe thirde. And þan Alexander gart sett
on his heuede a precious coroun, and þe kyngeȝ seruaundeȝ
spirrede hym what his name was. 'My name,' quoþ he, 'es wit-
24 owtten citee'. When Alexander herde þat he saide vn-till
hym: 'Thou noble wristiller,' quoþ he, 'whi arte þou callede wit-
owtten citee.' 'Wirchipfull emperour,' quoþ he, 'be-fore þat ȝe
werede þe emperours Dyademe, I hadde a citee full of folkeȝ
28 & of reches. Bot now, sene ȝe come to this astate & þis
dignytee, I am spoylede & priuede of my citee.' And when
[he] herde this, he wiste wele þat he ment of þe citee of
Thebe. And þan he garte his sergeanteȝ* make a crye that
32 [he] hadd giffen Clitomarus leue for to repairelle þe citee
of Thebes. Fra Corinthe, Alexander and his oste remowed till
a citee þat highte Platea, of þe whilke a man þat highte Scrassageras was prynce. And Alexander went to þe temple of Diane,
36 and fande þare a woman preste, þe whilke was a mayden, & scho
was araied lyke presteȝ of þat tymme. And when [scho] sawe
Alexander, scho saide vn-till hym: 'Alexander,' quoþ scho, 'þou

[1] Five half lines space with miniature A, with knight within.

Side notes:
an oracle of Apollo as to whether their city should ever be rebuilt. The answer is, it shall be rebuilt by a three-fold victor. Alexander is invited to a wrestling. He asks who will begin. Clitomarus begs the favour of so doing. He wins once. Alexander's promise. He wins twice. He wins thrice. Crowning him they ask him his name. He answers, 'One without City.' How it befell with his answer.

* Leaf 12.

From Corinth they go to Platea and the Temple of Diana. The maiden Priestess *and her prophecy.*

Scrassageras curses the priestess, but it avails him nothing.

He falls from his Lordship and flees to Athens, and prevails on them to help him.

Alexander marches on Athens.

The letter of Alexander to the Athenians, telling of his deeds and conquests.

He asks of them but ten philo-

arte welcomme. Þou schall conquere all þe werlde.' One þe morne Scrassageras went to þe same temple, and alsone als þe preste sawe hym, scho saide vn-till hym: 'Scrassageras,' quoþ scho, 'what thou wit-in a schorte while þou schall be priued' of 4 þe lordchip þat þou now hase?' And when he herde þis he was righte wrathe wit hir, & saide, 'þou arte no3te worthy,' quoþ he, 'for to be preste here. Alexander come to þe 3isterdaye, and þou prophicyed' hym gude; And to me þou sais, þat I schall lose all 8 my lordechipe.' And scho ansuerd', & saide, 'Bee3 no3te angry to me,' quoþ scho: 'for all þis buse be fulfilled', and nathynge þare of lefte ne ouerhippede.' A littill after it felle þat Alexander was gretely angrede at Scrassageras, and tuke fra 12 hym his lordchipe, & Scrassageras went to þe cite of Athene3, and sare wepande he complenede hym to þe cita3enes of Athene3 & talde þam how þat Alexander hadd' priued' hym of his lorde-chipe. And þan þe Atheneanes ware wonder [wrathe] towardes 16 Alexander, and made grete boste & manace, þat þay schold' ryse agaynes hym, bot if he restorede Scrassageras agayne till his lordechipe. Alexander remowed' his Oste fra Platea to þe citee of Athenes, and when [he] herde telle þat þe Athenens ware 20 wrathe till hym-warde, and manaced' hym, he wrate vn-to þam a lettre þat spak one this wyse.

'¹ Alexander, þe son of Philippe and of qwene Olympias, vn to the Athenenes, gretynge. Fra þe tyme þat oure Fadir was 24 dedde, & we were sett in þe Trone of his dingnytee, we went into þe weste Marches, whare all þe folke3 þat duelle3 thare for þe maste party 3alde þam vn-till vs wit-owtten stresse. Fra þe citee of Rome to þe weste see occyane, all men sub- 28 mytte þam vn-till vs þat wit oure awen fre will we hafe taken þam ² till oure grace. And thase þat walde no3te submytt þam till vs wit fairenes, we hafe distruyed³ þam & þaire cite3, and doungen þam down to þe erthe. And now þis oþer 32 daye as we went fra Macedoyne & passed thurgh Asye: bi þe cite of Thebe, þe Thebeyens despysed' vs, & lete as þay sett no3te by vs. Bot onane we garte þair pryde falle, and de-

---

¹ Four half lines space with miniature A.
² Here the scribe first has written 'to grace' and then erased it, substituting as in text.
³ The *uy* in *distruyed* has been substituted for *uu* by the same scribe.

The Speech of Demosthenes. 33

struyed᾿ bathe þaṁ & thaire citee. And þare-fore we write
vn-to ȝow; that ȝe sende vs teñ philosophres þat be wyse, *by
þe whilke we may be encensede and conselled᾿. For oþer thyng
4 wiłł we nane aske ȝow, Bot ałłe anely þat þe halde vs for ȝour
lorde & ȝour kynge. And ȝif ȝe wiłł noȝte submytt ȝowe vn-
tiłł vs, ȝow buse oþer be strangere þañ we, or ełłs submytt yow
to sum lordechip̄, þat be strangere þañ oures.'
8 ¹ The Athenyenes redd᾿ þis lettre and þan þay bigan to crye
one highte. And ane, þat highte Eschiłłe, stode vp amangeȝ
þaṁ, and said᾿: 'It es fully my consełł,' quoþ he, 'þat we oñ
na wise assent [to thise] wordeȝ of Alexander.' Alle þe folke þañ
12 þat was gadirde þare, prayed þe philosophre Demostines, þat
he walde tełł þaṁ his conselle, as touchynge þat matere. And he
stude vp, & badd᾿ ałł meñ be stiłł. And þañ he said᾿ vn-to þaṁ.
'Sirs,' quoþ he, 'I pray ȝow takes tent vn-to my wordeȝ &
16 herkenes gudly what I sałł say. If ȝe fele ȝow of power, for
tiłł agayne-stande Alexander, & to supprise hym, þañ feghtes
wit hym manly, and obeys noȝte tiłł his wordeȝ. And if ȝe
suppose ȝe be noȝte strange ynoghe to feghte wit hyṁ þan
20 hereȝ hyṁ, and obeys vn-tiłł hyṁ. Ȝe knawe wele, þat als
oure eldirs telles vs, Ȝerses was a grett kynge, & a myghty,
and many victories he gatt. And neuer þe lesse in Ellada he
suffrede grete meschefe. Bot he, this Alexander, hase done
24 many batailłes, in þe whilke he suffrede neuer disese bot alwaye
had þe ouerhande. Þe Thirienes, I pray ȝow, ware [þai] noȝte
balde knyghtes and strange, and ałł þaire lyfe hade bene excer-
cysede in Armes? And whate profitede þaṁ þaire strenghe?
28 Þe Thebienes also þat were so wyse, and so grete exercyse hadde
in armes, fra þe firste tyme þat þe citee was bygged, whare-off
seruede þaire grete witt þaṁ, and þaire grete strength, wheñ
Alexander assailede þaṁ? Þe Poliponiens faghte wit Alexander,
32 bot þay myghte na while agayne-stande his men of armes. Bot
alsoñ þaire ² ware disconfit and slaeñ. It es noȝte vnknawen
vn-to ȝowe, how many citeeȝ castełłs & towneȝ for fere submittis
þaṁ vn-tiłł hyṁ wit-owtteñ any assawte gyffyng. Þarefore,
36 it es noȝte my consaile þat ȝe be heuy, ne wrathe tiłł Alexander

sophers to
teach him
* Leaf 12
bk.
rendering
homage to
him; or else
must it
either be
stronger
than Alex-
ander or
dependent
on some
stronger
state.
The speech
of Aeschy-
lus against
Alexander.
The Athe-
nians beg
counsel of
Demos-
thenes.
He tells
them if
they feel
themselves
strong
enough to
resist, but
if not then
let them
submit.
He com-
pares Alex-
ander and
Xerxes to-
gether.
He nar-
rates Alex-
ander's
victorious
campaign.

He advises
them not to
be froward
towards
Alexander.

---

¹ Four half lines space with miniature   recurs on p. 55, l. 29. Cf. Icelandic þeir.
T.   There is nothing left out nor is it a mis-
² MS. reads 'þaire' for þay. This form   print.

3

34 Alexander's letter to the Athenians.

Alexander is a wise and reasonable man, neither would he have put Scrassageras out of his Lordship except for treason against him.

The Athenians commend this

*Leaf 13.

counsel greatly and sent tribute but no philosophers.

He hears of the speeches of both Aeschylus and Demosthenes. He writes them a letter.

The Letter of Alexander to the Athenians. He had purposed a philosophic dispute with them, and have shown them his friends. But their deeds showed otherwise. Whoso of them rises against him, he will make an example of. They, as knaves, think ill and fear ill.

He had put S. out of office for treason. They have despised his demand for ten philosophers.

for Scrassageras. For all men knawes wele þat Alexander es a wonder wyse man & a warre, & a man þat gouernes hym by reson; and þare-fore ȝe may wele wete, he walde noȝte putt Scrassageras oute of his lordechipe upon lesse þan forfett vn- 4 till hym.' When þe Athenyenes had herde þir wordeȝ, þay commedid gretly the conseille of Demostines, and than they ordeyned a coroun of golde þe weghte of ·l· pounde, and sent Messangers þarewit, and wit tribute vn-till Alexander, bot 8 philosophres sent þay nane. * And when þire Messangers come till Alexander, þay gaffe hym þe coroun, and þe tribute, þat þe Athenyenes sent hym, and talde hym þat þay had highte hym a grete nowmer of catelle. And when Alexander had herd þam, 12 he vnderstode wele þe concell of Eschilus þat concelid þe Athenyenes to agaynestand hym, and also þe concell of Demostenes that concellde þam þe contrary, and þan he wrate a lettre to þam whare-of the Tenoure was this. 16

[1] ' Alexander þe son of Philippe and quene Olympias, for þe name of kynge will we noȝte take apon vs, before we hafe oure enemys vnder oure subieccion: vn-to þe Athenyenes gretyng. It es noȝte oure entent to come in ȝour citee wit oure oste, 20 Bot allanly to come & dispuyte wit ȝour philosophres, and to asche þam certane questyons, Oure purposse was also to hafe declared for oure trewe leggeȝ & oure gude Frendeȝ. Bot ȝour dedeȝ proues þe contrary, as it [2] done vs till vnderstande. Oure 24 goddeȝ we take to witnesse, þat whilke of ȝow so ryseȝ agayneȝ vs, we sall take swilke wreke apon hym þat oþer men sall take ensample þare-by. Bot ȝe als schrewes, and euyll men, euer mare troweȝ ill, and thynkes ill. Wate ȝe noȝte wele þat 28 þe Thebienes þat raise agaynes vs, hadd þaire mede als þay disserued. And ȝe haffand in vs a wrange consayte, blameȝ vs, For we putt Scrassageras owte of his Office the whilke [3] forfett gretly agaynes oure maieste. We sent vn-to ȝow bi 32 lettre for ten philosophres, bot ȝe, noȝte knawande oure grete powere & oure myghte, despysed oure maundement and walde noȝte fulfill it. Neuer þe les if all ȝe hafe offendid agaynes

---

[1] Four half lines with miniature A.
[2] The reader must probably here supply ' hase ' between ' as it ' and ' us till understande', but as it occurs several times it may be a syntactical peculiarity.
[3] The reader must probably supply was or dede between þe whilke and forfett, but see previous notice.

Alexander and the Lacedemonians. 35

vs whider-towarde and bene disobeyande tiƚƚ oure maiestee, we
forgiffe ʒow aƚƚ ʒour gilt, and þe greuance þat ʒe hafe don vs,
so þat ʒe be obeyande vn-tiƚƚ vs, fra þis tyme forwarde. Com-
4 forthes ʒow þarefore & beeʒ mery, for of vs ʒe schaƚƚ hafe na
greuance ne na disesse be-cause ʒe did after þe conceƚƚ of
Demostynes.'

[1] Wheñ þe Athenyenes herd þis lettre redd, þay ware riʒte
8 gladd, and þañ Alexander & his Oste went fra thethyñ vn-to
Lacedoyne. Bot þe Lacedouns walde one na wyse obey vn-tiƚƚ
Alexander, bot said ilkañ of þañ tiƚƚ oþer, 'latt vs noʒte be
lykke þe Athenyenes,' quoþ þay, 'þat drede þe manaschynge,
12 and þe boste of Alexander bot late vs schewe oure myʒte, and
oure strenghe and manly defende *oure citee agayneʒ hym.'
Wheñ þay hadd saide, þay spered þe ʒates of þe cetee faste,
and went manly to þe walles. And a grete nowmer of þañ
16 tuke þañ schippeʒ & went to þe see, a grete nauy, to feghte
wit Alexander are he come to lande. And wheñ Alexander
saw this, he sent a lettre to þañ sayand on this wyse.

[2] 'Alexander þe soñ of Philippe and of þe quene Olympias
20 vn-to þe Lacedounes we sende. We conceƚƚ ʒow, þat þat, that
ʒour elders hase lefte ʒow, ʒe kepe hale & sound & in sauetee[3]
and lyfteʒ noʒte ʒour hende ouer hie to þe thyngeʒ þat þe may
noʒte reche to. And if ʒe desire for to hafe ioy of ʒour strenthe,
24 dose swa þat ʒe be worthy to hafe wirchipe of vs. Þarefore
we comande ʒow, þat ʒe turne agayne wit ʒour schippeʒ, and
leueʒ þañ, & gase to lande by ʒour awenñ fre wiƚƚ; or sekirly
I saƚƚ sett fire in thañ & brynne þañ. And if ʒee dispice oure
28 commandement, blameʒ na mañ bot ʒour selfe, if we wreke
vs one ʒowe.'

[4] 'The Lacedounes redd þis lettre, and wheñ it was redd, þay
ware wonder heuy. Noʒte for-thi þay redied þañ to feghte.
32 Bot Alexander arryued in an oþer coste, and come to þe citee
are þay wiste and vmbylapped þe citee one ilke a syde, and
assaillede it strangly & dange þe Lacedouns of þe walles &
slewe many of þañ & woundeď many, and sett fyre in þaire
36 schippeʒ & brynt þañ. Þe remanant of þañ þat ware lefte

Nevertheless he will forgive them if they be good for the future, since they followed Demosthenes' advice.

Alexander goes thence into Lacedemonia. But they would in no wise submit to

Leaf 13 bk.

him. But despising him the Athenians manned the walls. Yet others of them fled over-seas, and others went to meet him in fight.

The Letter of Alexander to the Lacedemonians bidding them return and submit.

Alexander arrives by an unforeseen way and surrounds them.

He attacks the city

---

[1] Three lines space miniature W.
[2] Four half lines with miniature A.
[3] MS. *sauetee* with *u* written over another letter.
[4] Four lines space with miniature T.

3—2

Darius takes counsel.

[Sidenotes: fiercely till they surrender. Alexander tells them they would not receive him peacefully, therefore are they come to this great harm. Alexander reproaches them with overgreat conceit and quotes a homely proverb. *Leaf 14. They thought in vain to have done to him as their forefathers did to King Xerxes. Darius hears of the coming of Alexander. He is greatly terrified and holds a council. The speech of Darius. He bewails that he has underrated him, and sees that they must now look to their safety. He fears that God's Foresight helps Alexander so that he may eventually conquer Persia.]

appon lyfe, when þay saw this grete meschefe come owte of þe citee vn-till Alexander, & felle doun at his fete, & besoughte hym of mercy & of grace. And Alexander ansuerd, 'I come to ȝow,' quoþ he, 'meke & mylde, bot in þat degre ȝe walde noȝte 4 ressayffe me, þarefore now are ȝour schippeȝ brynned, and ȝour citee distruyed, & ȝour folkeȝ slayne. Warned I noȝte be-fore þat ȝe schulde noȝte heue ȝour handeȝ ouer-hye to þe sternes, to þe whilke nane erthely man may wynn. For wha so euer 8 clymbeȝ hier, þan his fete may wynn to sum halde, he sall falle onane doun to þe grounde. And þarefore es þare a commone prouerbe: þat "wha sa hewes to hie, þe chippes will falle in his egh." Ȝe wende hafe done till vs as ȝour eldirs 12 didde sumetyme till kynge ȝerses, bot ȝour wenyng dessayued ȝow. For ȝe myghte noȝte agayne-stande vs when we assaillede ȝow.' Whan *he hadd saide on this wise, he gaffe þam leue to gaa whare þay walde. And than he remouede thethyn & went 16 to-warde Cicill. And when þe emperour Darius herd tell of þe comyng of Alexander, he was gretly abaiste and sent after all his princeȝ, Dukes & Erles, & oþer grete lordes, & went till a consaile. And he saide vn-to þam, 'I see wele,' quoþ he, 'þat 20 he, this Alexander, þat gase thus abowte werrayand, waxeȝ gretly in wirchipe, and ay-whare whare he commeȝ he hase þe victory. I wende he hadd bene a theeffe & a robbour, þat hadde went till cuntreȝ þat ere wayke & feble, and durst noȝte agayne- 24 stande hym, & robbed þam & spoyled þam. Bot now, I see wele, he es a doghty man of Armes, & a noble werrayour. And ay þe mare þat I hafe depraued hym and despysed hym; þe mare ryseȝ his name, & his wirchipe. I sent hym a balle, a toppe, 28 & a scourge, for to lere barne-laykes; bot hym þat I called a disciple, he semeȝ a mayster & whare-so-euer he gase, Fortune gase wit hym. Þare-fore vs byhoueȝ to trete of oure hele, & of oure popleȝ, and pute awaye all pride & all foly : & 32 namare despisse Alexander, saynge þat he es noghte, by cause we are emperour of Perse. For his littillnes waxes and oure gretnes decresseȝ. I hafe grete dowte, þat goddeȝ forluke helpeȝ hym, so þat whils we ere abowte, and weneȝ to putte hym 36 out of Ellada, we be spoyled, by hym, of þe rewme of Perse.'

[1] When Darius hadd said thir wordeȝ, his broder Coriather

---

[1] Four lines.

Darius consults his councillors. 37

ansuerd, & said, 'þou hase here,' quoþ he, 'gretly magnified' &   Darius'
commendid Alexander, in that, þat þou sais he es mare feruent   brother advises him
for to come in-to Perse, þan we in-till Ellada. And þarefore   to lead his own men
4 if it be plesyng vn-to ʒour maiestee, vse ʒe þe maners of   in the van as Alex-
Alexander, and so sall [ʒe] wele & peysably welde ʒour empire   ander does.
& conquere many oþer rewmes. Alexander, when he gase to
bataile and sall feghte, he lates [nane] of his pryncez ne his
8 oþer lordez gaa be-fore, &[1] hym selfe come by-hynde, bot
he gase bi-fore þam alle, and so risez his wirchip & his
name.'
Quod Darius, 'wheþer awe me to take sa ensample at   Darius demurs.
12 Alexander, or Alexander at me.' A prynce ansuerde & saide,
'Alexander,' quod he, 'es a warrer[2] man & a wyse, & hase   A prince tells him of
trespaste in na degree & þarefore he duse manly by hym selfe   the person of Alex-
all þat he doez. For he hase taken þe fourme of þe lyonn.'   ander, and
16 'Whare-by knawes þou þat,' quoþ Darius, *and he ansuerd, &   *Leaf 14 bk.
saide, 'whate tyme,' quoþ he, 'þat I was sent to Macedoyne for   advises him to
til aske tribute of kyng Philippe, I saw, bi his Figure & his   gather a tremen-
wise ansuere, þat he schuld be a passyng man, bathe of witt,   dous force
20 & of doynges. Thare-fore, if it be plesyng vn-to ʒow, I consell   that Alex-
þat ʒe sende till all þe landez & cuntrez þat langez to ʒour   ander's
empire, þat es to say to Parthy & Medy, Appollamy, Mesopo-   heart may fail him.
tamy, Ytaly, Bactri, and till all þe remenant for þay ere
24 subietez vn-to ʒow a hundreth : c. and fifty l. of dyuerse[3] folke.
To þe lordes of[4] all thire, I rede ʒe sende commandyng þam, þat
þay come to ʒow, in all þe haste þat þay may, with all þe men
þat þay may gett whilk ere able to ga to werre[5]. And when
28 þay [ere] all sembled to gedir late vs beseke oure goddis of
helpe. And þan Alexander when he seez swilk a multitude
of folke agaynes hym, his hert sall faile hym, and his mens
also. And owþer he sall for fere turne hame agayne till his
32 awen cuntree, or ells submytt hym vn-to ʒow.' And þan   The counsel
ansuerd anoþer prynce, & sayde, 'This es a gud concell,' quoþ   is commended
he, 'bot it es noʒte profitable. Wate þou noʒte wele þat a wolfe   but for the

---

[1] & is written in above the line in the MS. by the same scribe.
[2] Perhaps the abbreviation is here really a mere flourish, and we should read *warr*, though the contraction mark is well made.
[3] In MS. *deverse* was at first written, and *y* substituted by the same scribe.
[4] *af* written and crossed out between *lordes* and *of*.
[5] *were* at first written and changed to *werre* by the scribe.

38 Alexander and his Physician.

cowardice of the Persians and the wisdom of the Greeks.

chase3 a grete floke of schepe & gerse þam̄ sparple. Righte so, and þe wysdome of þe grekes passe3 oþer nacyons.'

[1] In this mene tym̄, Alexander sembled' a gret multitude of folke3 to þe nowmer of cc of feghtynge men̄, and remewed to 4

Alexander gathers his host. He bathes in a cold river and gets a fever, to the great alarm of his army.

warde Perse, & come till a reuere þat es called' Mociona, of whilke þe water was wonder calde, & faire, & clere. And Alexander hadd' a grete lyste for to be bathede þare-in, and went in-to it & bathed hym, & waschede hym þare-in, and also son̄ 8 he felle in a feuer and a heued-werke þare-wit, so þat he fure wonder ill. And when̄ þe Macedoyns saw þaire lorde so grefe seke, þay were wonder heuy and reghte dredand', and said amanges selfe: 'And Darius,' quod þay, 'wete þat oure lorde 12 Alexander be þus seke, he sall come & falle apon̄ vs sodaynly, & fordo vs ilkan̄. For, and we hadd' þe hele of oure lorde Alexander, we hadd' comforth ynoghe & dredde no nacyon̄.'

Alexander summons Philip his Physician.
* Leaf 15.

Than kyng Alexander called' till hym his Phicisiene þat 16 highte Philippe & badd' hym ordeyne hym a Medcyne for his sekenes. Þis ilk Phicisiene was [2] * bot a 3ong man̄, bot he was a passyng kunnyng man̄ and a sotell in all þe poyntes þat langed to phisic. And he highte Alexander, þat [by] a certane 20 drynke he sulde onane make hym all hale. Nowe fell it, þat was wit Alexander a prynce, þat highte Parmenius & was

But another Lord is jealous of him and warns Alexander that Philip would poison him being in Darius' pay.

lorde of hermony. This prynce hade grete envy to þis phicsiene, bi-cause þat Alexander luffede hym so passandly 24 wele & belyfe he wrate till Alexander, and warned' hym þat he schulde be warre wit Phillippe his phicisiene, and on na wyse resayfe þat drynke þat he walde gyffe hym. For he said', þat Darius had highte to giffe hym his doghter to wyffe & his 28 kyngdom̄ after his dissesse if swa ware, þat he myghte be any crafte make ane ende of hym̄. When̄ Alexander hadde redd' þis lettre he was na thynge trubbled', so mekill he tristede of þe conscience of his phisician. 32

The Physician comes to Alexander.

In þe mene tyme, þis Phisician come till Alexander wit þe forsaid drynke, and Alexander tuk þis drynke in a hande & þe forsaid lettre in his oþer hande and biheld' þe Phisician in þe vesage ri3te scharpely. To whome þe Phisician saide: 36

---

[1] Five lines space with miniature I.
[2] At bottom of leaf 14 obv. is written 'ff (fecit?) Sereu. Ser.'

Alexander puts his Physician to the test.

'wirchipfull Emperour,' quoþ he, 'be na thyng fered bot drynke
þe medcyne baldely,' and þan onane Alexander tuk this drynke,
& schewed Philippe þe lettre. And when Philippe had redde
4 þe lettre, he said till Alexander: 'Now for sothe, my lorde,'
quoþ he, 'I take oure goddes to witnesse þat I ne am noȝte
gilty of this treson, þat here es wretyn.' Alexander þan was
all hale als euer he was, & called vn-till Philyppe his phisician
8 & enbraced hym in his armes & said: 'Philippe,' quoþ he,
'knawes þou how mekill luffe & triste I hafe in the. Firste
I dranke thi medecyne, & syne I schewede þe þe lettre þat
was sent me agaynes the.' 'Mi lorde,' quoþ Philippe, 'I be-
12 seke ȝow þat ȝe wolle vochesaffe to send after myn accusour,
and do hym come bi-fore ȝour presence þat þis lettre sent vn-to
ȝow, and hase lered me for to do[1] swilk a hie treson. Be-lyfe
þan gerte Alexander send after Parmeny for to come vn-till
16 hym, and gerte þe sothe be serched, & fande þat he was worthy
þe dede. And þan he gert girde of his heued.

[2] Fra þeine kyng Alexander remowed his Oste till hermony þe
mare & onane he conquered it, & put it vnder his subieccion.
20 And fra þeine he trauailed many a day *wit his Oste, and at þe
laste come till a cuntre wonder drye, & full of creuesceȝ of
cauerneȝ, & alde cisternes whare na water myghte be funden.
And Fra þeine þay passede thurgh a cuntree, þat es called
24 Andrias, to þe Reuere of Eufrates. And þare þay lugede þam.
Þan Alexander garte brynge many grete treeȝ, for to make
a brygge of ouer þat water, appon schippeȝ, and garte tye þam
Samen wit chenys of Iren & iren nayleȝ. And when þe brigge
28 was all redy, he badde his knyghtes wende ouer apon it. Bot
when þay saw þe grete reuer ryne so swiftely and with so
a grete a byrre, thay dred þam þat þe brygge schulde falle.
For þay supposede þe chenys schuld breke be-cause of grete
32 weghte. And, when Alexander saw þam dredand on this
wyse, he gert hirde-men, þat were þare kepand katell, wend
ouer before, and warnede þat þe Oste schulde folowe þam.
Bot ȝit þe knyghtis ware ferde & durste noghte wende ouer.
36 Than was Alexander riȝte wrathe and callede vntill hym all
his prynces, & grete lordeȝ, and firste he went hym selfe ouer

marginalia: Alexander takes the drink given him, and shows the Physician the letter. Alexander declares to him his great trust. The trial of the accuser. Alexander conquers Armenia. *Leaf 15 bk. the Greater and marches through deserts to the Euphrates. He builds a bridge of boats and logs, but his knights fear to cross it because of the fierceness of the current. Alexander sends herdsmen over, yet the knights durst not follow. Alexander then goes

---

[1] MS. repeats *for to do* twice.   [2] Three lines with miniature F.

40 Alexander's trouble with his men; the Battle with Darius.

first over the bridge with his princes. Then the army follows. Alexander destroys the bridge behind him. The knights murmur thereat, fearing disaster.

þe bryges, & aH his prynceȝ folowed' hym, and sythen aH þe Oste. Twa grete ryuers rynnes thurgh Medee, Mesopotamy and Babiloyne, þat es to say Tygre & Eufrates, and soo rynneȝ in-to þe reuere¹ of Nilus. When Alexander & aH hys Oste 4 ware past ouer Eufrates, he gert smyte sonder þe brygge þat he hadd' gert make bifore, and dissolue ilk a pece þare-off fra oþer. And when his knyghtis sawe that, þay ware reghte heuy and murnede gretly þarefore, and said' emanges þam selfe, 'What 8 saH we now doo,' quoþ þay, 'when we are harde by-stadde wit oure enemys & walde flee. For ouer þis reuere may we noȝte wynn.' And when Alexander perceyued' þat murmoure of his folke, he said vn-to þam. 'What es þat,' quoþ he, 'þat ȝe say 12 amangeȝ ȝow, "If it faHe þat we flee owte of þe bataile."

Alexander's speech to his men. Let them all perish or conquer, for they shall never see home again till they have overthrown all their enemies.

Sothely, I late ȝow wele wite, þat þis is þe cause whi I garte for-do þis brygg, þat I gert make; For-thi, þat owþer we schulde feghte manly or eHs if [we] walde flee, we schulde aH perische at 16 anes and aH drynke of a coppe. For-whi þe victorye es noȝte aretted' to þam þat flieȝ, Bot to þam þat habydeȝ, or folowes on þe chace. Þare-fore comfortheȝ ȝow wele, & bese balde of hertis, and thynke it bot a playe stalworthly to feghte. For I say 20 ȝow sekerly; we ne schaH neuer see Macedoyne, be-fore we hafe ouercomen aH oure enemys, And þan wit þe victorie we saH tourne hame agayne.'

Darius gathers a great force Leaf 16. *to meet Alexander upon the river Tigris. But his men flee.*

²In þis mene tyme, kyng Darius gadirde a grete multitude 24 of men agaynes Alexander, and ordeyned' ouer þam fyve-hundreth * chyftaynes of grete lordes and luged hym wit his men apon þe reuere of Tygre. And one a day thir twa kynges wit þaire bather Ostes mett to-gedir apon a faire felde 28 and faughte to-gedir wonder egerly. Bot sone Darius men hadd þe werre & ȝode to grounde thikkfalde, slayne in þe felde. And when þe remenante saw þat, þay tuk þam to þe flighte.

The brave Persian who dares alone try to take Alexander's life in disguise for the sake of the

In Darius oste was a man of Perse, a doghety, & a balde; 32 to whaym Darius highte for to giffe his doghter to wyfe, if so were, þat he myghte, by any way, sla kyng Alexander. This man gatt hym clethyng and Armour like vn-to þe macedoyns, and went amangeȝ þam, as þay faghte, ay tiH he come by-hynd 36 kyng Alexander. And alson als he come nere hym, he lifte his

¹ Scribe first wrote *rerere* here, and then wrote a *y (ryrere)* over it. The process is quite plain.
² Two lines with small miniature I.

The brave Persian; who alone dares against Alexander. 41

swerde on heghte, & lete flye at hym̄ wit aft þe myghte þat he
hade, and hitt hym on þe heued so fercely, þat he perched[1] his
bacenett, and drewe þe blode of hym. When Alexander knyghtis
4 saw that : þay tuke hym anone, & broghte hym bifore Alexander,
and Alexander, supposyng þat he hadde bene a macedoyne, saide
vn-till hym. 'Wirchipfuft man,' quoþ he, '& doghety & strange
what ayled þe at me, for to giffe suylke a strake, knewe þou
8 noȝte wele þat it was I, Alexander ȝour helpere & ȝour allere
seruande.' And [the] Percyene ansuerd, & said, 'Wiete þou
wele wirchipfuft emperour,' quoþ he, 'I ne ame na macedoyne,
bot I am a man of Perse; and this dede I didd. For kyng
12 Darius made me a promysse of his doghetir to wife, if I myghte
brynge hym thi heid.' Than kyng Alexander called bi-for hym
all his knyghtis and askede þam what þam thoghte was for to
do wit this man. Sum ansuerde & saide þam thoghte it beste
16 to gerre smyte of his heid, Sum for to putt hym to þe fire for to
brynne, Sum to gare drawe & hang hym. And when Alexander
had herde þaire conceft, he ansuerd & said : 'Sirs,' quoþ he,
'what wrange or what defawte can ȝe fynde in þis man, Seꝝ he
20 hase besied hym tift obey tift his lordes commandement, and at
his power fulfilled it. Whilke of ȝow, so demeȝ hym worthy to
be dedde, es worthy in tyme commynge to hafe þe same dome.
For if I commande ane of ȝow for to ga & sla Darius, þe same
24 payne, that ȝe deme þis man for to suffre, ware ȝe worthy for to
suffre ȝourselfe of Darius, if ȝe myȝte be getyn.' [2] And * þan he
commanded þat he schulde wende hame to his felawes wit-owtten
any harme. When Darius herde þat his lordes ware slayne in
28 grete nowmer, he gadered a grete multitude of knyghtis and of
fotemen, and went vp on a hift þat es called Taurisius, and thare
he made his mustre of his men, supposynge þat he schuld ouercome Alexander thurgh multitude of folke. Bot alson als þay
32 mett wit þaire bathere osteȝ, and bigan for to fighte, Darius
men fledd and hymselfe also. And Alexander persuede hym
vn-to þe citee of Bactrian, and þare he luged hym, and offerde
Sacrafice tift his goddeȝ. And on þe morne he garte assaile þe

King's daughter.

Alexander asks him why he did this. He answers.

Alexander asks counsel of his knights, what shall he do with this man? Alexander speaks to them, and shows this man forth to them as an example. And then he utters his will.

* Leaf 16 bk.

Darius gathers his men again to the fight, but yet again is he overcome.

Alexander pursues him. He conquers Bac-

---

[1] The scribe wrote first 'perceed,' altered afterwards, in a very rough way, to 'perched.'
[2] MS. reads 'and he commanded' at bottom of first side of leaf 16 and '. þan he commanded' on the top of second side of the same leaf.

citee, and wanne it on werre. And in þe cheffe place þare-of he sett his trone. And aft þir oþer cite3 þat were abowte it, he wanñ þam̃ o werre, & putt þam̃ vnder his subieccioñ. In þis ilke citee of Bactriañ, he fande tresour wit-owtteñ nowmer, and also his moder, and his wyfe.

[Sidenote: trian, taking great treasure together with Darius' mother and wife.]

[1] And in þe mene tyme, whils Alexander lay at Batran: þare come a prynce of Darius oste vn-tiff Alexander, & said vn-tiff hym̃, 'Wirchipfuff emperour,' quoþ he, 'I hafe a lang tyme bene a knyght of Darius, and done hym grete seruyce; and 3itt to this day I had neuer na reward' of hym. And þare-fore if it like vn-to 3owre maieste; take me teñ thowsande of 3our meñ of armes; and I hete 3ow, for to brynge to 3our hande kyng Darius, & þe maste parte of his oste.' And wheñ Alexander had herde þis, he said vn-tiff hym. 'Frende,' quoþ he, 'I thanke þe mekiff of thi faire promys. Neuer þe lesse, I late þe wite my meñ wiff no3te beleue þat þou wiff feghte agaynes thyñ oweñn peple.' In þe mene tyme a Prynce of Darius oste sent vn-till hym a letter, of whilk þis was þe tenour.

[Sidenote: A Persian prince offers to betray Darius to Alexander if he will grant him ten thousand knights. Alexander's answer.]

[2] 'To Darius, grete kyng of kynges, his lordes whilke he [3] hase ordeyned cheftaynes vnder hym Sende3 meke seruyce. Oftymes be-fore this hafe we wreteñ to 3our maieste, and now agayne we writte vn-to 3ow, & late3 3ow wite þat þe macedoynes & kyng Alexander, as wode lyouns ere enterde * oure lande3, and aff oure strenthes, as a wilde raueschande beste he hase destruyed: & oure knyghtes slayne. And oppressed we are wit so grete tribulacionns, þat we [may] na lengare suffre his mawgree, ne his malece bere. Whare-fore, mekly we be-seke 3our benyngne maiestee, þat 3e wiff drawe to 3oure mynde oure meke seruyce, and swilke socoure vouchsaffe to send' vs, þat we put off and agaynestande þe violence & þe malice of oure fore-said enemys.' Wheñ Darius had redde þis lettre, on ane he gert writte a lettir to kyng Alexander, sayand on þis wyse.

[Sidenote: Letter of one of Darius' princes to Darius beseeching help. *Leaf 17.]

[4] 'Daryus kyng of Perse and kyng of kynge3, vn-to my seruande Alexander, I say. Now late þare es commeñ tiff oure eres tythynge3: þat þou wene3 to eueñ thi littilhede tiff oure heghe magnificence. Bot Señ it es inpossible tiff a heuy asse, wit

[Sidenote: Darius to Alexander, reproaching his vain ambitions, thanking]

---

[1] Three lines with miniature A and knight's head within.
[2] Three lines space with miniature T.
[3] MS. repeats 'he' twice.
[4] Three lines space with miniature D and a man's head within, much faded.

owttenꝺ wenges, or oþer instrumenteȝ of flying, for to be lifte vp
to þe sternes, late noȝte thyñ hert be raysede to hye in pride
for þe victories þat þou hase geteñ. We hafe wele herd tell þat
4 þou hase done gentilly, and schewed grete humanytee till oure
moder, oure wyfe, & oure childre, and þarefore I late þe wele
wite þat, als lang als þou dose wele to þam̃, þou sall fynde me
naue enemy to the. And if þou do ill to þam̃ þou sall hafe þe
8 enemytee of me, and þare-fore spare þam̃ noghte, bot do to þam̃
as þe liste. For somtyme þou sall see & fele þe sentence of oure
ire lighte apoñ thi heghe pride.' When Alexander hadd redde
þis lettre he wrate hym Anoþer agayne whare-off þe tenour
12 was this.

him for his kindness to his wife and children, and enjoining him to continue his courtesy to them.

¹ 'Alexander þe soñ of Philippe & qwene Olympias to Darius
kyng of Perse we write. Pride & vayne glorie hase oure goddeȝ
all way hated; and takeȝ vengeance of dedly meñ þat takes
16 apoñ þam̃ þe name of immortalitee. Bot þou, als I wele see,
cesseeȝ noȝte ȝitt hider-to for to blasfeme in all þat þou may.
Bot of that þat þou blameȝ me for þe benygnytes that I schewed
þi moder, þi wyfe, & þi childre; þou ert moued on a lewed
20 fantasye. For I late þe wele wyte, I did it noȝte * for to be
thanked of the, ne for to hafe thi Beneuolence þare-fore. Bot
it come of a gentilnes of oure awenñ hert, fownded in vertu. Of
thee victories also whilke þe forluke of godd hase sent vs, ere
24 we na-thyng enpriddede. For we knawe wele þat oure goddis
alwaye helpes vs, whilke þou ilk a daye dispyseȝ & setteȝ at
noȝte. And this sall be þe laste letter þat I sall writte vn-to
þe. Beware if þou will, For I say the sekerly, I come to þe
28 onane.' Þis lettre gaffe Alexander to þe messangers of Darius
and many grete gifteȝ þare wit. Seyme,² he sent anoþer lettre,
till his prynceȝ & his lordeȝ, of þis tenour.

Alexander to Darius, reproaching him with assuming to himself the character of deity, spurning *Leaf 17 bk. *his proffered thanks, and leaving the decision of the matter to the gods.*

³ 'Alexander, þe soñ of Philippe & of þe quene Olympias vn-
32 to þe prynceȝ & þe lordeȝ vnder our subieccioñ in Capadoce,
In laodice, or ells whare duelland, gretyng, & gude grace.
We charge ȝou & commandeȝ ȝow straytly þat ilkañ of ȝow
ordayne vs in all þe haste þat ȝe may jᵐ nete-hydes barked, &
36 send þam̃ till Alexander, þat we and oure knyghtis may gere

Alexander writes to his Lords, ordering commissariat materials.

¹ Three lines space, miniature A, with king's head (much faded).
² MS. clearly reads *seyme*, it may be for 'seyine' (=seine).
³ Four lines space, red capital A, much smudged; a small *a* written beside it in the margin.

make vs of þaṁ clethyng, & schoees; And wit cameles þat 3e haue at Alexsander gerre cary þaṁ to þe water of Eufrates.' In þis mene tyme a prynce of Darius, Nostande by name, wrate to Darius on þis wise. 4

One of his barons writes to Darius, telling of his own defeat and the treachery of others.

¹ 'To Darius þe wirchipfull grete godd his seruande Nostand law seruyce. Me aughte no3te to sende swylk tythynge to 3our ryalle maiestee, bot grete nede gers me do it. Þare-fore be it knaweñ vn-to 3our hie lordchipe, þat twa grete prynce3 of 3ours, & 8 I, hase foghteñ wit kyng Alexander, And hyṁes falleñ þe victorie, & slayne he hase thir twa worthy prynce3, & mekitt oþer folke, and I fleed greuously wonded. And many worthi knyghtis of 3ours hase for-saken 3our lordchipe & ioyned þaṁ titt Alexander 12 oste, þe whilk he hase wirchipfully, and hase giffen grete lord-chipes of 3ours.' And wheñ Darius had redd þis lettre, he sent in haste titt Nostand, and commanded hym for titt ordeyne a grete Oste; and manfully agaynestande þe folke of Macedoyne. 16 He sent also a lettre to Porus kyng of Ynde, prayng hym to helpe hym agaynes Alexander, and Porus wrate agayne in þis manere.

Darius writes to him, order-ing him to gather a great force, and to Porus, King of India, ask-* Leaf 18. *ing help. Porus re-plies that he is at that time grievously sick, but that he will come as soon as possible with ten legions of knights.*

²' Porus, kyng of Ynde, vn-to Darius, kyng of Perse, gretyng. 20 For þou hase prayed vs to come to the in helpynge *of ³ the agaynes thyn enemys, we late the wete, þat we are redy & alwaye hase bene, for to coṁ to helpe 3ow. Bot as at þis tyme we are lettede to coṁ to 3ow, be-cause of grete seknesse þat we 24 ere stadd in, Neuer þe lesse, sekerly, it es ri3te heuy vn-titt vs, & greuous, vn-titt [vs to] here of þe grete injury þat es done vn-titt 3ow. And þarefore we late 3ow wite, þat wit-in schorte tyṁ, we satt come for to helpe 3ow wit teñ legyouns of knyghtis.' 28 Bot wheñ Rodogorius, Darius moder, herd tette þat Darius hir soñ ordayned hym for to feghte agayne wit kyng Alexander scho was ri3te sory and wrote a lettre vn-titt hym þat contened this sentence. 32

Darius' mother writes to him, coun-

'To ⁴ kyng Darius, hir moste biloued son, Rodogorius, his modir sende3 gretyng & ioy. I hafe vnderstandeñ þat 3e hafe assemblede 3our meñ, & mekitt oþer folke also, for to feghte

---

¹ Four lines with red capital T, much smudged; a small t written beside it in margin.
² Two lines with smudged capital P; a small p written in margin.

³ On leaf 17 *of þe*, on leaf 18 *of the*.
⁴ *Rodorius* scratched out. Four lines with large capital T in red; small t in mar-gin beside.

Darius' mother. Alexander's vision.

eftsones wit Alexander. Bot I late þe wite it wiłł availe þe
nathynge. For þoghe ȝe hadd' gadirde to gedir alle þe men in
þe werlde duellyng, ȝit ȝe ware vnable to agayne-stande hym.
4 For þe foreluke of godd' mayntene ȝ hym, & vphaldeȝ hym. And
þarefore dere son, it es my conseł, ȝour heghenesse of herte
ȝe lefe, & fałł sumwhate fra ȝour glory, and bese fauorable to þe
gretnes of Alexander. For better it es to forga þat at ȝe may
8 noȝte halde, and haffe in pesse þan þat at ȝe may halde, þan for
too couett ałł and be excluded' & for-ga ałł.' When Darius
redde þis lettre, he was gretly troubbled' and weped' bitterly,
command' vn-tiłł his mynde, his moder, his wyf, & his childer.
12 [1] In the mene tyme kyng Alexander remowed' his oste, and
drew nere þe cite of Susis, in þe whilke Darius was lengand'
the same tyme, so þat he myȝte see ałł þe heghe hilleȝ þat ware
abownn þe citee. Þan Alexander commanded' ałł his men, þat
16 ilkan of þam suld cutte downe a brawnche of a tree, and bere
þam furth wit þam & dryfe bi-fore þam ałłe manere of besteȝ þat
þay myȝte fynde in þe way. And when the Percyenes saw þam
fra þe heghe hilleȝ þay wondred' þam gretly. And Alexander come
20 wit his oste to þe citee of Susis and luged hym nere besyde þe
citee. And than he called' his prynnceȝ & his oþer lordeȝ and
said vn-to þam, 'Late vs,' quoþ he, 'send a messangere to kyng
Darius & bidd' hym [2] owþer & com feghte wit vs or ełłs *submyt
24 hym vn-tiłł vs.' The nexte nyghte after, Godd' Amon appered
vn-tiłł Alexander in his slepe bryngand' hym þe figurre of Mercuri
& a mantiłł, and anoþer manere of garment of Macedoyne, and
saide vn-tiłł hym. 'Alexander, son,' quoþ hee, 'euer mare when
28 þou hase nede, sałł I helpe the. And þarefore luke þou sende
noghte to Darius þat messangere þat þou spake off. For I wiłł
þat þou thi selfe clethe thee wit my figure & wende thedir þi
selfe; if ałłe it be perilous for to do, Dred þe na thynge, for
32 I sałł be thi helpe, so þat þou sałł hafe na maner of disesse.
On þe morne when Alexander rase fra slepe, he was gretly
comforthed' of his dreme & called tiłł hym his prynceȝ and
talde þam alle his dreme, and þay assentede ałłe, þat he schulde
36 wende to Darius in his propir person. And onane he called' vn-
tiłł hym ane of þe princeȝ, þe whilke highte Emulus. This

selling him
to lower
himself
somewhat
and yield
to Alex-
ander's
greatness
rather
than
lose all.

Alexander
comes to
Susa, driv-
ing before
him a
crowd of
beasts. He
decides to
send a mes-
senger to
Darius.

*Leaf 18
bk.

The Vision
of God
Amon in
the night,
who tells
Alexander
to go
alone to
Darius in
his figure.

---

[1] Four lines with large red capital I;
small i written in margin.

[2] hym inserted afterwards in left-hand
margin.

Alexander rides with a single knight to the River Grancus which was frozen over.

prynce was a wyghte man, & an hardy & wonder trewe till Alex*ander*. And þan Alex*ander* bad hy*m* lepe one a horse, and brynge w*it* hy*m* a no*þer* horse & folow hy*m*. And he didd so. And when þay come to gedir to þe wat*er* of Graunte, þat in þe langage of Perse es called Struma, þay fande it frosen ou*er*, and Alex*ander* onane chau*n*ged he[1] wede, & lefte þe foresaid prynce w*it* twa horse at þe wat*er*-syde and hy*m* selfe, w*it* þe horse þ*at* he satt apon, went ou*er* þe wat*er* apon þe Ysȝ, towarde þe citee of Susis. And his prynce besoghte hy*m* þ*at* he walde suffre hy*m* wende w*it* hy*m*, ne *per*auent*ur*e any disesse felle hy*m* by þe waye. And Alex*ander* ansuerd & sayde, 'Habyde me here,' q*uo*þ he, 'For he sall be my helpere, wham in dremeȝ I sawe appere vn-to me.' This ilke wat*er* I spake of bi-fore, all þe wynt*er* seson ilke a nyghte was frosen all ou*er*; bot tymely in þe mornynge als sone als þe warme son smate apon it, þan it dissoluede agayne, & ran wonder swiftely; þe brede of þ*at* wat*er* es þe space of a furlange. When Alex*ander* come to þe ȝate of þe citee the P*er*ciens, when þay saw hy*m*, hadd grete wonder of his figure, and wend he hadd bene a godd, and onane þay asked hy*m* what he was? And he ansuerd, and said he was a messang*er*e sent fra kyng Alex*ander* to þaire lorde Dari*us*, and be-lyfe þay broghte hy*m* til hy*m*. Dari*us*, when Alex*ander* come bi fore hy*m*, said vn-til hy*m*. 'Whethyn ert þou,' q*uo*þ he? 'I ame,' q*uo*þ Alexander, 'sent vn-to þe fra kyng Alexander to wiete where to þou taries to come till hy*m* to gyffe hy*m* batelle. Owthir come & feghte manfully w*it* thyne enemys or ells submitte þe till hym & * pay[2] hy*m* tribute.'

He will not allow his knight to fare further with him.

The river ever freezes in the night and thaws in the morning.

The Persians are amazed at him. Alexander comes to Darius and summons him to give tribute or fight.

* Leaf 19.

And Darius heard him and said, 'Art thou then the Alexander who with such madness shaped thy speech, for I see thou holdest thyself not from words as a messenger doth, but art bold as a king. Yet know that by thy words I am not frightened at all. Come dine with me this day.' And with these words, he reached out his hand to him and took him by his right, and led him into the palace. And Alexander, musing, began to say: 'A right good token hath this barbarian wrought me when he clasped my right hand and drew me into

[1] MS. reads '*he*'. We ought perhaps to substitute '*his*'.

[2] *Pay him tribute* is written at the bottom of leaf 18; between that leaf and what is now leaf 19 a whole leaf is missing.

(From the Latin) Alexander and Darius.

the palace, because, as the gods say sooth, ere long the palace shall be mine.' And going in, Darius and Alexander lay by a table, and the daintiest feast was laid out. And Darius' marshall gazed hard at Alexander face to face. And the table was wreathed in cleanest gold. But the Persians, seeing Alexander's shape, yet knew nothing of what wisdom, doughtiness, and strength lurked in this small body. The dishes and tables and seats were wrought of the finest gold. The cup-bearers bore cups in golden vessels and rarest jewels. And when a cup was handed to Alexander, he hid it in his breast. And another cup was brought to him and he did the same, and thus too with a third. And those who bore the cups, seeing this, gave the news to the Emperor Darius. And he, hearing of it, rose up, saying: 'Friend, what is this that thou doest, hiding the cups in thy breast?' And Alexander: 'In our king's feasts the guests are wont, whenever they will, to take their drinking-vessels. But, as this seemeth to you unworthy, I will give them back forthwith.' And with these words he gave them back to the cup-bearers. But the Persians who sate at the feast said each to each, 'a good custom, indeed, and one to be praised.' And some lords, too, praised this way and exalted it. But one of the Princes of Darius, called Anapolus, sitting at the feast, gazed hard at Alexander and his face. For he had seen him when, at Darius' bidding, he went into Macedonia to take tribute of Philip. He, knowing his voice and looking on his face, began to think to himself and say : 'Is this not Alexander?' And rising at once he drew near to Darius, saying: 'This messenger whom thou beholdest is Alexander, the son of Philip of Macedon.' And Alexander, seeing them with each other in talk, knew they were speaking of him and he was known. And at this he rose up from his place and leapt away from the board. And taking a blazing torch from a Persian's hand, himself mounted his palfrey, which he found ready outside Darius's palace, and fled in the swiftest flight. And the Persians seeing this, taking weapons, mounted their steeds with a mighty stir, and quickly followed after Alexander. And in the darkness of the nightfall, they began to stray, some scratched their faces by the tree-boughs, some falling into ditches. But Alexander, bearing his blazing torch in hand, fared straight

The Feast of Darius and its magnificence.

Alexander hides the golden cups in his breast. Darius chides him. Alexander answers by giving them to the cup-bearers.

Alexander is recognized by one who had been in Macedon. He tells Darius.

Alexander flees away and is pursued by the Persians. He escapes in the darkness.

48 Alexander's Flight—His harangue to his men.

Darius on his throne sees the golden image of Xerxes break, which foretokens the end of the Persian Empire.

forward. Now, Darius sate on his throne and thought of Alexander and how great his daring was. He saw a statue of gold of Xerxes the Persian king, who sate below the high-seat in the hall. And at once the statue broke and was all scattered 4 asunder. And Darius seeing this was smitten with heaviness of heart and began to weep sorely and long. And he said: 'This foretokeneth the wasting of my life, and the utter downfall of the Persian kingdom.'

Alexander swims the river, but his horse is lost.

Alexander, however, coming to 8 the river Grancus, found it swollen, and leapt athwart it. But ere he was over the stream burst its banks, and swept his horse away; with great hardship Alexander escaped and met Eumulus, his lord. And thus he went back to his army and 12 told them of Darius, how he had dealt with him, and the torch with which he had fled away.

How Alexander put Heart into his Host anew.

Alexander gathers his army.

And on the following day, he gathered his army, which told two hundred and twenty thousand of weaponed men. And 16 he went up

* * * * * * *

* Leaf 19. Alexander's harangue to his men, telling them to have trust in their own bravery.

*on a hye place & comforthed his meṅ and said͛ vn-to þaṁ: 'Þe multitude of þe p*er*cienes,' quoþ he, 'may noȝte be euend to þe multitude of þe g*r*eckes. For sewrly we are ma þan þay. And 20 if þay were ane hundreth sythes maa theṅ wee, late noȝte ȝo*ur* hertis faile ȝow þa*re*fore. For I telte ȝow a grete m*u*ltitude of flyes may do na harme tilt a fewee waspes.' And wheṅ þe Oste had herde thire wordes þay com*m*endide hy*m* halelely wit a 24 voyce.

Darius crosses the river Grancus with a mighty army and meets Alexander in battle.

[1] Thaṅ þe emp*er*our Darius removed͛ his oste, and come to þe reu*e*re of Graunt on þe nyghte, and went ou*er* on þe ysȝ, and þar he luged͛ hy*m*. The Oste of Darius was wonder grete and 28 strange. For þay had͛d͛ in þaire oste X^m cartes ordaynd͛ For þe werre, and grete m*u*ltitude of Olyfanteȝ, w*i*t towres of tree oṅ þaṁ, stuffed͛ w*i*t feghtyng meṅ. And sone aft*er* appoṅ a day thir twa kynges w*i*t þaire osteȝ mett sameṅ 32 on a faire felde, Darius w*i*t his meṅ, and Alex*a*nder w*i*t his men.

---

[1] Four lines with large cursive ornamental T of new type and decorative style.

The great battle between Darius and Alexander. 49

Than Alexander lept apoñ his horse, þat highte Buctiphalas, and rade furthe bi-fore aff his oste, and houed in þe myddes waye bi-twene þe twa ostes. And wheñ þe Percyenes saw hym,
4 þay had grete wonder of hym, and ware riʒte ferde for hym, by cause he was so vggly. Neuere-þe-lesse þay trompeď vp & went to-warde Alexander. And sone þe bateff ioyneď, & faghte to-gedir fersely, and many meñ dyeď on ayther party; þare was so
8 thikke schott of arowes, þat þe ayer was couerde, as it had bene wit a clowde. Some faghte wit swerdeʒ, sum wit speres, sum wit axes, & sum̃ wit arowes. Þe felde lay fuff of folke, sum̃ dede, sum̃ halfe-dede, & sum̃ greuously wondeď. Thay begañ
12 for to feghte at þe soñ-rysynge, and faghte to þe soñ-settyng. Bot þare dyeď many ma of þe percyenes þan þare dide of Macedoyns.

And wheñ Darius sawe his meñ faffe so thikke in þe felde, he
16 lefte þe felde, and fledď, and þe percyenes seyng that, þay fledď also. Bot þañ þaire cartes of werre rane amange þe percyens & slewe of þam̃ folke wit-owte nowmer & namely of fote-meñ. For by þat tyme it was myrke nyghte, and þay ne myʒte noʒte see
20 for tiff eschewe þam̃. Wheñ Darius come* to the foresaiď watere he fande it froseñ, and ouer he went. And wheñ he was ouer, þe oþer lordes of perse went appoñ þe ysʒ, so grete a multitude þat þay couerde þe ysʒ fra þe taa banke to þe toþer,
24 & þat a grete brede, & þañ onane þe ysʒ brake als sone als Darius was paste ouer, & aff þat ware on þe ysʒ ware perischte, ilk a moder soñ, & drownede in þe water. Þe remanaunt, wheñ þay come to the water, þay myʒte noʒte wyñ ouer. And þañ þe
28 Macedoynes come, & dange pam̃ downe. In this bateffe þare was slaen of þe percyenes cccm wit-owteñ thase þat were drownned.

Kyng Darius fledď to þe citee of Susis, & went in tiff his
32 palace, & feffe downe to þe grounde, & sigheand & wepande wit a sare hert, he saiď theis wordes: 'Allas, fuff wa es me, vnhappye wriche, þat euer I was borne, for þe ire & þe indignacioñ of heueñ es falleñ one mee. For I Darius þat lifte
36 my selueñ vp to þe sternes, Now am I broghte lawe to þe erthe. Now es Darius, þat conquerede aff þe Este nacyons, & made þam̃ subiecte & tributaries vn-tiff hym, fayne for to flee fra his enemys and submytte hym vn-to þam̃. And it ware

4

knawenn vn-to þe wreched mann, what schulde falle till hym after-wardeȝ, he schulde hafe littill thoghte of þe tyme presentt, bot one þe tyme to come solde his thoȝte be. In a poynte of a daye it falles, þat þe meke es raysede vp to þe clowddeȝ, and þe prowde es putt to noȝte.' And whenn he hade saide thir wordes, he rase vp, & satt & wrate a lettre vn-till Alexander, sayande on this wyese.

¹ 'Till his lorde Alexander, kyng of Macedoyne, Darius, kyng S of Perse, gretyng & Joy. We hafe wele vndirstanden by þat that we hafe herde of ȝowe and sene, þat ȝe hafe in ȝow grete wysedom & a hye witt: so þat noȝte allanly ȝe knawe thynges þat are present or passede, bot also thyngeȝ þat ere for to come, and þare-fore all thyngeȝ, þat ȝe doo: ȝe do it wit-owtenn any lakke or repreue. Neuer-þe-lesse hafeȝ in mynde þat riȝte as wee ware, so ware ȝe getenn & borne of a fleschly woman. And þare fore rayse noȝte ȝour herte to hye bi-cause of ȝour prowesche & ȝour doghty dedis, so þat ȝe forgete ȝour laste ende. For ofte tymes we see þat þe lattere end of a mann discordes wit þe firste. It sufficeȝ till a wer-ryoure for to gete þe victorye of his enemys, þofe all he schewe noȝte alle þe malice þat he may. Remembre ȝow of þe wirchipfull kyng ȝerses oure progenytour, þat many victoryes gatt & schane in alle prosperiteez, Be-fore he rayseḋ his hert in pride passande mesure. Alle þe wirchippe þat he hadd wonn be-fore, he loste in Ellada, þare-fore remembre ȝow, þat all þe wirchipes & þe victoryes þat ȝe hafe getenn by þe forluke of ² godd'

* * * * * * *

ye got this victory. To us then who beseech grant your mercy. Yield us our mother, our sons, and wife, and we will render vnto you the treasures we have in Aydem and Susa and Batram, the which our fathers hoarded and hid in earthen cellars. And we will give you the kingship of the Medes and Persians, that thus ye may have and keep what victory Jove the all-mighty hath granted you.'

---

¹ Four lines space with decorated miniature T.
² 'by þe forluke of godd' is written at the bottom of leaf 18 bk. Between this leaf and what is now numbered leaf 20 a whole leaf is missing; and we are plunged into the middle of quite a different letter of Darius on leaf 20, which is addressed to Porus.

Alexander's answer. The burying-places of Persia.

How the Messengers of Darius gave Alexander the Letter, and his Answer.

The messengers of Darius coming then to Alexander gave him the letter, which Alexander read soon before them all. Then one of his chieftains, called Parmerion, said to Alexander: 4 'Most mighty emperor, take all the wealth which Darius covenants unto thee, and give back to him his wife and sons.' And, hearing this, Alexander called to him the messengers of Darius, and before all spoke thus, saying: 'Tell ye to your 8 emperor we wonder first that he misdeemed his mother, wife, and sons to be betrayed by our hands. If he be overcome, bid him not promise us a reward. If he bow himself to our yoke, all his honours and the majesty of God shall be laid 12 bare to our sway. If he be not overcome, let him do us battle once again.' This said, he gave them rich gifts and sent them forth away. Then he bade the soldiers take up and gather the bodies of the dead and bury them in graves: 16 and he bade them heal those that were wounded.

A noble of Alexander counsels him to accept these terms. But he will not. But bids Darius either submit himself or do battle.

He orders the dead to be buried.

How Alexander encamped by the stream Grancus.

Then he encamped with his host by the stream of Grancus, and wintered there some days. And there he offered up victims to the gods. And about the river there were palaces, 20 and they were the fairest, raised up with greatest skill, and Xerxes the King of the Persians had built them. Alexander, seeing them, bade them be burned. And soon after this, stirred by ruth, he gave word none should dare touch them. 24 And there too was a most fair and very wide field in which the Kings and Deemsters of Persia were of old buried. And digging into this field the Macedonians found in the graves gemmed vases. And there they found the grave of Ninus the 28 King of Assyria and Persia, which was hollowed out of a single amethyst, and engraven on the outside with palm-leaves and sundry kinds of birds. And so bright was the amethyst that even from the outside the man's body appeared whole. 32 And in this place was a narrow and evil tower on which stood many men, some with cut legs, some with broken thighs, some with torn hands, and some blinded. They hearing

He encamps with his army by the Grancus and sacrifices. Alexander commands the palaces to be burnt. The burying-place of the Kings and Judges of Persia, wherein treasure is found. The grave of Ninus and its wonders. The Tower of the Maimed Men.

Darius writes to Porus; the evil plot.

They beseech mercy of Alexander, who restores them to their own.

the noise of the armed men cried out to Alexander, who hearing their cries, bade them be taken thence. And seeing them was struck with ruth and wept, and bade each one be given ten thousand drachmas, and be restored every one to his own.

For they were nobles dispossessed by Darius.

For Darius kept them in prison, since they were of noble birth, and awarded all their possessions to his thralls. In the meantime the messengers from Alexander to Darius told all that Alexander had said. And Darius hearing this began to get ready for the fight. And he wrote another letter to Porus King of India, which runneth as follows:—

Darius' letter to Porus, King of India. He asks him again for help against Alexander, since he has resolved to fight to the very death. For it is better to die in the field than to see the end of his kingdom and people.

The Letter sent by Darius to Porus King of India.

'Darius King of the Persians to Porus King of Our Indians joy. We asked but lately of you, and again we ask you to come and help against those who strive to overthrow our palace. We know well also that the like harm will light on you. For this Alexander, who fighteth thus, hath an unquenchable and wild soul, which like a lion ceaseth not, and is like the sea when stirred by mighty winds. Furthermore, unwillingly though it be, we have gathered numberless races, and we have taken our counsel to fight with him to the very death.

* *Leaf 20.*

Darius writes to Porus succour him for the sake of himself, his dynasty, and his people, promising him help and the spoils of Alexander. He warns him that as Alexander had done to him, so would be done to Porus.

* better vs es for to dy manly in þe felde þan for to see þe mescheffe of oure pople & þe dissolacioñ of oure rewme. Whare-fore, hafand reward and compassioñ of oure disesse, we be-seke ȝow, þat ȝe late oure prayeres satteľl in ȝour hert, & helpe for to succour vs now at oure nede, hafand in ȝoure mynde þe grete noblaye of oure progenytours. And I seure ȝow þat [I sall] giffe ilke a fote-man þat comeȝ wit ȝow, thre peceȝ of golde, And ilke a horse-mañ, fyve peceȝ of golde, And also mete & drynke ynoghe to ȝow & all ȝour meñ. And whare so ȝe lugge ȝow, we schalľe fynde ȝow a hundreth & fourscore tentes curyously wroghte. And also we schalľ gyffe ȝow Alexander horse Buktyphalas, and alľe appairailľ, & þe araye þat langes till Alexander hallely schalľ be ȝours and also all þe spoylle of his folke sall be dalte amangeȝ ȝoure folke. Where-fore we beseke ȝow þat also soñ als this

The slaying of Darius. 53

lettre comme3 to 3ow, 3e haste 3ow tiƚƚ vs in aƚƚ þat 3e may.
For wite 3e wele for certayne, that ri3te als he done tiƚƚ
vs, so he purpose hym in tyme commynge for to do to 3owe.'

4 ¹In the men tyme, certane meñ of Darius went fra hym
& come tiƚƚ Alexander, & talde hym, þat Darius purposede *Alexander*
hym for to feghte wit hym eftesones, and had sent tiƚƚ Porus, *hearing of this*
kyng of Inde, for to come in grete haste, for to helpe hym. *through treachery*
8 Wheñ Alexander herd þis, be-lyfe he remowed' his Oste to *marches*
ward' Darius, thynkand in his herte þat he wolde on na wyse *against Darius.*
take apoñ hym þe name of Emperour be-fore he hadd' wonñ
Darius and his rewme one werre. And when Darius herde
12 of þe commyng of Alexander, he dredd' hym gretly & þe
percyenes also. Bot þare was two prynce3 of Darius, of þe *Two nobles*
whilke þe tane highte Bisso & þe toþer Ariobarsantes, thir *of Darius conspire to*
twa wheñ þair² herd' of þe comyng of Alexander, conspyred' *slay him that they*
16 to-gedir for to slaa þaire lord' Darius, supposyng for tiƚƚ hafe *may have*
a grete thanke of Alexander, and a gret reward' for þaire dede. *reward of Alexander.*
And ayther of þam̃ ware sworne tiƚƚ oþer. And thañ thay
went to þe kynges palace, and come intiƚƚ his chamber wit
20 draweñ swerdes in þaire hande3, and fand Darius bi hym
ane. And wheñ Darius saw that, he trowed' wele þat þay
wolde sla hym̃, And said vn-to þam̃: 'Dere frende3, hedir *Darius see-*
to warde3 hafe I called 3ow my seruaunde3, bot now I call 3ow *ing them begs for*
24 my lordes. What ayles 3ow at me þat 3e wiƚƚ sla me? Haes *mercy, and foretells*
Alexander cheriste þe macedoynes mare þañ I hafe done 3ow? *the future*
Hafe I no3te sorow & disese ynoghe of enemyse wit-owtteñ? *vengeance of Alex-*
Bot if 3e conspire agaynes me for to sla me wit owtteñ gilt, *ander. But*
28 I say for sothe, & 3e sla me *thus preuelye, And Alexander *they slay him.*
may gete 3ow, he wiƚƚ take mare crueƚƚ vengeance one 3ow, theñ *Leaf 20*
on any theues. For sothely it es na comforthe ne lykyng tiƚƚ *bk.*
ane Emperour to fynd an oþer Emperour murthered wit his aweñ
32 meñ.' Bot þay were na-thynge stirrede to petee, ne tendernesse,
ne mercy, thurgh his worde3, Bot went tiƚƚ hym and wit grete
cruelnesse smate hym, & al-to magle hym, and went faste þaire
waye, & lefte hym for dede.
36 ³And wheñ Alexander herd' teƚƚ þat Darius was slayne he *Alexander hearing of*

---

¹ Five lines space with a capital I.
² MS. þair for þay, just as on leaf 34, l. 23. Cf. Icelandic þeir. There is no mis-
take here, as the two spellings vary þaire and þair on leaves 34, 54.
³ Four lines with red capital A.

54 Alexander comes to Darius.

his death enters Susa without resistance.

went ouer þe water of Graunt, and all his Oste wit hym, and come to þe cetee of Susis. And alsone als þe percyenes saw hym, Thay Opened þe ʒates of þe citee, & rescheyued hyṁ wit grete wirchipe. And wheñ þe prynceʒ þat slewe Darius wiste 4

The conspirators hide themselves.

þat Alexander was comeñ iñ-to þe citee þay went & helde þaṁ in hidils ay till þay myʒte gete knaweynge of Alexander will,

Alexander goes to the room where Darius lies dying.

as towchand þat that þay hadd done to Darius. Alexander þañ went in-to þe kynges Palace, and as he went þare-in he 8 merueyled hym gretly of þe biggyng þare-off. For Cirus þe kyng of Perse gert bigg it ryally. And the pament þareoffe was made of stanes of dyuerse colours, & þe walles all enueround wit fyne golde & precyous stanes & sternes lyke to þe firmament, 12 and pelers of golde þat bare vp þe werke. Wheñ Alexander saw all this curious werke, he meruailed hym gretly. And thañ he went to þe chambre þare Darius laye halfe dede.

Alexander has pity on Darius and promises him all he once had if he will but live.

And alsone als he saw hyṁ he hadd grete rewthe & compassioñ 16 of hym, and he tuke off his aweññ mantill & couerd [hym] þare-wit, & went and graped his wondes and wepid for hym riʒt tenderly, & said un-til hym. 'Rise vp, sir Darius,' quoþ he, '& be of gude comforthe. And als frely as euer þou reioysede thyñ 20 Empire, so mot þou ʒitt do, And be als myghty, & als gloryouse als euer þou was. I swere the here by oure myʒty goddes & by

Alexander says he would rather give his own Empire to Darius than behold him dead.

þe faythe in my body, þat here I resigne vn-to the all thyñ empyre, desyrand souerayngly for to hafe þe lyfe of the, as þe 24 soñ of ¹ þe Fader, For sekerly it es vnfittand & unsemly till ane émperour for to be reioysede of an oþer emperours mescheffe & disesse, wheñ fortune hase forsakeñ hym. Telle me, sir, what þay are þat hase thus fareñ wit the, and I sewre þe als I am 28 trew mañ I sall venge the to þe uttereste.' And * wheñ

* Leaf 21.

Darius embraces Alexander.

Alexander had said this & mekill mare, Sare wepand Darius putt furthe his hande, and layde his arme abowte Alexander nekke, and kyssed his breste, his nekke, & his hande, & saide 32

Darius' speech to Alexander on the worthlessness and unsteadfastness of

thir wordeʒ, thare that here folowes. ² 'A, dere soñ Alexander,' quoþ he, 'als thi heghe witt knawes wele, all this werlde es corupt and sett in malice. For þe souerayne forluke of godd, all thyngeʒ knawande fra þe begynnyng, and hafand felyng 36 of þe wirkyngeʒ for to come, made mañ in that wyse, at þe

---

¹ þe is written in above the line in the MS.

² Four lines miniature with ornamented red capital A.

The dying speech of Darius. 55

begynnynge, þat nathyng es in hym stable ne faste. So þat all all earthly
thynge3 þat ere passande & werldely, fra þat he faile of things,
gouernance, tournes alsoñ till hym in contrarye. For if godd'
4 hadd' ordeyned' all thynge3 esy to mañ and alwaye wit-owtteñ
chaungynge sent hym prosperitee, mañ schulde be lyftede vp
so hie in pryde & in vayne glorye, þat he solde no3te arett alle
his wele-fare & his welthe vn-to godd, bot till his awenñ desert
8 & his awenñ vertu. And so schulde meñ gaa fra þaire makare.
On þe toþer syde if þe heghe wyssedoñ of godd' hadd' made
þe werlde oñ þat wyse þat all illes and infelicytes fell apoñ mañ
wit-owtten any maner of gudenesse, so many freletese sulde folow
12 þe kynde of mañ, þat we schulde all be draweñ in-to þe gilder
of disparacioñ, so þat we solde hafe na triste in þe gudnes of
godd. And þarefore grete godd' wolde so wisely skifte all
thynges, þat, wheñ a mañ full of felicitee, thurgh his heghe
16 pride will no3te knawe his makere, Fra þe heghte of pride in-to
þe pitte of mekenes & lawnes he moñ be plungede. So þat he
þat thurgh pride & felicite forgatt his godd, thurgh fallynge in
wrechidnesse & disesse hafe mynde of his godd. Reghte als þou with par-
20 may see bi me, my dere soñ Alexander, þat was raysede vp so ticular
hye in pryde & vayne glorye, thurgh reches & prosperitee þat to him-
felle vn-to me, þat I trowed no3te þat I was goddes creature self.
bot goddes Felawe. And þañ, thurgh blyndeness of pride,
24 I couthe no3te see that, þat now, thurgh scharpenesse of mekenes
and mescheffe, I see clerely & knawes. Bot if it happeñ þat any On the pre-
mañ be vmbilappede wit grete infilicitee, so þat he, despairand' sumption
of þe grace of godd, supposse na remedy, ne nane lukes eftere ; who have
28 *þañ oure lorde godd' rayse3 hym vp to þe heghte of prosperitee, *Leaf 21
so þat þañ he, þat bi-cause of wrechidnes & infilicitee, my3te great
no3te see godd' ne knawe hym, thurgh felicite & prosperitee wealth.
knawes þat he, þat may bryng a mañ to lawe state, may rayse
32 a mañ till heghe degree. And he þat may rayse a mañ till On the
heghe degree, may putt hym to lawnesse agayne, wheñ hym lyst, God to put
and þare-fore, soñ, late no3te thy hert ryse to hye in pride, for þe down the
victoryes þat godd' hase sent the, if all þou may do now whate þe from their
36 list ri3t as [¹ þou] were a godd. Bot alway thynke on thy laste seats, and
ende. For þou ert a dedly mañ, and ilk a day if þou be-halde them of
graythely þou may see thy dedd' bi-fore thyñ eghne. Consedirs low degree.

¹ þou may have been left out by the scribe beginning a new line.

56 *Darius dies. His burial.*

> þou noȝte how oure lyffe may be lykkened to þe werke of Eranes, þat so sotelly makes þaire webbes? Bot alsoñ als a little blaste of wynde puffes apoñ þam̃, þay breke, & falles to grownde. Behalde & see how glorius I was ȝisterday & how wrechede I am̃ to-day, & how law I am broghte. I was lorde nerehande of all þe werlde, & now I hafe na power of myñ aweñ selfe. Now I be-seke the, soñ, þat þou wiħ bery me wit thy benynge handes. And suffre for to come to myñ exequise bathe þe Macedoynes and þe persyenes. And fra this tyme forwardeȝ, þe empire of Macedoyne & þe empire of perse be bathe ane. Haffe recomend vn-to the my Moder Rodogoñ, & trete hir wirchipfully as thyñ aweñ Moder. And I be-seke þe also, þat þou be Mercyable to my wyfe. And if ¹it be lykynge to þe, take Rosañ my dogheter to thi wyfe. For semely it es, þat ȝe be ioynede to-geder þat er comeñ of so wirchipfuħ progenitours, For þou of kyng Philippe, and scho of kyng Darius. And of ȝow twa may a wirchipfuħ & a noble fruyte sprynge.' And riȝte as he had saide thir wordeȝ he swelt in Alexander armes. Kyng Alexander, þañ, after þe custom̃ was for to bery emperours, gert araye Darius body als ryally as he couthe. And wit aħ þe solempnyte and wirchipe þat myghte be done, he helped hym selfe for to bere þe bere, sare wepande, and gert þe Macedoynes & þe Percyenes gaa bi-fore þe bere. The persyenes also weped wonder faste, noȝte allanly for þe dede of Darius, bot for petee of þaire hertis, þat þay saw Alexander wepe so enterely. And wheñ Darius was beried Alexander went agayne to þe palace.

> ² And one þe morne Alexander went and sett hym in a trone aħ of golde & precyous stanes, the whilke Cyrus sumtyme gert *make þat was kynge of Perse. And the Macedoynes and þe Persyenes sett apoñ his hede a coroune þat was Darius, þe whilke was so precious, þat meñ knewe nane like it in na lande. For aħ þe palace schane thurgh bryghtness of þe precyous stanes, þat were sett þare-in. And þe trone was aħ of golde, & of precious stanes, & of þe sege þare-offe was vii seueñ ³ cubeteȝ heghe fra þe grounde, and a grece of seueñ greeȝ was made

4

8

12

16

20

24

28

32

36

Sidenotes: Darius asks burial of Alexander, and that both peoples should come thereto. And wills thereto that both empires be one. He bids him be merciful to his widow, and take his daughter Roxana to wife. He dies.
Alexander buries Darius in royal state. He bears the bier himself. The Macedonians and the Persians go before it. Alexander seats himself on the
*Leaf 22.
throne of Cyrus, and is crowned with the crown of Darius.
The throne of seven steps with its mystic meanings inwrought.

---

¹ *it* written in above by the scribe.
² Two lines space with miniature A.
³ 'vii' occurs at the end of one line, and '*seven*' at the beginning of the next.

The throne of seven steps. 57

þare-to, whare-by kynges ascended þare-to. And thir gree3 were made wonder craftyly & curyously. The firste gree was of ane amatist. The seconde gree was of a Smaragd. The thredd 4 gree was of a Topa3. The ferthe gree was of a granat. The fifte was of ane adamand. The sext was of fyñ golde. And the seuennt was of clay. And thay ware no3t [1][wit-o]wtteñ grete cause3 ordeyned one þis wyse.

8 For þe first gree w[as a]ne [2] amatist, for amange all oþer stanes it hase this vertu, that it represses & halde3 donne þe fumositee of wyne & þe myghte þare-offe, & suffers no3te a mañ þat bere it [3] oñ hym be troubbled in his witt ne in his mynde 12 thurgh drownkeness. And, on þe same wise, solde ilke a kyng be of perfite witt & mynde, & thurgh nane occasioñ do na mysse. The secund gree was of a Smaragd, þe whilke clarifye3 & kepe3 þe sighte of hym þat beres [it] apoñ hym, and so schulde 16 a kynge hafe clere sighte of his hert, wysely for to see & discerne that þat es spedfull & profitable bathe for hym selfe & for þe comoñ profit. The thirdd gree was of a Topa3, þe whilke es so clere, þat & a mañ bi-halde hym selfe þare-in, it sall seme 20 till hym, as his hede ware tournede downwarde3, and his fete vpwarde3; And it be-takenes þat a kyng schulde alway take hede till his laste ende. The ferthe gree was of a Granat whilk passe3 all manere of precious stanes in reedness: & betakens 24 þat a kyng suld be schamfull for till consent till any thynge þat es vnlefull. The fifte was of ane Adamande. Þe Adamande es so harde þat it may no3te be brokeñ nowþer with yreñ ne wit stane, bot if it firste be enoynted wit gayte blode. On þe same 28 wyse a kyng suld be of so grete constance & sadnesse þat, for na prayere, ne for na worldely gude, he solde no3te bewgh fra þe way of ryght-wisnesse. The sexte gree was of fyne gold: for ri3te as gold passe3 all maner of metalle in bewtee, & in pre- 32 cioustee; ri3te so a kyng awe to be [4] preferred before oþer meñ & gouernours of þam. * Þe seuent was of Clay, till þat entent þat a mañ þat es raysed vp to þe dingnyte of a kyng sulde alway vmbythynk hym þat he was made of erthe, & at þe laste

*The first step of amethyst, that a king be not drunken but walk soberly and steadfastly. The second of emerald, that a king see well those things which belong to his rank. The third of topaz, which reminds him of his latter end, showing him upside down. The fourth of garnet, which makes him shame to do unlawfully. The fifth of diamond, which means that a king should be righteous. The sixth of gold, to show the greatness of kings. * Leaf 22 bk. The seventh of clay, to*

---

[1] Piece gone in MS. Reads —*wtten*. The beginning of a *w* occurs before the hole, and the latter half of an *o* after it— so it must clearly be read '*witowtten*'.

[2] MS. *w* and a gap follows as above;

[3] read, of course, '*was a-*'.

[3] *it* written in above line.

[4] MS. has in another hand in bottom of margin '*preferred before*' written over again.

58 Alexander's letter to all countries.

show him above all he is but dust and deathly.

to þe erthe he saíd agayne. When Alexander was sett apon this trone, coronnde wit his diademe, & þe Macedoynes & þe persenes standyng abowte hym: be-fore þam aíte he gert write a lettre tiíl aíl cuntreeȝ, þat was of this tenour. 4

Alexander's letter to all lands—announcing that he sits on the throne of Darius. He orders that all things should be as they were before.

[1] 'Alexander the son of godd Amon & qwene Olympias kyng of kynges & lorde of lordes, tiíl aíte Dukes, Prynceȝ, Erles, Baronns, maisters, & tiíl aíl þe folkeȝ of Perse: ioy & grace. Sen it es plesynge to godd, þat I sitt one þe trone of Darius, & be 8 lorde of þe persyenes, grete cause I hafe for to be reioyist gretely þare-offe, ne were it for þe gret multitude of folke þat ere slayne. Bot sen it so es þat godd hase ordeynede me to be ȝour lorde,[2] and ȝour gouernour, þare-fore we commande ȝow þat in 12 ilke a citee, thurghowte þe lordchipe of Perse, ȝe ordeyne prynceȝ and gouernours as þare was in Darius tyme, to þe whilke we commande ȝow þat ȝe be obeyande as ȝe before-tymes hafe bene, and that þay do riȝte tiíl ilke a man at þaire powere. 16

He commands security of tenure to all, and free trade between Hellas and all Persia.

Also it es oure wiíl and oure commandement, þat ilke a man welde & reioyse paysabily his landes and his possessiouns. We commande alsoo, þat fra this lande of perse vn-tiíl Ellada, & fra thethyn to Macedoyne, be redy way & open so þat ilke a man 20 þat wiíl may passe bathe in and owte, wit merchandyse or any oþer erandes þat þay hafe at do, and Joy & pese be vn-to ȝowe.'

Alexander promises a fitting reward to them that slew Darius.

[3] Þan gert Alexander aíl men be stiíl, and said one this wyse: 'Whilke of ȝow so slew myn enemy Darius; comeȝ forthe be-for 24 me, and I shaíl giffe ȝow worthy mede, & conable wirchipe do þam, I swere bi oure goddeȝ þat ere Almyȝty, & bi my moste biloved moder Olympias, þat I saíl gyffe þam worthy mede.' When Alexander had saide thir wordes þe persyenes wepede 28 wonderly sare. And than þe twa man-morthireres Bisso and Aryobarȝantes come bi-fore Alexander, and sayde vn-tiíl hym: 'Wirchipfuíl emperour,' quoþ þay, 'we ere thase þat slew Darius thyne enemy wit oure Awenn hende.' And when 32 Alexander saw þam, he bade his knyghtes belyfe ga & take þam, & bynde* þam, & lede þam to Darius grafe, & þare smyte of þaire heuedes. And than þay ansuerd, & saide vn-tiíl Alexander: 'A, A, wirchipfuíl emperour,' quoþ þay, 36

They declare themselves.

* Leaf 23.
Alexander bids them be taken

---

[1] Ten lines blank space for a miniature.
[2] In MS. between 'be ȝour lorde' and and ȝour gouernour' is written '& lorde of þe persyenes', but it has been erased by the scribe.
[3] Three lines space with red capital Þ.

He punishes the murderers of Darius. 59

'swore þou noȝte tiłł vs, bi oure goddeȝ þat ere Almyȝty,   *and be-*
& bi þe hele of thi moder Olympias, þat þou solde gerre do vs   *headed.*
na harme, bot þat þou solde giff vs a worthi reward.' And   *They plead his own*
4 Alexander saide agayne vn-to þam͂: ' So aughte me wele for to   *words.*
swere, for to gette knawyng of þe slaers of Darius. For I solde   *But it avails them*
neuer hafe getyn͂ knawyng þare-offe had I noȝte sworne so. And   *nought.*
ȝitt I sałł safe myn͂ athe wele ynoghe. For it was al-way myn͂
8 entent, þat if I myȝte wete what þay ware, þay solde hafe
swilke a rewarde. For þay þat slaes þaire awenn͂ lorde it es
a taken͂ þat þay witt hafe na conscience to sla anoþer man͂.' And
when þe perseyenes herde this þay by-gan͂ to prayse Alexander
12 & to commende hym and blysse hym as he had bene a godd.
Þan͂ kyng Alexander gert hede tha twa homycydes. And ałł   *They are*
þe rewme he sett in gouernance of certayne lordes. Amanges   *slain. Alexander*
oþer þare was ane alde lorde was eme to Darius, þe whilke   *makes Darius'*
16 highte Climitus, þat was gretly luffede wit þe persyenes; And   *uncle*
Alexander at þe request of ałł the persyenes ordeyned hym for to   *governor of the*
be chefe gouernour vnder hym of ałł perse. And one þe morne   *Persians.*
Alexander sett hym in his trone, wit his coroun͂ on his hede,
20 and efter þe biddynng of Darius he commande to brynge bi-fore   *Alexander*
hym Rosan͂, Darius doghter, wit a coroun͂ on͂ hir hede, sett futt   *weds Roxana,*
of precious stanes. And þare, as þe maner was of þe persyenes,   *Darius' daughter.*
he tuke hir to his wyfe, and made hir to sitt wit hym in his
24 trone & command ałł men͂ to wirchipe hir als quene. And
þan͂ þe persyenes were wonderly glade, & onane þay broȝte
þaire goddeȝ bi-fore Alexander, and bi-gan͂ to wirchipe hym, &   *The Per-*
loue hym riȝte als he hade bene a godd, and said vn-till hym,   *sians worship Alex-*
28 hallely wit a voyce, ' þou thi selfe es a godd, For that þat es   *ander as a god.*
plesande tiłł oure goddes alway þou dose.' And when͂ Alex-
ander saw this, he was gretly troubled & riȝte ferde & said
vn-to þam : ' Wirchipfułł sirs,' quoþ he, ' I pray ȝow þat ȝe   *He chides*
32 wirchipe me noȝte as a godd, for sothely I am as ȝe are, a   *them for it.*
corupteble & a dedly man͂, and in me þare es na parcełł of the
godhede. And þarefore, I beseke ȝow, cesseȝ of this wirchipe
þat ȝe do me.'
36   [1] Þan gert Alexander write a lettre tiłł Olympias his moder &   *Alexander*
tiłł Arestotle his maister, makand mencyon͂ of ałł þe bataylłs &   *writes to his mother*
þe disesseȝ þat he hadd suffred in Perse, and of þe grete reches   *and to Aristotle.*

[1] Five lines with large capital Þ.

The march against Porus.

He commands an eight days' feast for the marriage.
*Leaf 23 bk.

þat he fande þare, of þe whilke he & aƚƚ his meñ ware made riche. And also he wrate vn-to þam̃,* þat þay scholde make grete solempnytee lastyng aghte dayes be-cause of þe weddynge of Alexander & Rosañ Darius doghter. And so did' Alexander, 4 in Perse, wit þe maceydoynes & þe persyenes, many a daye.

Alexander marches against Porus of India, through waste country, with great rivers and caverns. The Macedonians murmur at the continued wars and marches, and against Alexander's ambition. They fain would leave him.

[1] Afftẽr this kyng Alexander sembled' a grete Oste, bathe of macedoyns & of persyenes, and went towarde Inde for to werre apoñ Porus, kyng of Inde, þe whilke ordeynede hym for to 8 come & helpe kyng Darius. And, when Alexander was entered in-tiƚƚ Inde, he went thurgh wildernes & waste cuntree, whare in ware grete reuers and many grete caues & cauernes. And þan Alexander & his meñ wex wery, & irkede riʒte sare. And 12 þe pryncez of macedoyne & of grece murmourede amangeʒ þam̃ gretly, & saide ilkañ tiƚƚ oþer: 'It myʒte hafe sufficed' tiƚƚ vs, þat we hafe ouer-sett kyng Darius, & conqerred' þe kyngdom̃ of Perse. Where-be seke we forthire in-tiƚƚ Inde, þe whilke es 16 fuƚƚ of wilde besteʒ, and leues oure awenñ landeʒ. Ne þis Alexander nane oþer thyngeʒ desyreʒ, .bot for to wende abowte and thurgh werre to brynge aƚƚ þe worlde vndere his subieccion. For werre & debate unrescheʒ his body so fer furth þat, and he 20 ristede any lange tyme witowteñ werre, riʒte als it were for defaute of mete he schulde faile & dye. Leue we hym þarefore, and turne we agayne vn-tiƚƚ oure awenñ cuntree, and late hym wende furthe wit the persyenes, if he wiƚƚ.' When 24

King Alexander divides the Macedonians and the Persians.

Alexander herde þis, he garte aƚƚ þe Oste habide, and he went and stodde in ane heghe place amangeʒ þam̃, & sayde one this wise: 'Departis ʒow in twaa, so þat þe persyenes be by þam̃-selfe and þe Macedoynes and þe grekes bi þam̃-selfe.' 28

Alexander rebukes the Greeks that they would leave him alone with rebellious Persians. He reminds them of what he has done

And wheñ þay hadd' so done, Alexander saide to þe Macedoynes and þe grekes: 'A A, myne owenñ dere knyghtis,' quoþ he, 'wele [ʒe] knawe þat thir persyenes, vn-to þis day, hase bene contrary & rebeƚƚes vn-to ʒow & to me, and ʒe wiƚƚ now lefe me 32 here wit þam̃, and tourne agayne to ʒour awenñ cuntree. Wele ʒe wate, þat when ʒour hertes were troubblede, & fered', for þe wordes þat ware conteneď in Darius lettres, I thrugh my speche & my conseƚƚ comforthed' ʒour hertis. And afterwarde, when we 36 come in-to þe felde agaynes oure enemys, I went bi-fore ʒow aƚƚ.

---

[1] Four lines with miniature A with a barrel drawn within on its side, and a tree springing from it. Small *a* written in the margin beside it.

Alexander exhorts his mutinous army. 61

And I by myñ ane was þe firste mañ þat entrede þe batayle. *for them,*
And ȝitt more-ouer, as ȝe wele wate, I tuke apoñ me for to be *and what they will*
ȝoure allere messangere vn-to kynge Darius. And þare, for *do to-gether.*
4 ȝow, I putt my selfe in many grete *perilℓs. And þarefore, **Leaf 24.*
witteȝ wele for certayne, þat, riȝte as hedirtowardeȝ, we hafe *But what-*
ouercomeñ oure enemys and hade þe better of þam̄, riȝte so fro *ever they do, he will*
heþein-forwardeȝ, thurgh þe helpe of oure goddeȝ we saℓℓ ouer- *go on-wards.*
8 come oure enemys, & hafe þe victorye of þam̄. And þare-fore I
say ȝow forsothe, þat, aℓℓ if ȝe will tourne agayne to grece &
macedoyne, I saℓℓ noȝte tourne agayne oñ na wyse, þat ȝe may
knawe þat, wit-owtteñ gouernance of a kynge, nane Oste may
12 wynne na wirchipe.' Wheñ Alexander had said' þus, aℓℓ þe
prynceȝ of Macedoyne and of þe grekes schamede gretely, and *They be-*
askede mercy & forgifnesse, sayande one this wyse: 'Moste *come ashamed of*
wirchipfuℓℓ emperour, oure lyfe lyes hallely in ȝour hande. *themselves and beg for*
16 Whedir so euer ȝe wiℓℓ goo we wiℓℓ gladly felowe ȝour hye *forgive-*
maiestee; þofe we schulde aℓℓ dye for ȝow oñ a daye, we saℓℓ *ness.*
folow ȝow & neuer lefe ȝow.' And þañ þay remowed fra þeinne [1] *They con-*
and come in-tiℓℓ a cuntree of Inde þat es called Phisiaceñ, in þe *tinue their march and*
20 laste ende of July. And þare mette hym þe embassatours of *meet the ambas-*
Porus kyng of Inde, and broghte hym lettres fra Porus, þat said *sadors of*
oñ this wyse. *Porus.*

[2] 'Porus kyng of Inde: vn-to þe theeffe Alexander, þat thurgh *Porus'*
24 thifte & robbery many citeeȝ wynneȝ, biddyng we send'. Señ *letter to Alexander.*
þou ert dedely: wharto weneȝ þou þat þou ert of powere to
agaynstande godd' þat es vn-dedely. A grete fole, me thynke,
þou ert þat hase eghne, and cane nott see. Trowes þou we be lyke
28 vn-to þe percyenes þat þou hase made subiecteȝ vn-to the? Þou *He tells*
hase foughteñ hedir-towarde wit softe meñ & cowardeȝ, & for *him of the superiority*
þou hase ouercomeñ þam̄, þou weneȝ, þat thi littillness saℓℓ *of the Indians to*
brynge oure hye maiestee vnder thi subieccion; þe whilke es *the Per-sians.*
32 vnpossyble for to bee, bot if goddeȝ submytt þam̄ vn-to meñ,
and þe erthe be euen lyke to þe heueñ. I late the wiete, þat I *The gods*
may noȝte be ouercommeñ for noȝte allanly meñ bot also goddeȝ *also fight for India.*
doeeȝ seruyce to my name. Wate þou noȝte wele, þat ane *The Indians*
36 Dynise, þe fader of Bachus, come in-tiℓℓ Inde, wit a grete Oste *overcame*
for to feghte, bot onane he tournede þe bakke & fledd', for he *Dionysius.*

---
[1] MS. reads þeiñe.
[2] Four lines space for miniature P. P written in the page beside it.

62 Alexander comforts his knights. His letter to Porus.

He advises him to go back again to Macedonia.

was noȝte of powere to agaynstande þe vertu of men of Inde. And þarefore, or any schame or mischeffe com to þe; we consell the & commandeȝ the, þat in all þe haste þat þou may, þou tourne hame agayne to thyne awen lande. Fore wele þou 4

Before Xerxes' time the Macedonians gave tribute to India, but the Indians recked

knawes, þat, bi-fore ȝerses was kynge of Perse, þe macedoynes gaffe tribute till Inde. Bot, by-cause þat þaire lande es barayne & vnprofitable, & na thyngeȝ þer-in plesande till a kynge: þe men of Inde sett noȝte þare-by. For ilke a man, 8 desyres mare a large lande & a plenteuous: þan *a strayte lande

* Leaf 24 bk.

& a barayne. And þarefore, ȝitt the thirde tourne, I comaunde the that þou tourne hame to thyne awenn lande. And neuer, in thi lyfe, couette to hafe Lordschipe þare þou may nane gete.' 12

naught of Macedonia, for it was a barren and little land.

¹ When þis lettre was comen till Alexander, he gerte rede it be-fore all men. And when his knyghtis hadd herde þe tenour of þis lettre, þay were trublede. And Alexander sayde vn-to þam: 'My wirchippfull knyghtis,' quoþ he, 'late noȝte ȝour 16 hertis be trublede ne fered' for Porus lettre. Hafe ȝe noȝte in mynde, wit how grete pride Darius wrate vn-till vs dyuerse tymes? I say ȝow sotheley þat all þe folke of thyse Este parties hase þaire hertis & þaire wittis lyke vn-to þe bestes þat þay 20 duelle wit-all, þat es at say, Tygres, Pardes, & oþer wilde bestis, whilke full selden ere slaenn of men, and þare-fore þay triste all in þaire strengthe.' And when Alexander hade said thir wordes, he garte writte a lettre vn-to Porus kynge of Inde 24 whare-of this was the tenour.

Alexander's knights are troubled at the letter.

He tells them Eastern folks are like wild beasts trusting but in their strength.

Alexander's letter to Porus. Porus' words have stirred on the Greeks to win so great and fruitful a land as India, as well as to crush Porus' pride. For Porus is but a

² 'Kyng of kynges and lorde of lordes, Alexander þe son of godd' Amon & þe quene Olympias, vn-to Porus we sende. Þou hase scharpede oure wittes, & gyffen vs hardynesse for to feghte 28 agaynes þe, whare þou says þat macedoyne es bot a littill lande & barayne of all thyng þat gude es. And Inde, þou says, es large, & plenteuous of all gudeȝ & reches. And þare-fore we sall enforce vs to feghte wit the at all oure myghte, for to con- 32 quere thi landeȝ þat, þou sais, es so full of reches. And, for þou haldeȝ vs pouer, & of na reputacion, þare-fore we desire for to ascende to þe heghte of thi majestie. And also þare þou says, þat noȝte allanly vn-to men, bot also vn-to goddeȝ þou erte 36 emperour, I sall come to the, for to feght wit þe, as wit an

---

¹ Three lines with miniature W and small w written alongside in the margin.
² Eleven lines blank space without either miniature or small letter at side.

The battle with Porus' army. 63

haytheñ mañ fuɫɫ of Pompe & pride and vayne glory, & noȝte *heathen man full of pride.*
as wit a goddˀ. For aɫɫ þe werlde may noȝte ¹agaynstandˀ þe
wrethe of a goddˀ. Þer-fore, señ þe elementis of this aere, þat *He threatens him with the wrath of the gods.*
4 es at say Thunners, leuenyngeȝ and water, may noȝte bere þe
indygnacion of goddeȝ, how schulde þañ dedely meñ mowe
agaynstande þaire wrethe? And þare-fore I late the * wele ** Leaf 25.*
witte þat þi founde proudde speche trubbleȝ me noȝte ne moueȝ
8 me neuer a dele.'
²Wheñ Porus haddˀ this lettre, he was wondere wrathe & *Porus is angered at the letter and gathers a great army with elephants. Its numbers and array.*
assemblede a grete Oste of meñ, and a grete multitude of
Olyphanntes wit þe whilke þe meñ of Inde ere wount for to
12 feghte, and went agaynes Alexander. This Oste of Porus was
riȝte grete & strange, for þare ware þer in xiiij. cartes of were
and viijᶜ Oliphannteȝ, and ilk an Oliphante haddˀ a toure of tree
apoñ his bakke, & in ilke a toure xxx meñ. Þare ware also
16 oþer feghting meñ on horse and on fote wit-owten nowmer.
And wheñ þe Macedoynes and þe persyenes sawe þe grete *Alexander's allies are startled by the appearance of the elephants and the Indian army.*
multitude bathe of meñ & of Olyphaunteȝ, þay were feredˀ, &
gretely stonayde. Neuer þe lesse, bathe þe partyes ordaynedˀ
20 þam̃ to bateɫɫ, and arayedˀ þaire bateɫɫs, Alexander on his syde,
and Porus on his syde. And Alexander lepe vp-oñ his horse
Buktiphalas & prikkede bi-fore aɫɫ his meñ, and comandedˀ,
þat þe Medoynes & þe persyenes sulde firste begynñ to feghte.
24 And so þay didˀ; & hym selfe wit þe grekes, and þe macedoynes
stode on þe toþer syde, redy to succour þam̃ wheñ myster ware.
And for þe Olyphaunteȝ also, Alexander gert make suylke añ *Alexander's device for overcoming the elephants.*
ordynance. He gert make xxiiij ymageȝ of brasse, and gert fiɫɫ
28 þam̃ fuɫɫ of dry wodde. And he gerte make also cartes of yreñ,
for to bere thir ymageȝ before þe Olyphaunteȝ and wheñ þe
Osteȝ came nere to-gedir he gert sett fyre in þe woddˀ þat was in
þe ymages. And wheñ þe Olyphaunteȝ saw þir ymages, þay
32 wende þat þay haddˀ bene meñ and schott owte þaire groynes,
as þay were wount for to do for tiɫɫ hafe weryed þam̃. And
alsone thurgh þe grete hete, þay were brynnedˀ and thañ thay
gaffe bakke, & fleddˀ for drede to brynne þayre groynes. And
36 þare-fore þe meñ þat were aboweñ in þe toures myghte noȝte
wyñ to for to feghte. And wheñ Porus saw that he was reghte

¹ *agaynstand* written in the margin, with a mark of insertion over against it in the text.   ² Four lines space with red capital *W*. Small *w* in margin next it.

64 *The palace of Porus.*

<small>The allies begin the battle and fight for thirty days.
When exhausted they are re-
*Leaf 25 bk.
placed by the Greeks and Macedonians.
Utter defeat of the Indians and flight of Porus.</small>

sary. Þan þe Medoynes & þe persyenes, with arowes and speres & oþer dyuerse wapynes of werre, slewe thykfalde of þe men of Inde. And thus þay faghte contenuelly xxx^{ti} days, & mekill pople of bathe þe parties ware dede. And at þe laste þe 4 Medoynes, & þe persyenes, began faste for to fayle. And when Alexander saw that, he was wondere wrathe, and entrede in-to þe batelle, sittand on his horse Buctiphalas, *and faghte mannfully, & þe grekes & þe macedoynes with hym. And his horse 8 also helped hym gretely. And than belyfe þe Indyenes began gretely for to fayle. And when Porus saw that he turned þe bakke & fledd. And þan þe Indyenes þat ware lefte on lyfe fledd also. And Alexander luged hym thare wit his Oste and 12 made Sacrafice till his goddez and commaunded for to bery þe dedd bodys, bathe of Indyenes & of þe persyenes & þe Macedoynes.

<small>Siege and capture of Porus' city.
The riches of Porus' palace.</small>

[1] Sone after, apon a day, Alexander ensegedd Porus citee & 16 wann it, and went in-till Porus Palace, whare-In he fande [2] mare reches þan any man will trowe. For he fande þare-in xl pelers of Massy golde, ilkan of a grete thiknes & a grete lenthe, with þaire chapytralles. And bitwene þe pelers of golde, 20 ware hyngande venettez of golde & syluere, wit leues of golde. And þe brawnchez of this venett ware sum of cristalle, sum of Margaritez, sum of Smaragdes, & sum of Onyches, and þay

<small>The walls were plated with gold an inch thick.</small>

semed as þay hade bene verray vynes. Þe walles also of þe 24 palace ware couerde all ouer wit plates of golde, þe whilke when þe Macedoynes cutte in soundre & brakke, þay fande þat þay ware a gret ynche thikke. And þir walles ware sett full of diuerse precious stanes, þat es at say, of charebuncles, Smaragdes, 28

<small>The palace gates were of ivory and ebony.</small>

Margarites & Amatistes. And þe ȝates of þe Palace ware of Euour wonder whitt, & þe bandez of þam, & þe legges of Ebene. Þe chambirs, also, of þis Palace, were all of Cipresse, and þe beddez in þam ware sett full of Margaritez, Smaragdez, & 32

<small>The wonders of the hall. The golden birds that sang as though alive.</small>

charebuncles. Þe haull, also, of þis Palace, was sett full of ymages of golde, & bi-twix þam stode perlatanes of golde, in þe branches of whilke þare were many manners of fewles & ilke a fewle was colourede, & paynted after his kynde asked, þe 36 bekes of þam, & þe clowes ware all of fyne golde. And ay,

<small>
[1] Four lines with red capital ornate S, and small s in margin beside.
[2] MS. repeats *he fande* twice.
</small>

Alexander and the Queen of the Amazons. 65

wheñ Porus liste, thir fewles thurgh crafte of music walde
synge after þaire kynde askede & was. He fande also in þat   The riches
Palace veselles wit-owteñ nowmer, sum̃ of golde, sum̃ of Cristalle,   of the treasury.
4 Sum̃ of oþer maneres of precyouse stanes, sum̃ of Suluere, and   There is but little
þat all maner of vesell þat meñ sulde be serued' offe. Bot þare   silver.
were bot fewe of þam̃ of Siluere.
  ¹Fra thethyñ, Alexander remowede his Oste & come to þe
8 ȝates of Caspee, and þare he luged' hym̃. It was a noble lande
& a gude. Bot þare ware þare-In many maners * of nedders   * Leaf 26.
and of wilde besteȝ. Fra þeine Alexander sent a lettre till
Talifride quene of Amaȝoñ, of þis tenour.
12   ²'Kyng of kynges, and lorde of lordes, Alexander, þe soñ of   Alexander's
godd' Amoñ, & þe quene Olympias, vn-to Talifride þe quene   letter to
of Amaȝoñ, ioy. The grete Batayltes þat we hafe hadd' wit   the Queen of the
kyng Darius, & how we hafe conquered' all his rewme, and his   Amazons
16 lordchipes, we trowe be noghte unknaweñ vn-to ȝow. And also   mentioning his
how we hafe foghteñ with Porus þe kyng of Inde & his cheeffe   victories and de-
citee wonneñ. And also wit many oþer folkes, & þay ware   manding
neuer of powere to agaynestande vs, þe whilke we suppose   tribute.
20 be noȝte vnknaweñ vn-to ȝowe. Whare-fore we sende ȝow
worde, & commandeȝ ȝow, þat ȝe sende vs tribute, if ȝe will þat
wee com̃ noȝte to ȝow to do ȝow disesse.'
  And vn-to this lettre Talifride made ansuere by lettre one this   The answer of the
24 wyse.   Queen of
  ³'Talyfride quene of Amazoñ wit oþer grete ladys of oure   the Amazons. She
rewme, vn-till Alexander, kynge of Macedoyne, joy. We hafe   has heard
wele herde telle of þe hye witt þat es in the, thurgh whilke þou   of his victory.
28 hase in mynde thyngeȝ þat ere passede, and disposeȝ thynges   She warns him of the
þat ere present, and knaweȝ thyngeȝ þat ere to come. Avyse   danger of
the wele þarefore are þou come till vs, what trebulacionneȝ   attacking the
& disesse may falle the in thi commynge. For þare was neuer   Amazons.
32 nane ȝit þat werreyed agayneȝ vs þat ne he had' schame þare-
offe at þe ende. And þare-fore take hede to thi last ende. For
grete schame it es till a wyse mañ thurgh indiscrecioñ to falle
in mescheffe. Bot if it be lykynge to þe, to knawe our con-   She describes
36 uersacyoñ, and oure habitacioñ, we declare it vn-to þe be oure   their land

---

¹ Three lines with miniature capital *F*   ³ Twelve lines space for miniature which
and small *f* beside in the margin.   is lacking. Written in the margin is
  ² Four lines with ornate capital *K* and   'Regina Talibus cum duabus astantibus'.
small *k* in margin beside.

5

The Amazons.

and their manners.
They are in an island girdled round by a river. The men dwell on the other side of the river.
How they breed their kind.

* Leaf 26 bk.

How they ride to war.

Their husbands honour them at their return. They will fight Alexander, who will get no honour through victory over women, but rather if he be overthrown, to the women shall it be great honour, to him great shame.

Alexander laughs and sends them another letter, telling that he has conquered three parts of the world and never been withstood.

present lettres, þat oure habitacioñ es in ane Ile, þat es closede abowte wit a grete reuer þat noþer hase bygynnynge nor endynnge. Bot on a syde we hafe a strayte entree. And the nowmer of womeñ þat duelleȝ þer-in es ccxiiii^m þat ere noȝte 4 filed wit meñ. For oure husbandeȝ duelleȝ noȝte amangeȝ vs ne no noþer mañ, Bot on þe toþer syde of þe reuer. And ilke a ȝere we make a solempne feste in the wirchipe of Iubiter xxx days. And þañ we go till oure husbandes, and duelleȝ 8 wit þam̃ oþer xxx dayes & hase oure luste and oure disporte *to-gedir as kynde askes. And if any of vs consayfe & bere a childe if it be a male þe modere kepis it seueñ ȝere and thañ sendeȝ it to þe fadere. And if scho bere a maydeñ 12 childe þe moder haldeȝ it wit hir & techeȝ it oure maners. Wheñ we goo to werre agayne ȝoure enemys we ere c^m rydand' one horse wele armede. And sum̃ of vs hase bowes & arowes, and sum̃ speres, and oþer diuerse wapyne. And þe remanent 16 kepeȝ oure Ile. And wheñ we come wit the victorye oure husbandeȝ does vs grete wirchipe. And þare-fore if þou come agaynes vs we late the witt þat we will feghte wit the at all oure myȝte. And if it happeñ þat þou hafe þe victory of vs, 20 wirchipe sall it nane be to the bi-cause þou hase discomfit womeñ. And if we discomfit the, it sall be an heghe wirchippe till vs, þat we may discomfit so wirchipfull an emperour; and to the it sall be a hye reproue. Where-fore we sygnifie vn-to 24 þe by oure lettres þat þou come noȝte agaynes vs for sekerly þare may grete dysese come þare-offe, þat perauenture þou knaweȝ noȝte now offe at þis tymme.'

Wheñ Alexander hadd' redd' þis lettre, he begañ to lawghe. 28 And onane he garte writte anoþer lettre, and sent it to Talyfride, whare-offe þe tenour was this.

[1] 'Alexander kyng of kynges and of lordeȝ, the soñ of godd' Amoñ & þe qwene Olympias, to Talyfride quene of Amaȝoñ 32 and þe oþer ladys of þe same rewme : ioy. We late ȝow weite þat thre parties of þe werlde, þat es to say, Asye, Affric, & Europe we hafe conquered' and made subiects vn-till vs, & þare was neuer nane of þam̃ þat myȝte agaynstande oure powere. 36 And if we now suld noȝte be of powere, to feghte with ȝowe it ware ane heghe schame till us. Neuer-þe-lesse for als mekill

---

[1] Thirteen lines blank space for a miniature.

Alexander marches against Porus through a desert. 67

als we lufe ȝour conuersacioñ we conseƚƚ þat ȝe come¹ forthe of   He sum-
ȝour Ile & ȝour husbondeȝ wit ȝow, and appere in oure   mons them
                                                         before him
presence.   For we swere ȝow bi god' Amoñ oure Fader, & by   and ad-
                                                             vises them
4 aƚƚ oure goddeȝ þat ȝe saƚƚ hafe na disesse of vs.   Bot gyffeȝ vs   to give tri-
sumwhat in name of tribute and we schaƚƚ fynd ȝow and ȝoure   bute.
Amaȝonns þat come *wit ȝow horse ynowe.   And wheñ ȝou   *Leaf 27.
listees for to wende hame agayne, ȝe schaƚƚ hafe gude leue.'
8 And wheñ þe Amaȝons hadd' redd' þis lettre, þay went to   The Ama-
conseƚƚ, and thoghte it was beste for to ascent vn-tiƚƚ hym.   zons assent
                                                              to the
And þañ þay sent hym x stedes þe beste þat myȝte be fundeñ   terms of
in any cuntree, and x oþer horse þe beste þat myȝte be geteñ,   the letter.
12 and a grete suñ of golde.   And Talifride hir selfe and oþer
ladys wit hir went un-tiƚƚ hyñ, and accorded' wit hym, and
went hame agayne, wonder glade and blythe.
   ²In þe mene tyme it was talde Alexander, þat Porus, þe kyng   Alexander
16 of Inde, was in Bactriceñ. and assembled' a grete Oste for to   moves his
                                                                  army
feghte eftsonns wit hym.   And wheñ Alexander herde this, he   against
                                                                Porus
remowede his Oste, and chese owte c.l of duyercs þat knewe þe   through
                                                                the desert
cuntree, for to hafe þe gouernance of his Oste, and to lede þañ   in the
20 seurly thurgh þat strange cuntree.   In þe Monethe of Auguste,   month of
                                                                    August.
wheñ þe soñ es maste hate, þay bigañ for to take þaire iournee.   The desert
And thay went thurgh a dry cuntree, sandye, & wit-owtteñ   is waterless
                                                           and full of
water.   And nedlyngeȝ þañ byhoued' wende armede, þare was   snakes and
                                                             wild beasts,
24 so grete plentee of neddirs, and crueƚƚ ³ wylde bestes.   For   for the
thies forsaid gydeȝ ware mare fauorable to Porus, þañ tiƚƚ   guides were
                                                             favourable
Alexander & his Oste, and þare-fore þay ledd' þañ thurgh   to Porus.
                                                           Alexander
swilke barrayne and perilous cuntreeȝ.   And wheñ Alexander   then re-
28 saw it schope thus, and that his conseƚƚ byfore had sayd þe sothe,   mь..
                                                                      the wise
þat es at say, bathe his awnñ frendeȝ and meñ of Caspy, þat   words of
                                                              his council.
conseld' hym þat he suld noȝte hye hym ouerfaste, ne triste to   They all go
mekiƚƚ to stranȝgers; þan he commanded' þat aƚƚ meñ schulde   armed, so
                                                               that the
32 wende armed': & so þay did'.   And þañ aƚƚ þe Oste schane riȝte   whole
                                                                    army
as it had' bene sternes, for sum of þaire armours ware of golde,   gleams like
suñ of siluer, and suñ of precious stanes.   And wheñ Alexander   the stars,
                                                                  with ban-
saw þe araye of his Oste, and þaire baners bi-fore þañ   ners and a
                                                         shining
36 Schynande so faire, he was riȝte gladde.   Neuer-þe-les grete   mail.
disese he hadd', þat nowþer he, ne his meñ, myȝte fynde na water.

¹ MS. *cone.*   its foliage three-quarters of the margin.
² Six lines with miniature *I*, covering with   ³ *wh* turned into *wy.*

5—2

A Macedonian knight finds water in a hollow and brings it to Alexander in his helmet. Alexander refuses it lest he alone of all go refreshed. He
Leaf 27 bk.
casts it down upon the rocks and goes without, so that all his followers are comforted as though they had drunken water. On the morrow they come to a river with reeds on its banks as high as pine trees. They drink of the water; it slew many of them with a flux. Alexander is greatly distressed, not only for his knights but also for the many beasts of burden that bear their things, and the flocks and herds that go with them.

So it felle þat a knyghte of Macedoyne þat hyȝte ȝephilus fand' water standynge in an holle stane, þat was gadird' þare of þe dewe of þe heuen͡, the whilke þis forsaide knyghte putt in his Bacenett, & broȝthe it till Alexander for to drynke. And þis water, sall þe Macedoynes & þe persyenes be any thynge refreschede þareby, or I sall hafe all þe refreschyng be my selfe.' And he ansuerd, & saide, 'Þou all ane lorde,' quoþ he, ' sall be comforthed þareby.' Quoþ Alexander þan͡, 'And' * if ȝe¹ sall all perische trowes þou þat it solde be lykand' to mee, for to lyfe in sorowe & disese seynge þe dedd' of þe Macedoynes & þe persyenes ?' And be-lyue he garte helle downn͡ þe water on þe erthe be-fore all his men͡. And when͡ his knyghtis saw that, þay were hugely comforthede þare-by riȝte als Ilkan͡ of þam͡ hadd' dronken͡ a grete draughte of water, and þan͡ went furthe þaire waye. And on͡ þe morne, þay come till a reuere whase bankes was growand' full of grete redys & þay ware als hye as pyne-treese; ȝa, for þe maste partie of xl fote lange. Than badd' [he] that þay drawe of þe water and brynge to þe Oste. Bot all þat dranke þare-offe it keste þam͡ in-till a flux, and slewe a grete hepe of þam. For þat water was wonder scharpe, and als bittire als any mekill gyrse. Bot þan͡ was Alexander gretly disessedd' & all his Oste noȝte allanly of þam͡-selfe, bot also for þaire horseȝ & þaire besteȝ þat þay ledd' wit þam͡ þe whilke bi-gan͡ for to faile for thryste. Alexander hadd' wit hym a thowsande Olyphanteȝ þat bare his golde, And foure hundreth cartes of werre and jᵐ & cc wayneȝ. He hadd' also in his Oste cccᵐ horse men͡ and muyles & camelles witowten͡ nowmer, þat bare þaire vetails, and oþer thyngeȝ þat was necessarye to þe Oste; also oxen͡ and kye, schepe and swyne, wit-owten͡ nowmer, þe whilke perischt for defaute of drynke. Sum͡ of Alexander knyghtes lykked' Iren͡, Sum͡ dranke oyle, & sum ware at so grete meschefe þat þay dranke þaire awen͡ stalynge. And thare was so grete habundance of nedders & oþer venymous besteeȝ, þat þam by-houed' nedeȝ trauelle armed', and þat was a grete nuy to þam & an͡ heghe disese. Þan͡ was Alexander wonder² sorye & namely for þe disese þat his Oste suffrede.

4

8

12

16

20

24

28

32

36

---

¹ On first side of leaf 27 ȝe *sall* is written, but on the second side ȝe *schal*.

² MS. undoubtedly reads *worder*, but one must substitute *wonder*.

The silent castle. 69

¹ Andˀ as þay went endlande þis reuere, abowte þe viii houre In what
of þe day, þay come till a castell þat stode in a littill Ile in þis fearful
                                                                       ways his
forsaidˀ ryuere; And this castell was made of þe forsaidˀ redeȝ. knights try
                                                                       to quench
4 Þe brede of this ryuer was foure furlange lenth. And in þat their
castell þay sawe a few men̄. And þan̄ Alex*ander* bad his men̄ thirst.
                                                                       Going
spirre þam̄ þat ware i*n* þe castell in þe langage of Inde whare along the
                                                                       banks they
þay myghte fynde any swete watir able for to drynke. And come to a
                                                                       little isle
8 also son̄ als þay spake to þam̄ þay with-drewe þam̄ & hiddˀ. with a
And Alex*ander* gerte schotte arowes in-to þe castell and þan̄ castle,
þay hiddˀ þam̄ wele þe mare. And when Alex*ander* saw *that * Leaf 28.
þay walde one na wyse speke w*i*t hy*m*, he haddˀ a certane of his wherein are
                                                                       men who
12 knyghtes nakne þam & swyme oue*r* þe wat*er* to þe castell. And will give
                                                                       them no
þan̄ xxxvii balde knyghtis & hardy of Macedoyue naknedˀ þam̄, answer.
and tuke ilkan̄ of þam̄ a swerde in his hande & went in-to þe Alexander
                                                                       bids
wat*er* & swame it to þay were passede þe ferthe parte þ*are*-offe. certain of
16 And sodeynly thare rase oute of þe wat*er* a grete m*u*ltitude his knights
                                                                       swim the
of besteȝ, þat ere calledˀ ypotaynes, grettere of body than̄ an̄ stream.
olyphant, and deuoredˀ thir knyghtis eue*r*-ilkan*n*e. And þan̄ They swim
                                                                       the river,
was Alex*ander* riȝte sare greuede, and be-lyfe garte take þe but are de-
                                                                       voured by
20 forsaidˀ guydeȝ cl & caste þam̄ in-to þe wat*er*. And onane hippopo-
                                                                       tami.
þe ypotaynes deuoredˀ þam.   Alexander
    And Alex*ander* thoghte it was noȝte spedfull langare to stryffe throws the
                                                                       guides into
w*i*t thase monstres, and garte tromppe vp and removedˀ his the river
24 Oste fra þeine, and went so all þat day wondere wery for thriste. and they
                                                                       are de-
And also þay haddˀ grete disese & nuye of wilde ² Beste þat come voured
                                                                       also.
apon̄ þam̄, þat es to say, of lyon*es*, beres, vnycornes, tygres, They travel
and pardeȝ, w*i*t þe whilke þay faughte & grete trauell hade. onwards
                                                                       greatly
28 ³ And as þay went on̄ þis wyse w*i*t grete angere & disese worried by
aboute þe elleuedˀ houre þay saw a littill bate in þe riuere made wild beasts.
                                                                       At the
of rede and men̄ rowande þ*are*-in. And Alex*ander* gert spirre eleventh
                                                                       hour they
þam̄ in þe langage of Inde, whare þay myȝte fynde any fresche meet a
32 wat*er*. And þay talde whare & schewedˀ þam̄ a place a littill small boat
                                                                       whose crew
þeine whare-in þay saide þay scholde fynde a grete staunke of direct them
                                                                       to a great
swete wat*er* and gude. And þan̄ Alex*ander* & hys Oste went pond of
all aboute þat ryuere, & come till þis forsaidˀ stanke and lugedˀ fresh water.
                                                                       They camp
36 þam̄ aboute it. And Alex*ander* comandedˀ þat þay sulde felle round the

---

¹ Four lines with miniature *A* and small   ³ Four lines with red capital *A* and
a written in MS. margin beside.   small *a* in the MS. margin beside.
² *of* deleted by the scribe before *Beste.*

The adventures with wondrous beasts.

[Marginal notes:] pond. Alexander bids that they fell a great wood of huge reeds that grow around it. When the moon rises a great crowd of scorpions come down to drink. And there come snakes also and many-hued dragons. These have crested heads with *Leaf 28 bk. golden breasts and open mouths. Their breath slew any quick thing it smote upon and out of their eyes came fiery flames. Alexander comforts his frightened knights. Alexander shows how to fight them with nets, and slays many of them. How many men of Alexander fell thereby. The wondrous crabs that then attack them. Then come white Lions

a wodd' þat growed' faste þare-by three myle on lenthe, & aɫɫs
mekiɫɫ on brede. Þat wodde was aɫɫ of þe redeʒ þat I spak of
bi-fore, and þe stanke was a myle oñ lenth. Þañ Alexander
comanded' þat þay sulde make many fires in þe Oste, and gerte 4
trompe to þe mete. And alsoñ þe mone be-gañ to schynne
þare come a grete multitude of scorpyons to-warde þe stanke
for to take þam̃ a drynke. And þañ þare come oþer manere
of nedders, and dragones wonder grete of dyuerse colours. 8
And aɫɫ þat cuntree resounned' of þe noyse & þe hissʒingeʒ
þat þay made. Þir dragones come dounne fra þe hye mountaynes for to drynke of þe stanke, and þay hadd' crestis one
þaire heddeʒ & þaire bresteʒ ware bryghte lyk golde, & þaire 12
mowthes opeñ. Þaire aande slewe any qwikk thynge þat it
smate apoñ, and oute of þaire eghne þare come flammes of fyre.
And wheñ Alexander & his Oste saw þam̃ þay ware riʒt
*fered' for þam̃. For þay wende þay schulde hafe weried' þam̃ 16
ilkañ. And þañ Alexander comforthed' þam̃ and saide vn-to
þam̃: 'Mi wirchipfuɫɫ knyghtes,' quoþ he, 'bees noʒte agaste of
þam̃, bot does ilkane as ʒe see me do.' And þañ he tuk a nett
& sett it bi-twixe hym & þam̃ and tuke his schelde & his spere 20
& faughte wit þam̃ manfully. And wheñ his knyghtes saw þat
þay ware gretly comforthed' & be-lyfe tuke þaire wapynneʒ &
didd' als þay sawe Alexander doo, and slewe of þam̃ a grete
multitude, whatt thurgh dyuerse wapynneʒ, what in þaire fyres. 24
And of Alexander knyghtes þe dragones slewe xxti & xxxti
fotemeñ. After þam̃, þare come owte of þe forsaide wodde of
redeʒ, Crabbes of a wonderfuɫɫ greteness; and þaire bakkes ware
harder þañ cocadrilleʒ. And wheñ þe knyghtis smate þam̃ one 28
þe bakkes wit þaire speres, þay myʒte noʒte perche þam̃, ne na
harme do þam̃. Neuer-þe-lesse þay slewe many of þam̃ in
þaire Fires and þe remenant of þam̃ gatt in-to þe staunke. And
aboute þe sexte houre of þe nyghte þare come apoñ þam̃ whytt 32
lyones grettere þañ Bulles, and þay schoke þaire heuedeʒ at
þam̃ & grete manace made in þaire manere. Þañ þe knyghtes
keped' þam̃ in þaire nettis and slew þam. After this þare com̃
apoñ þam̃ þañ a grete multitude of swynne þat ware aɫɫ of a 36
wonderfuɫɫ mekilness, wit tuskes of a cubett lenthe. And wit
þam̃ þare come wilde meñ & womeñ of þe whilke ilkañ hadd'
sex hende. Bot Alexander & his knyghtes keped þam̃ in þaire

Wondrous beasts.

nettis & slewe many of þam̅. And on þis wyse Alexander & his greater than bulls.
Oste was gretly disesed. Þañ comanded' Alexander þat þay Then follow huge
schuld' make many fyres wit-owtten̅ þe Oste aboute þe stanke. swine with great tusks.
4 After this þare come apoñ þam̅ a wondere grete beste, grettere And with
& strangere þañ añ Olyphaunt, and he hadde in his frunte them six-
three lange hornes. And he was schapen̅ lyke a horse & he handed men and
was all blakke. And þis beste was called' in þe langage of Inde women.
8 'Anddontrucion̅'. And or he went to þe water at drynke, he They make great fires
assailled' þe Oste. Bot Alexander went here & þare amangeȝ þe around the pond. Then
oste & comforthed' þam̅. This ilke beste slewe of his knyghtes comes a horselike
xxviij and bare donne lij and at þe laste it felle in þe nettis and beast
12 was slayne. After þis þare come oute of þc redeȝ a grete multi- greater than an
tude of mysȝ als grete als foxes, and ete up þe dede bodys. Þare elephant.
was na qwike thyngeȝ, þat þay bate þat ne also soñ it dyed'. Alexander again
Bot harme did' þay nane *to þe oste. Þan̅ come þare flyande *Leaf 29.
16 amangeȝ þam̅ bakkes, grettere þam̅ wilde dowfes, and þaire rallies his men.
tethe ware lyke men̅-tethe. And þay didd' men̅ mekill disese It slays
and hurte many men̅. Of sum̅ þay bate offe þe nese; of sum many, but is at last
þe eres. In þe mornenynge arely þare come many fewlis als slain.
20 grete as wlturs, reed' of colour, and þaire fete & þaire bekes Mice as big as foxes
all blakke. Bot þay didd' na disese to þe oste, bot went to eat up the dead
þe stanke-syde & drewe fisches & eleȝ oute of þe water, & bodies.
ete þam̅. Whatsoever they
24 ¹ Þhan̅ lefte Alexander þir perilous placeȝ, and come wit his bit at once died.
Oste, in-to þe cuntree of Bactricen̅, þe whilke was full of Then come
golde & oþer reches. And þe men̅ of þe cuntree resayfed' hym bats greater
benyngly & wirchipfully and gaffe hym and his Oste grete giftes. than wild doves.
28 And þare he habade xxti dayes. In þat cuntree þay sawe They
trees þat, in-stedde of leues, bare wolle; þe whilke folkeȝ of march into Bactria
þe cuntree gaderd' & made clathe þare-offe. Þe knyghtes of where they are well re-
Alexander wex wonder balde & strange of hert because of ceived.
32 þe victoryes þay hadd' wonnen̅ of þe wilde besteȝ before The wool-bearing
neuenned. trees.
  The
² Fra thethyn, Alexander remowed' his Oste and come to þe knights
place whare Porus lay wit þe folke þat he hadd' assembled. take courage be-
36 And one þe morne bathe Alexander and Porus tuke þaire cause of the
grounde & arayed' þaire batells for to feghte. And than̅ strange beasts they

---

¹ Four lines with red ornate capital Þ, but small t scribbled in the margin beside.   ² Four lines space with red capital S and small s written in the margin beside.

72 The combat of Porus and Alexander.

[margin: have conquered. The armies of Porus and Alexander are arrayed against each other. The Indians fall heavily. Porus challenges Alexander to single combat. The kingship of the nations to abide by the outcome. For Porus being a great man scorned Alexander.]

Alexander lepped apoñ his horse Buktiphalas and went bifore his Oste & þaiñ þay trumpede up & þe batells joyned samen, & faghte to-gedir riȝte sare. Bot þe Indienes fell thikfalde in þe batell as corne dose in þe felde be-fore þe sythe. 4
[1] And wheñ Porus saw that, he went and stode bi-fore all his meñ, and cryed vn-till Alexander, & saide on this wyse: 'It sitteȝ noȝte till an emperour,' quoþ he, 'to lose his meñ þus in vayne. Bot it sitteȝ till hym for to determyne his 8 cause with his aweñn handeȝ. And þarefore late thi folke stand still on þe ta syde, & myñ on þe toþer & late the & me feghte to gedir hand for hand. And if it happeñ þat þou ouer-come me, my folke & I sall be subiecteȝ vn-to þe. And 12 if I ouer come the, thañ thou & thi folkeȝ be subiecteȝ vn-to me.' Thir wordeȝ said Porus dispysand Alexander, bi-cause þat he was a mañ of littill stature. For he was bot three cubites hye, & Porus was fyfe cubetes hye & mare. And þare- 16 fore he traysted hym all in strenghe of his body, noȝte knawande þe vertu & þe hardnes þat was hidd in Alexander.

*[margin: *Leaf 29 bk. Porus hits Alexander on the head.]*

*And than bathe þe ostes stode still ant lete þe twa kyngeȝ feghte sameñ, Porus gaffe Alexander a grete str[a]ke 20 oñ þe hede, & was in poynte to hafe felled hym. And then Porus knyghtes sett vp a grete Schowte. And Porus tourned hym to þam-warde for to reproue þam for þaire schowttyng.

[margin: Alexander slays Porus by a trick. The Indians fight on for their dead king. Alexander chides them for fighting when their leader is dead.]

And Alexander went till hym manfully & tuke his swerd in 24 bathe his handeȝ & lete flye at hym & hitt hym fullbott one þe heued & slew hym. And wheñ þe Indienes saw that þay bi-gan scharply for to fighte wit Alexander & his oste. Vnto whayme Alexander spake & sayde: 'Wrechis,' quoþ he, 28 ' wharto feghte ȝe señ ȝour kynge es dede. Wate ȝe noȝte wele that thare na gouernour es þe folke are sparpled be-lyfe als schepe þat ere wit-owtteñ ane hirde.' Þe Indienes ansuerd & saide : ' Vs es leuer,' quoþ þay, 'fighte manfully, and dye in the 32 felde, þan for to see þe dissolacioñ of oure folke, and oure lande

[margin: Alexander bespeaks them peace and surety. They are right glad and wor-]

be distroyed & wasted.' ' Leues ȝour feghtynge,' quoþ Alexander, ' & wendeȝ hame to ȝour howseȝ pesaybly & seurely. For I swere ȝow bi oure goddeȝ, if ȝee will do so, ȝe sall hafe no harme, ne 36 ȝour lande sall noȝte be distroyed ne spoyled, bicause þat ȝe hafe foghten so manfully for ȝour kynge.' And wheñ þe Indienes

---

[1] *Robert Louson* is scribbled here in the right-hand margin.

Alexander and the Gymnosophists. 73

herde thir wordes þay keste fra þam̅ þaire wapyne3 & thanked̛ Alexander and wirchiped̛ him ri3te als he hadd̛ bene a godd̛. Than kyng Alexander luged̛ hym þare & his Oste wit hym,
4 & he command̛ to bery þe dede corse3 þat ware slayne in þe Batell, and offred̛ sacrafice till his godde3. Also he garte Entere Por*us* þe kynge of Inde wirchipfully.
  ¹Fra thethyn̅ Alexander remowed̛ his Oste & come till a cuntree
8 þat was called̛ Oxidraces. The folkes of þat cuntree are wonder Symple men̅, and no3te prowde, & þay are called̛ Gumnosophiste. Þay feghte neu*er* mare ne stryfes. Þay ga alway naked̛, & citez ne townnez hafe þay nane, Bot duellez in luge3 & in
12 caues. When̅ þe kyng of þis folke herd̛ tell of þe commyng of Alexander he wrate a l*ett*re, & sent vn-till hym whareoffe this was the teno*ur*.
  ²*'The coruptible Gumnosophist vn-till Alexander a man̅ wee
16 wryte. We here tell þat þou comme3 to werre apon̅ vs, whare of we merueylle vs gretly. For wit vs sall þou fynd nathyng þat þou may spoyle vs offe. For we hafe na thyng elles amange3 vs, bot allanly whare with we may sustene oure wafull
20 bodys. What may þou þan̅ take fra vs. Bot if þou come for to feght wit vs, feghte on̅. For I late the wele witt, þat oure symplenes will we on na wyse lefe.' When̅ Alexander had redd̛ this l*ett*re he sent ane ansuere agayne on̅ this wyse. 'Paisably,'
24 quoþ he, 'will we com̅ to 3ow and no violence do 3ow.' And þan̅ he wente in-to þe cuntree whare þay duelled̛. And he saw þam̅ ga naked̛ & duelle in luges & in caues, & þaire wyfes & þaire childre away fra þam̅, walkand̛ wit wilde beste3.
28 And he hadd̛ grete m*a*rueylle, & asked̛ þam̅ if þay hadd any oþ*er* howse3. And þay ansuerde & said̛, 'Nay. Bot in thir holette3 duelle we alwaye & in þir caues.' And Alex*ander* commendid̛ gretely þaire symplenesse, and bad þam̅ aske hym̅
32 whate-so þay walde. And þay ansuerd̛ & sayde, 'Gyffe vs,' quoþ þay, 'vndedlynesse, so þat we mow no3te dye; for oþ*er* reches couet we nane.' Quoþ Alex*ander*, 'I am dedely my selfe, how þan̅ may I giffe 3ou vndedlynes?' And when̅ þay
36 herd̛ hym say soo þan̅ þay ansuerd̛ & sayde on̅ this wyse. 'A, A, wreched̛ man̅,' q*u*oþ þay, 'whare to wende3 þou þ*us*

Side notes: ship Alexander as a god. King Alexander offers sacrifice and buries Porus worshipfully. King Alexander comes to the Gymnosophists, a strange people. *Leaf 30. The letter of their king to Alexander, telling him he has naught to win of them. Alexander commends them and comes peaceably to them. He sees them leading the life of nature. He admires their ways greatly and offers them a boon. They ask for deathlessness. They chide him for his ambition when they

---

¹ Five lines with red capital *F* and small *f* written in the margin beside. ² Four lines with red capital *T*.

74   *The pillars of Hercules and the uttermost islands.*

<small>hear he also must die.

He says he is driven on to conquer by the might of God, which will not allow him to rest. He goes thence.

He comes to the pillars of Hercules, which are statues,

* Leaf 30 bk.

one of gold and one of silver. He finds them hollow and puts money therein. He marches thence into a cold and mirky wilderness. They come to a great river, on the other side of which are fair women foully clad, who bear weapons of silver since other metal have they none. There were no men amongst them.</small>

aboute, & quelleȝ so many meñ, & soo many ilke dediȝ dooes sen þou wate wele þat þou saƚƚ dye.' 'For sothe,' quoþ he, 'þe cause whi I do it es of þe prouydence of godd. For hys mynystre I am̃, doand' þe commandement of hym. ȝee wate 4 wele þat þe see es noȝte trubbled' of hym selfe. Bot wheñ þe wynde entres in-tiƚƚ hym, þan̄ it stirreȝ hym & trubleȝ hym. I walde hafe ristedd' and lefte aƚƚ werre. Bot þare es anoþer spyryte & suffres it noȝte be in reste.' And wheñ Alex*ander* 8 hadde said' thir wordeȝ he lefte þam̃ & went tiƚƚ anoþer cuntree.

¹ Anoþer day, he come wit his Oste tiƚƚ a place wharee twa ymageȝ ware, þe whilke Ercules gart make & sett in þat place. 12 And þe tane of þam̃ was of fyne golde and þe toþer of fyne Siluere, & the lenthe of aythir of þam̃ was twa cubettis. Wheñ Alex*ander* saw þir ymageȝ, * he gert perche ² þam̃ for to witt, wheþer þay ware holle or massy. And he fand' 16 þat þay were a party hoƚƚe. And he garte stoppe þe hole agayne and putt in þam̃ a thowsande nobles, & fyve hundreth. And fra þeine he remowed his Oste, and entrede in-tiƚƚ a wildirnesse calde & myrk, so þat þay myghte vnnethes an̄ 20 knawe anoþer or see anoþer. And fra thythiñ þay went seueñ daye iournee and entred' in-tiƚƚ a wildirnesse, and come tiƚƚ a grete reuere. And bi-ȝonde þat riuere þay saw wonder faire & wele vesaged' womeñ cledd' in foule clethyng & horrible; and 24 þay hadd' in þaire handeȝ wapne made aƚƚ of siluere, bicause þay hadd' noþer Ireñ ne stele. And þay rade one horse. And men saw þay nane amangeȝ þam̃. And wheñ þe Oste walde hafe passede ouer this ryuere, þay myȝte noȝte be cause it was 28 riȝte brade and fuƚƚ of dragones and oþer monstres.

³ Fra thethin þay went aboute towardeȝ þe lefte party of ⁴ Inde and come till a dry Marras fuƚƚ of gret redeȝ. And as þay passed thurgh þat Marras, be-lyue þare come owte of þe 32 redeȝ a beste lyke ane ypotayne, whase breste was lyke to þe cocadriƚƚe, and his bakke lyk a sawe, and his tethe wonder grete, & als scharpe as a suerde; bot in his gangyng he was

---

¹ Three lines with red capital *A* and small *a* in the margin beside.
² Bottom of leaf 30 right-hand side reads as above *gert perche*; top of leaf 30 turning over to the left-hand side reads *garte perche.*
³ Four lines with red capital *F* and small *f* written in the margin beside.
⁴ MS. *of* twice.

Adventures with wild beasts and wondrous folk.

als slaw als a snyle. And, in his oute-come, he slew twa knyghtis of Alexander. This ilke beste my3te þay on na wyse perche wit þaire speres. Bot wit mellis of yreñ þay slew it.
4 ¹And fra þeine þay trauelde thritty day iourne3 and come to þe vttermaste iles of Inde, & þare þay luged' þam̃ beside3 a ryuere þat es callede in þat langage of Inde Hemmahurer. And aboute þe Eleuend houre þar come owte of þe wodde3 a grete
8 multitude of Olyphante3 & come apoñ þam̃ wit a gret birre & þaire groynes opyñ. And onane Alexander lepe apoñ his horse Buktiphalas and busked' hym agaynes þam̃ and badd' þe macedoynes þat þay solde tak þaire horse and ilk a mañ a swyne in
12 a bande, & wende agaynes þe olyphantis. And wheñ þe oliphantes saw þam̃, þay come gapande wit þaire groyne3 redy te tak þam̃. And wheñ þe Macedoynes saw þat þay ware fered' and durste no3te go to þam̃. And Alexander saide vn-to þam,
16 'My wirchipfull knyghtes,' quoþ he, 'bese of gud comforthe and drede3 3ow na-thynge. For, and 3e will gare 3oure swyne crye faste *3e schall see all þir Olyphantes flee anoñ.' And alsone als þe Olyphantes herde þe crye of þe swyne, and þe
20 noyse of þaire trompes, þay fledd' and durste no3te habyde. And Alexander & his meñ pursued' tham̃, and what wit nettis, whatt wit swerdes & speres, þay slewe of þam̃ a grete multitude, and come agayne to thaire tentis.
24 ²Anoþer day þay removed' þeine, and trauelde thurgh the same wodde3 of ³Inde. And þay fande þare womeñ with berdis rechande downñ to þaire pappes, & þaire heuede3 playne abownne, and þay ware cledd' all in skynnes. Þay chasede thir
28 womeñ and sum of þam̃ þay tuke & broghte þam̃ till Alexander. And he gart spirre þam in the langage of Inde, how þay liffed in thase woddes, whare na duellyng was of meñ. And þay ansuered' & said, 'We lyffe all,' quoþ þay, 'wit venysoñ þat we
32 take in thir woddes thurgh huntynge.'
⁴Wheñ þay ware passed' oute of thir wodde3 þay come in-till a faire felde vn-till a place whare this forsaid' riuere rañ. And þare þay fande bath meñ & womeñ all naked. And þay ware

They come to a dry morass and meet a terrible beast.
They come to the uttermost isles of India.
There come a great multitude of elephants against them. But Alexander overcomes them by a trick.
He bids his men take swine against
Leaf 31.
them and makes the swine squeal.

They march thence through the forests of India and come upon wild women with long beards.

And they find also other tribes of wild men

---

¹ Four lines with red capital *A* and small *a* beside it in margin.
² Four lines with capital *A* in red, and small *a* beside.
³ Þnde altered into Inde.
⁴ Four lines with red capital *W* and small *w* written in the margin beside.

[Sidenote: and women.] als rugħe of hare as þay hade bene bestes. Whase kynde & custoᵐ it was als wele to be in þe water, als oᴺ þe lande. And als sone als þay saw Alexander Oste onane þay fledd' to þe water,
[Sidenote: They go thence fifteen days till they meet the Cynocephali whom they overcome.] and dowked in-till it. Fra þeine þay traueld' xv day iourneє, 4 and entred' in-till woddes þat ware full of cynocephals, þe whilke als soᴺ als þay saw Alexander & his oste onane þay assaillede þam. Bot Alexander & his meᴺ, what wit arowes whate wit speres & nettes slew a grete multitude of þaᵐ, and 8 þe remenaunt of þaᵐ fledd' here and thare in þe woddeȝ.

[Sidenote: They march forty days to a barren land with no hills, and a terrible east wind blows over it and causes fires and disease throughout the camp. They fear it is because of Alex-]

*[Sidenote: * Leaf 31 bk.]*

[Sidenote: ander's ambition. He tells them it is because of the Equinox. Then they go thence twenty-five days to a green valley where is fearful cold. They light fires against the snow-storms. Rain comes and the snow stops, but five]

¹ Fra thethyᴺ þay went fourty dayes & come in-till a champaynne cuntree, þat was all Barayne, and na hye place ne na hilles myghte be sene on na syde. And as it ware aboute þe xj 12 houre of þe day, þare bigaᴺ so grete a wynde to blawe oute of þe Este þat it blew doune to þe erthe all thaire tentis & þaire luges. And þare was grete disese ymang þe oste. For þe wynde tuk fire-brandes oute of fyres þat þay hadd' made, and 16 smate dyuerse meᴺ & brynte þaᵐ. And þaᴺ Alexander knyghtes mournurede gretly & said amangeȝ þam, 'Þe wrethe & þe wreke of oure goddeȝ,' quoþ þay, 'falleȝ apoᴺ vs, Bicause we seke to ferre towarde þe soᴺ rysynge.' 'My wirchipfull 20 knyghteȝ,' quoþ Alexander, 'bese * of gud comforthe and no thyng ferde for this tempeste es noȝtee falleᴺ thurgĥ wrethe of oure goddes bot be-cause of equinox of heruest.' Wheᴺ þe wynde was cessed' þay gadirde to-gedir þat þe wynd' hadd' 24 sparpled'.

²Fra þeine þay went xxv days and come in-till a grene valay, and þare þay luged' þaᵐ. Than commanded' Alexander þat þay schuld make many fyres. For it begaᴺ for to be vn- 28 sufferable calde. And thare be-gan for to falle grete flawghtis of snawe, as þay had bene grete lokkes of wolle. Wheᴺ Alexander saw that, he was ferde þat it schuld' noȝte hafe cessed' sone, and bad his meᴺ þat þay suld tred douᴺ þe snawe & full 32 it wit þaire fete. And þaire fyres also helpe þaᵐ gretly. Neuerþe-lesse þare ware fyve hundrethe of þe Oste dedd' thurgh þat snawe, þe whilk Alexander gart bery. Þaᴺ þare felle a passand' grete rayne, and þe snaw cessed. Wit þe rayne, also, þare 36 come so thikke a myste, þat contenually three days to gedir þay

---

¹ Four lines with red capital *F* and small *f* in margin beside.
² Four lines with red capital *F* and small *f* in the margin beside.

Alexander and Dindimus, King of the Brahmans. 77

saw na sonñ. And oute of þe clude þat hange abowñ þamꝺ þer
felł as it hadd˙ bene grete fyrebrande3 þe whilk brynt many of
thaire tenttis and of þaire luges. And onane Alexander offred˙
4 sacrafice tiłł his godde3 and bad his knyghtis put alde ryueñ
clathe3 wate bi-fore þe fire, and he made his prayere. And also
soñ the whedir wexe clere & faire.

¹ Fra thethin, þay remowed˙ and come tiłł a grete ryuere þat
8 es called˙ Ganges & þare þay luged þamꝺ. And as þay luked˙
ouer on the toþer syde, þay saw twa or thre meñ walke up &
downñ þare. And Alexander badd˙ his meñ spirre þauȝ in þe
langage of Inde what þey ware. And þay ansuered˙ & said˙.
12 'We are Bragmayns,' quoþ þay. Alexander hadd˙ grete desyre
to speke wit þe Bragmayns. Bot he my3te no3te wynñ ouer
þe water; it was so depe & so brade Bot if it had bene in þe
monethe of July and Auguste. And also it was fułł of ypotaynes
16 & scorpyones and cocadrilles, out takeñ in þe forsaid˙ monethes.
And wheñ he saw þat he myghte on na wyse wynñ ouer he was
re3te heuy. And belyfe he garte make a lyttiłł bate of redis, &
couerde it wit nowtte hydis & gerte pykk it wele bathe wit-in &
20 wit-owtteñ. And wheñ þe bate was made, he gert a knyght of
his gang in-to it, and gaffe hym a lettre wit hym for to bere
* to Dindimus, þat was kyng of þe Bragmayns, of whilk lettre þis
was þe tenour.

24 ² 'Kyng of kynges and lorde of lorde3, Alexander þe soñ of
godd˙ Amoñ & of þe quene Olympias, vn-to Dindimus kyng
of Bragmayns, ioy. Euer señ we were comeñ to þat age þat
we couthe discerne by-twix gud & iłł we hafe desyred˙ soueraynly
28 for to hafe wysdomme & konnyng, & for to putt away fra
vs ignorance & vnconnynge. For as þe wise techynge of oure
philosoþres declares opynly, Eloquence wit owtteñ witt & wis-
domꝺ dose ofte-sythes mare skathe þañ gude. Þarefore we hafe
32 wele vnderstandeñ by relacioñ of dyuerse meñ, þat 3our lyfe &
3our maners are diuised˙ and diuerse fra ałł oþer meñ; so þat
noþer oñ þe See ne on þe lande 3e seke na helpe and þat 3e
3eme anoþer manere of doctryne þañ we hafe lerende of oure
36 doctours. Whare-fore we pray 3ow þat 3e wiłł certyfye vs bi
3our lettres of 3our lyffe and 3our maners and 3our doctryne. For

---

¹ Four lines with capital *F* and small *f*   ² Four lines with capital *K* in red,
written in the margin beside.   and small *k* in the margin beside.

hundred have died. Then comes a great mist with the rain, out of which fall firebrands. Alexander offers sacrifice to his gods and the weather becomes clear. They come to the Ganges, on the other side of which are the Brahmans. They cannot cross because of the dangerous beasts. He sends a knight over in a boat with a letter to Dindimus, king of the Brahmans. Alexander's letter to Dindimus, asking the Brahmans the reason for their strange manners, since he fain would learn wisdom of them.

*Leaf 32.

perauenture we may take þare of sum̃ gud Ensample, and ȝour wysdome & ȝour gudnesse neuer be þe lesse. For it es na harme till a man̄ thurgh his gudnes to make anoþer man̄ gude as he es. The whilk I may proue bi this simylitud̃—I supposse a man̄ hadd̃ in his hand̃ a lyght candill, many oþer candills may be lyghted̃ þare at, & it lose na-thynge of his lyghte. And riȝte so it es of þe gudnesse of a man̄. For many men̄ may take gude ensample of hym & his gudnesse be na thynge enmenuste þareby. Where- fore ȝitt eft-sons we pray ȝow þat wit-owtten̄ any taryinge or delay, ȝe schowe vs þe maners of ȝour lyffyng.' Than kyng Dindimus resaffed̃ þis lettre wirchipfully and wrate anoþer agayne of this tenour.

[1] ' Dyndimus maister of þe Bragmayns vn-to kyng Alexander ioy & gretynge. We hafe wele vndirstanden̄ by þe tenour of thi lettres, þat þou desyres gretly for to hafe verray connynge and perfitt wysdom̃; þe whilke are mekill better þan̄ any kyngdom̃; for þay may neuer be boghte wit na pryce, wharefore I comend̃ þe gretly, knawyng þat þou arte a wyse man̄. For ane Emperour wit-owtten̄ * wisdom̃, es noghte lorde of his subiectis, Bot his sugettis ere lordes of hym. ȝe wrate vntill vs, praying vs for to schewe ȝowe oure maners of lyffynge, ilke a poynte efter oþer, þe whilke we halde inpossible for to doo. For oure maner of lyffynge es full ferre dyuerse fra ȝours. For noþer we wirchipe þe goddes þat ȝe wirchipe, ne ledis þe lyfe þat ȝe lede. And if I writte ȝowe oughte of oure maner of lyffyng, ȝe may hafe na sauoure þare in, be-cause ȝe are besily ocupied̃ wit dedis of armes. Neuer-þe-lesse þat ȝe say noȝte þat I layne oure lyfe fra ȝow for envy, Als mekill as comeȝ to my mynde at þis tyme I sall writt vnto ȝow of oure maners.

[2] ' We Bragmayns ledeȝ a symple lyfe & a clene and þe wirchipyng of many goddes we eschu. We do na synnes ne we will hafe na mare þan̄ reson̄ of kynde asches. All thyngeȝ we suffer & þat, say we, es necessary & ynoghe, þat es noȝte ouermekill. We tille na lande, ne eryes, ne sawes, ne ȝokes noþer ox ne horse in plughe ne in carte. Ne nett caste we nane in þe see, for to take fysche; Ne hunttynge ne fewlynge vse we

---

[1] Four lines with capital *D* in red, and small *d* in margin beside.

[2] Three lines with red capital *W*, and small *w* in margin.

Dindimus' letter to Alexander.   79

nanne. Mete & drynke hafe we ynoghe, and oþer mete seke we nane, bot þat þe erthe oure allere moder wit-owtten mannes labour brynges furthe. Wit swilke metis we fill oure wambes,
4 whilke nuȝes vs noȝte, ne na harme dose. And ȝit of swilke metis we fill noȝte oure bodis to full. For amangeȝ vs it es an vn-semely thynge & an vn-leefull to see a grete-belyed man. And þare-for ere we all oure lyfe tym wit-owtten sekenesse
8 & lyffeȝ lang & alwaye are in gude hele till oure lyffes ende. We vse neuer-mare na medcyns ne sekes na helpe for þe hele of oure bodys. At a terme of deede endes oure lyfes, for ane of vs leues na langere þan an-oþer, Bot efter þe order of þe birthe of
12 man, þe terme of deede comes till ilke a man. Thare comeȝ nane of vs at na fire for na calde, ne clatheȝ comeȝ þare nane apon vs, Bot alway we ga naked. We fulfill neuer þe desyres of oure bodys. Thurgh pacyence we suffree all thyngeȝ. All
16 oure inwarde enemys we slaa, So þat we drede nane enemys wit-owtten. For lightlyer es a citee or a castelle taken þat es ensegged bathe wit inwarde enemys & wit-owtten, þan þat þat es ensegged allanly wit owtwarde enemys. Bot þou, emperour,
20 feghtes agaynes owtwardeȝ enemys for [to] foster & nuresche thyn inwardeȝ enemys, þe whilke ere fendes of helle. We Bragmayns has slayne all oure inwardeȝ enemys and þarefore we drede nane owtwarde enemys ne nane helpe sekes for to hafe agayneȝ þam*
24 noþer be see ne be land. Bot we ere always sewre ynoghe, and lyffeȝ wit-owtten any drede. Oure bodys we hill wit þe leues of trees and þe fruyte of þam we ete. We ete mylke also and drynkes water of a gude ryuere or of swete welles.
28 We wirchippe a godd, and till hym alwaye we ȝelde lonyngeȝ. We desire þe life of þe werlde þat es to come, and vs liste noȝte here þe þyng þat turneȝ to na profett. We spekke noȝte mekill, Bot when we ere artede for to speke we say noȝte bot
32 þe sothe, and onane we halde vs still. Reches luffe we noȝte. Couetise es a thynge þat may noȝte be filled, þe whilke ofte-sytheȝ bryngeȝ a man till a mescheuous ende. Wrethe ne envie es þare nane amangeȝ vs, ne nane of vs es strangere þan
36 anoþer. Of the pouert þat we hafe we ere riche, for we hafe it in comon. We strife neuer mare, ne beres neuer wapen. We bere peesse ilkan till oþer of custom, noȝte thurgh vertu. Domes hafe we nane amanges vs, for we do nane ill, whare-fore

to mother earth. They use such meats as do them no harm, nor do they eat too much, and there are no great-bellied men amongst them. They have no sickness nor medicines. They live the fixed term of life. They have no fire for cold. They conquer themselves. Alexander conquers others and is conquered by his inner enemies. Therefore do the Brahmins   * Leaf 33. dread no foes. They are clad in leaves and drink water. They worship one god and desire eternal life. They love not long speech nor covetousness. They are all of equal might and riches, and bear no weapons. Neither have they dooms, for they do no ill.

Dindimus' letter to Alexander.

[Marginal notes:]
Neither need they mercy.
They have no avarice, adultery, or lechery, and have therefore no penance or sudden death.

They are arrayed in no bright clothes.

They always keep to the same trades.
They use no baths.
They will make no other man serve them.
They have no houses nor vessels, but live in caves and crags.
They sleep on the earth.
* Leaf 33 bk.
Their houses become their graves.
They sail not the seas for trade.
They seek no eloquence but rather simplicity of speech. They have no philosophers, for such are liars and of unsteadfast speech.
But in their schools they learn wisdom and righteousness.
They love not plays.

[Main text:]
we schulde be called'vn-to dome. A law þare es þat es contrary til oure kynde. For we do na mercy, bi-cause we do no thyng whare-fore we sulde aske mercy. We do na labour þat pertene3 to couetise or auarice. We giffe no3te oure bodyse to lechorye, we do nane advowtrye, ne we do na synn whare-fore vs sulde nede to do penance. We fynde na fawte in na thynge, For we all does that þat righte es. We dye na sodeyne dede, For thurgh foule dedis we corupte no3te þe ayere. We vse na clathes þat are littede of dyuerse coloures. Oure wiffes ne are no3te gayly arayed' for to plese vs. Ne wit þam we comon no3te bi-cause of luste of lecherye, bot bi-cause of childre getynge. Our wyffes sekes na noþer clethynge, þan þe forluke of godd' hase granted' þam. And whaa dare take apon hym for to chaunge his wirkynge, an heghe syn vs thynke it ware till any man for to presume to do it. Baththis vse we nane, ne warme water to wasche oure bodys wit all. Þe Son mynistres vs hete, and þe dewe of þe ayer ministre3 vs moyster & wete. We hafe na thoghte of na thynge, ne we schewe na lordechipe abownn oþer men þat ere lyke vn-till us. For a grete crueltee we halde it to constreyne a man to serue vs, whayme kynde & þe forluke of godd' hase made oure broþer als fre als we are. We brynne na stanes for to make lyme off and þare-wit to make vs howses at duelle in, and curiouse palase3 : ne vessell make we nane. In caues or creuyce3 of cragges we duelle, whare thare come3 na noyse of wyndes * ne whare vs thare drede na rayne. On þe erthe we slepe wit-owtten any besynesse. Swilk howses we hafe; in þe whilke, whils we lyffe, we duelle, and when we dye, þay ere oure graues. We sayle no3te in þe see aboute na merchandyse, in þe whilke þay suffre many perills þat sayles þarein & many meruaylles can tell offe. The crafte of Eloquence & faire speche, lere we no3te for to polishe oure wordes; Bot thurgh þe sympilnesse þat we hafe þat suffres vs no3te to lye, all oure speche we speke. Scoles of philosophres haunt wee no3te, whase techechynge3 es alway discordand & na thynge certayne, ne stabill diffines, bot for þe mare partye lyes. Bot þa scoles we haunte in þe whilke we lere to lyffe vertuosly and also thynges þat teches vs for to do no wrange to no man. Bot after verray rightwisnesse to helpe ilk man at oure powere. Plays lufe we nane.

[Line numbers: 4, 8, 12, 16, 20, 24, 28, 32, 36]

Dindimus' letter to Alexander.   81

Bot if vs liste hafe any disporte we take & redeȝ þe lyfes But they rather read of the lives and deeds of their forefathers and weep if there be any cause for laughter.
& þe dedis of oure Auncestres, and oure predicessours. And
if we fynde any thynge in þaṁ þat es cause of laughtre
4 þar-at we wepe & makes dole. Neuer-þe-lesse we behalde
oþer thynges of þe whilke oure hertis ere gladdide and grete
lykyng has, þat es at say, heueṅ-schyne wit sternes wit-owt
nowmer; þe soṅ faire & bryghte, of whase bryghtnesse aħ
8 þe werlde takes lyghte and hete. The see we se alwaye They are glad in the brightness of nature and its delights.
of purpour coloure, and wheṅ tempesteȝ ryseȝ þare-iṅ it dis-
truyes noȝte þe land' þat es nere it, as it does in ȝoure
partes. Bot he embraceȝ it as his sister and gase aboute it. He will tell Alexander a little of their doctrine. Alexander has conquered the world, and made the sun pale. The visages of his men grow thin and hungry. They offer their children to Maumets. Alexander sows
12 And in þe se we see many dyuerse kyndeȝ of Fisches,
Delphines & porpaseȝ layke þaṁ. We hafe lykyng also for
to bihalde faire feldes alouer florescheď wit flores of þe whilke
a swete reflaire enters in-tiħ oure noseȝ, in þe whilke
16 a sensible saule hase maste delite. Also we delit vs in faire
placeȝ of woddeȝ & of swete welles whare we here swete
sangeȝ of fewles. This customs hafe we al-way, þe whilke, &
þou walde halde noȝte bot a while, we trowe þou suld thynke
20 þaṁ riȝte hard'. Blame noȝte me, for aħ þat þou requerede
me be þi lettres I send þe wretyṅ. Neuer-þe-less, and it
sulde noȝt displese the, I walde teħ þe a littiħ of oure
doctryne þe whilke makes oure lyfe to seme harde vn-to þe.
24 ȝee hafe wit-in a schorte while conquered' & made sugete
vn-to ȝour empire aħ Asy, Europe, & Affryke. As ȝour selfe
hase¹ sayde * ȝe make þe lighte of þe soṅ to faile, wheṅ ȝe * Leaf 34. discord between kings and ever desires more ground. The gods of the Greeks do ill deeds and they are fools that serve such. The Greeks fain con-
seke þe termes of his course thurgħ werre. Ȝe ete aħ manere
28 of thynges² þat comeȝ tiħ hande, And ȝour vesages semeȝ as
ȝe ware fastande & hungry. Ȝe slaa ȝour childre makande
sacrafice of þaṁ to Mawmetes. Ȝe sawe discorde bi-twix
kynges and thase þat schulde be meke ȝe stirre for to be
32 prowde. Ȝe make meṅ to thynke þat grete space of landes
suficeȝ þaṁ noȝte And so þay seke duellynge placeȝ of heueṅ.
'Also thurgħ ȝour goddes ȝe do many iħ dedis, as þay didď
þaṁ selfe, Ensample of Iubiter ȝour godď & of Proserpyna þat
36 ȝe wirchipe as a goddesse. For Iubiter defouled' many mens

---

¹ Scribblings at the bottom of leaf 33 bk. :—'P.', 'G.' below the P., then 'H. Amen. Do For'.
² Scribe originally wrote *thynkes*, but changed the *k* into a *g*, thus *thynges*.

6

The Brahmins to Alexander. Their betterness.

quer other men.

They change their laws, and do but hold with fine speech, loving gold and silver and rich things. The Greeks live in gluttony and fall sick.

The wisdom of the Brahmins surpasses all that of the Greeks. They burn the bodies of the dead and do not give back to earth what earth has given forth. The Brahmins slay no beasts in the worship of God, neither do they have gold nor silver nor precious things in His service, since for none of these things does God hear man, but only for his good works. Prayer is the word and the word is God. Therefore are the Greeks fools, holding themselves
* Leaf 34 bk.
heavenly and thinking they communicate with God whilst they defile

wyfes, and Proserpyna made many meɴ to do advowtry wit hir. Fuƚƚ wreched & fuƚƚ hye fules þay ere, þat swilke goddes wirchipes. ȝee wiƚƚ noȝte suffer meɴ lyfe in þaire awenɴ libertee bot makes þaɱ ȝour thralles & ȝour sugetes. ȝe deme 4 noȝte riȝtwisly, ȝe gerre ȝour iugeȝ change ȝour lawes as ȝow liste. ȝe say many thyngeȝ þat sulde be donne, bot ȝe do þaɱ noȝte. ȝe halde na maɴ wysse bot hym þat hase Eloquence of speche. ȝe hafe aƚƚ ȝour witt in ȝour tungeȝ, and aƚƚ ȝour 8 wysdome es in ȝour mouthe. ȝe lufe golde & siluer & gaders þam to-gedir and desyreȝ to hafe grete howseȝ & hye, and grete multitude of seruandeȝ. ȝe ete & drynk to mekiƚƚ, so þat oftymes ȝour stomake thurgh grete repleccioɴ es greued & many 12 sekenesse þare-thurgh ȝe faƚƚ in, & so ofte sythes dyes before ȝour tyme. ȝe wolde euer-mare halde ȝour reches and aƚƚ thyngeȝ þat ȝe may gete. Bot aƚƚ thyngeȝ at þe laste leues ȝow. Þe wysdoɱ allanly of þe Bragmayns passeȝ aƚƚ ȝour witt & 16 ȝour wysdoɱ. For, & we wele consedere, þe same moder þat broghte forthe stanes & trees, of þe same was bathe oure bygynnyng & ȝours. ȝe honowre ȝour Sepultours curyousely wit golde & syluer, and in vesseƚƚe made of precyouse stanes ȝe putt 20 þe asse of ȝour bodys, wheɴ þay ere brynned. And what may be werre þaɴ for tiƚƚ take þe banes, þat þe erthe sulde hafe, for to ga bryɴ þaɱ, and noȝte suffere þe erthe resayffe his element þe whilke he broghte forthe. 24

'We sla na besteȝ in þe wirchipe of goddeȝ. Nee temples make we nane, for to sett in ymageȝ of golde or of siluere in þe name of false goddeȝ, as ȝe do; ne awters of golde and of precious stanes. ȝe hafe swilke a lawe for to honoure ȝour 28 goddeȝ wit ȝour gudes for þat þay saƚƚ here ȝour prayers. Bot we vndirstande & wate wele þat noþer for golde ne siluer; ne for þe blode of calues nor gayte ne schepe Godd heres any maɴ. Bot for gude werkes þe whilke Godd lufes, and thurgh 32 þe wordes of deuote prayere. Godd wiƚƚ here a maɴ for þe worde. For thurgh worde we ere lyke to Godd. For Godd es worde,* and þat worde made aƚƚ þe werlde aud thurgh þat worde aƚƚ thyngeȝ hase beyng, Mouyng & lyfe. That worde wirchipe 36 wee and luffes & honowres. Godd es a spirite. And he lufes na-thyng bot þat that es clene. Whare-fore we halde ȝow fuƚƚ grete foles, that weneȝ ȝour kynde be heuenly, and þat ȝe hafe

The Brahmins to Alexander. Greek errors. 83

communicacioṅ with Godd͛, And neuer-þe-less files ȝour kynde
wit advowtries & fornicacions & seruyce of Mawmettis & false
goddis, and many oþer wikkede dedis : ilke a day þis ȝe do.
4 Þis ȝe luffe, anɑ þarefore wheṅ ȝe ere dede ye salt suffere tour-
mentis wit-owtteṅ nowmer. Ȝe wene þat Godd͛ wilt be mercyable
vn-to ȝow bi-cause þat ȝe offre hym blode & flesse of dyuerse
besteȝ. Bot we on þe contrarye wyse luffeȝ clennesse bathe of
8 Body & of saule, so þat we mowe hafe after þis lyfe ioy þat
neuer salt hafe ende.

'Ȝee serue noȝte a Godd͛ þat regneȝ in heueṅ, Bot ȝe do seruyce
to many false goddis. For als so many membris, als ȝe hafe oṅ
12 ȝour bodys, als many goddis ȝe wirchipe & serues. For ȝe calle
a maṅ þe lesse werlde, and riȝte as a maṅ here hase many
lymmes, so ȝe say þare are many goddes in heueṅ. Ȝe say Iuno
es godd͛ of þe hert, bi-cause he was wonder angry ; and Mars ȝe
16 say es godd͛ of þe breste, bi-cause he was prynce of Batells.
Mercury ȝe calle godd͛ of þe tung, bi-cause he was wonder
euloquent in spekyng. Hercules ȝe trowe be godd͛ of þe armes,
Bi-cause he did͛ twelfe passande dedes of armes. Ȝee trowe
20 Bacus be godd͛ of þe throtte, for he fande firste drounkynnesse.
Couetise, ȝe say, es godd͛ of þe lyuer, for he was þe firste lechoure
þat euer was. And ȝe say þat he hase in his hande a byrnand
fyrebrande whare-wit he styrres þe luste of lechery. Cereris
24 ȝe calle godd͛ of þe wambe, bi-cause scho was þe firste Fynder
of wheete. And Venus, be-cause scho was moder of lechery, ȝe
say scho es godd͛ of þe preuee membres of maṅ & womaṅ.
Mynerua, bi-cause scho was fynder of many werkes, ȝe say
28 wisdome risteȝ in her, and þare-fore ȝe calt hir godd͛ of þe heued͛.
And oṅ þis wyse alt þe body of maṅ ȝe deuyde in goddes,
& na party þareoffe ȝe lefe in ȝour aweṅ powere. Ne ȝe trowe
noȝte that a godd͛ þat es in heueṅ made ȝour bodys of noghte.
32 False goddes ȝe wirchipe þat salt brynge ȝow to thralledome
& schame & schenchipe, and to thaym̄ ȝe make sacrafice &
tribute payes. Vn-to Mars ȝe offere a Bare. To Bacus ȝe
offere a gayte; To Iune a pacoke; To Iubiter a Bulle; To
36 Appollo * a swane¹; To Venus a doufe; To Mynerua ane
owle; To Cereris floure; To Mercury hony. And Hercules ȝe
onowreṅ wit floures & grene brau*n*ches of treesseȝ. Þe temple

their own kind with foul sins and idolatry. When they die they shall suffer endless pain and their slain beasts avail them nought.

The Greeks serve not one God but many. They have for every human member a god. The account of all the Greek gods and their evil doings.

Thus they give all their body over to numberless gods, not worshipping the oneCreator, but rather false gods that bring them into
* Leaf 35.
thraldom. The sacrifices

---
¹ Bottom of leaf 34 *swanne*, top of leaf 35 *swane*.

6—2

The Brahmins to Alexander; the ills of Heathendom.

which they offer to their gods.
The gods become not their helpers but their tormentors, egging them on to all evils. Yet they must hearken to them.

of Couetyse ȝe enourne wit roseȝ. Alle ȝour myghte & ȝoure triste ȝe putt in þam þat may ȝow na-thyng helpe at nede. Now sothely ȝe pray þam̃ noȝte to be ȝour heipers, Bot ȝoure tourmentours. For it byhoues nedis be þat, als many goddes als ȝe wirchipe & gyffeȝ þam̃ powere of ȝour lymmes, als many tourmenteȝ ȝe suffere. Ane of ȝour goddes stirres ȝow to fornycacion. Ane oþer to ete & drynke to mekill, and anoþer to feghte & stryffe. All ere þay ȝour lordes, and to þam̃ ȝe obey & serues and wirchippes. So þat wonder it es þat ȝour wrechid' bodys fayles noȝte for þe many seruyceȝ þat ȝe do to so many goddes. And gud riȝte it es þat ȝe serue swilke goddes bi-cause of þe many wikkede dedis þat ȝe do.

Righteous punishment for the ill deeds of the Greeks.
The prayers of the Greeks are evil, so that they are harmed whether such be heard or not.

And for ȝe will noȝte cesse of ȝour ill dedis, þarefore ȝe serue swilke goddes till ȝour awenn̄ harme, For euermare þay desyre þat ȝe do ill. If ȝour goddes here ȝow when̄ ȝe pray to þam, þay do ȝow harme in ȝour conscience. For þat that ȝe pray fore es ill. And if þay here ȝow noghte, þan̄ ere þay contrarye to ȝour desyres. Whare-fore whethir þay here ȝow, or þay here ȝow noghte, euer-mare þay do ȝow disesse. Þise ere þa[1] tourmenteȝ þat oure doctours talde vs offe, þat here in this werlde tourmenteȝ ȝow as ȝe ware dede. For, and ȝe consyder wele, þare may no man suffere wers tourment þan̄ ȝe doo.

All the torments of hell are in the Greeks through their own vices.

For all þe takens þat oure doctours telleȝ vs ere in helle, and we see þam̃ in ȝowe.[2] Þare are many paynes in helle, ȝe suffre paynes when ȝe wake for to do advowtres, fornycacions, & thiftes, man̄-slawghters. And namely, þat ȝe bee filled' of werldly reches; ȝa, & of worldly rechesse. For oure doctours says, þare es in helle so mekill thriste, þat it may neuer be slokend'; and ȝe haue so grete Couetyse of worldely reches þat ȝe may neuer be full. Þay say also þat in helle þare es a hunde þat es callede Cerberus þe whilke hase thre heuedes; And if ȝee conseder ryȝte, ȝour wambes are lyke Cerberus.

And the bodies of the Greeks are a living hell.

For mekill etyng & drynkkynge, þay say also, þare es[3] in helle a maner of nedder þat es called' Idra. And ȝe for þe many viceȝ, þat ȝe hafe bicause of ȝour full wambeȝ may be callede Idra. Whare-fore & we bi-helde wele all þe illes þat

4

8

12

16

20

24

28

32

36

---

[1] MS. reads þa.
[2] in ȝowe inserted in the right-hand margin by the same scribe.
[3] MS. twice over, þare es.

are in heɫɫe, þay dueɫɫe in ȝow.* Waa es ȝow, wreches, þat swilke a mysbileue haldes; whare-fore after þis lyfe, ȝe moñ suffere paynes w*i*t-owtteñ nowm*er*.' Wheñ Alexander hadd' redd' þis
4 let*t*re, he was wonder wrathe, be-cause of iniury of his goddeȝ. Neu*er*-þe-less, be-lyfe he gart write anoþ*er* agayne of this teno*ur*.

¹ 'Kyng of kynges, and lorde of lordeȝ, Alex*ander* þe soñ of
8 godd' Amoñ and of þe quene Olympias, to Dindim*us*, kyng of þe Bragmayns, gretyng. If aɫɫ be fuñ trew amanges ȝow þat þou hase sent wretyñ in thy let*t*res, þañ allanly ȝe are gude meñ in þis werlde; for as þou says ȝe do nañ iɫɫ.
12 Bot wit þou wele² for certayne, þat þis maner of lyffyng comm*e*ȝ noȝte of vertu bot of custoɱ. Aɫɫ thyngeȝ þat we do, ȝe saye es synñ. And aɫɫ þe crafteȝ, þat ere amangeȝ vs on þe same wyse, ȝe say, þay ere sy*n*nes. Ȝe wiɫɫ distroye aɫɫ þe
16 customs þat mañ-kynde hedir-towarde hase hadd' & vsed.' Owther ȝe schew bi ȝo*ur* wordeȝ, þat ȝe are goddeȝ, or eɫɫs tiɫɫ goddes ȝe hafe envy. And þ*are*-fore ȝe say, as ȝe say, I may noȝt write to ȝow aɫɫ þe order of ȝo*ur* lyffyng. Bot als mekiɫɫ þ*are*-offe
20 als I may vnderstande at this tyme, I saɫɫ writte vn-to ȝow. Ȝee say ȝe vse noȝte for to tiɫɫ þe erthe, ne sawe na corne, ne plante na vynes, ne sett na trees, na to make na faire howseȝ. And þe cause here-of as it wele semes es for ȝe hafe na Ireñ.
24 whare-of ȝe myghte make ȝow tuyles for to wirke with-aɫɫe. And þ*are*-fore ȝow by-houes nedes ett herbes & lede an harde lyfe, ryȝte as besteȝ. For ȝe may nowþ*er* gette brede ne flesche ne fysche. Does noȝt wolfes oñ þe same wyse, þe whilke, wheñ
28 þay may noȝte gete þaire fiɫɫ of flesche, þay fiɫɫ þaire belys of þe erthe? And it ware lefuɫɫ or lykande to ȝow to come tiɫɫ oure cuntree, we sulde lere na wisdoɱ of ȝoure nede. And þ*are*-fore late ȝo*ur* hung*er* habyde at hame in ȝo*ur* awenñ cuntree.
32 Þat mañ es noȝte mekills at commend' þat alwayes lyffes in disesse. Bot he es gretly to commend,' þat in reches lyffeȝ attemp*er*ally. Bot and meñ schulde be commendid' þat are oppressed' w*i*t disesse, þañ sulde blynd meñ, leprouse meñ,
36 & oþ*er* swilke ou*er* aɫɫ oþ*er* be commendid'; þe blynde, for he sees noȝt at desyre; þe pou*er*, for he hase noȝte at do. And we walde make oure duellynge in ȝo*ur* cuntree we sulde suffere

¹ Five lines spaced red capital *K* with small *k* in the margin beside.   ² *Bot wit þou wele* repeated in MS.

do no ill, since their defect hinders them. Their chastity is due to want of food. But the Brahmins live as mere beasts.

The Brahmins seek no learning, having beastlike no feeling or delight in good. But men can rejoice through free will. The changes of the world and of the ages of man are even as the day brightens and darkens, even as a child is simple, youth presumptuous, and old age stable. Who will look for the opposite? The delights of the senses and of those things given us by earth, sea, and sky. Abstinence from this is

pouert & wrechidnes riȝte as ȝe do. Ȝe say also þat ȝour wyfes vseȝ na prowde aray for to plese þaire husbandeȝ, and þe cause es for þay hafe na noþer * thyng for tiłł araye þam̅ wit.[1] Also ȝe say ȝe do nane advowtries ne fornycacions. And þat es na meruaile! For-whi, how sulde þay hafe luste to lechery þat etes noȝte. Luste of lechery es noȝte comonly, bot yf it come of hete of þe leuer or ełłs of habudance of mete & drynke. Bot ȝe ete na-thynge bot herbes & roteȝ, as ȝe ware swyne, & drynkes water & vnnethes may ȝe sloken̅ ȝour hunger and þarefore ȝe hafe nan̅ appitite to women̅.

'Ȝe hafe na liste to studie aboute lerynge, ne ȝe seke na mercy ne dees nane tiłł oþer. And ałł this ȝe hafe in comon̅ wit besteȝ. For riȝte as besteȝ hase nowþer reson̅ ne discrecion̅, ne hase na felynge of gude, riȝte so þay hafe na delite in gode. Bot tiłł vs resonable men̅ þat has free wiłł of kynde ere many lykynges & blandeschyngeȝ granted. For it es im-possible þat þis werlde wyde & brade sulde noȝte hafe sum̅ chaungynge of gouernance; So þat ne after heuynes & sorowe, Ioy & myrthe sulde noȝte folowe.[2] For-why manes wiłł es variable & chaungeable þat chaungeȝ wit þe heuen̅ abownn̅. On þe same wyse manes hert es dyuerse. For when̅ þe day es clere, manes hert es gladde & blythe. And when̅ þe day es derke, manes wittis are derke & dułłe & heuy. Also men̅ chaungeȝ thurgh dyuerse ages. For barnehed reioyse it in sympilnesse, ȝouthede in presumptuosnes, And grete elde in stabilnes. For wha wiłł luke efter wysdome in a childe, In a ȝunge man̅ stabiłłnes, or in an alde man̅ wildenes? Many delitable thynges comeȝ tiłł oure mynde. For sum̅ we See wit oure eghne; Sum̅ we hafe thurgh herynge; Sum̅ we fele thurgh smellyng; Sum̅ thurgh tastynge; and Sum̅ thurgh towchynge. Sumtyme we hafe delite in salutacions & swete sangeȝ & melodys of dyuerse Instrumenteȝ. Of þe erthe we hafe al maner of gud fruyteȝ; of þe see we hafe habundance of fysche, and of þe ayere delyte of fewles of dyuerse kyndis. If þou abstene þe fra ałł thies owthir it es for pride or for envy. For pride, þat þou dispyseȝ swilke precyouse gifteȝ. For envy bi-cause þay ere noȝte gyffen̅ ȝow, as þat þay ere to vs. Bot efter myn̅ opynyon̅ I deme þat

---

[1] Leaf 35 *þam wit*; leaf 36 *þam wit*.
[2] The second vowel in *folowe* is difficult to read. It looks like *folewe*.

Dindimus to Alexander. Of the goodly ways of the Brahmins.

ȝour lyffyng and ȝour maners commes mare of foundnesse þan of wysdom. For sen ȝe are men ȝe schulde hafe þe vertuȝ of a resonable creature, and þat hafe ȝe noȝhte.' When Dindimus hadd redd þis lettre, onane he wrate anoþer to kyng Alexander of þis tenour.

due either to pride or peevishness.
He deems the Brahmins live so through folly.

[1] 'Dyndimus, þe mayster of þe Bragmayns, vn-till Alexander, gretyng. We hafe vndirstand þe tenour of þi lettres & þus we ansuere. We er noȝte * lordeȝ of this werlde, as we sulde euermare lyffe þare in. But we ere pilgrymes in þis werlde, and when dede commeȝ we wende till oþer habytacions. Oure Synneȝ greueȝ vs noȝte, ne we duelle noȝte in þe tabernacles of synners.[2] We do na thyfte. And for þe conscyence þat we haue, we gaa noȝte furthe in open. We say noȝte þat we ere goddes, ne nane envy hase vn-to þam. Godd þat made all þat es in þis werlde, he ordeyned many diuerse thyngeȝ. For warne dyuersitees ware of thyngeȝ þe werld myȝte noghte stande. Godd gaffe man fre will, for to discerne of all thyngeȝ þat ere in þe werld, and chese whilke hym lyste. Whare-fore he þat leues þe ill & cheseȝ þe gude, noȝte godd, but goddes frende he may be called. Be-cause þat we lyffe contenently, and in quiete & reste, ȝe say þat we ere goddeȝ, or elles þat we hafe envy to goddeȝ. But this suspeccion þat ȝe hafe of vs, perteneȝ to ȝow. For ȝe þat ere blawen full of þe wynde of pride ȝe aray ȝour bodys wit gloryous clethyng, and on ȝour fyngers, ȝe putt iowells of golde & precyous stanes.

Dindimus to Alexander.
* Leaf 36 bk.
Man is not lord of this world, but a pilgrim in it. The virtue of the Brahmins. God made things diverse so that the world might endure.
He gave man free will to choose of all that which him list. Not they, but the Greeks, seem envious of the gods.

'Bot I pray ȝow, what profit does þis ȝow : Golde and siluer saues noȝte a manes saule, ne susteneȝ noȝte mens bodys. Bot we þat knawes þe verray profitt of golde, and þe kynd þare-offe, when vs thristeȝ, & gase to þe ryuere for to take vs a drynke, if we fynde golde in þe way, we trede apon it wit oure fete. For golde noþer filleȝ vs when we hunger, ne slokens oure thriste, ne it heleȝ noȝte a man þat es seke. If a man thriste & drynke water, it putteȝ away his thriste. Also if a man hunger & ete mete, it does away his hunger. Bot and golde ware of þe same kynde, als son als a man hadd it, þe vice of Couetyse suld be slokynde in hym. Be þis cause es golde ill.

Gold and silver save none. They despise it as useless, quenching neither hunger nor thirst.
Neither does it slack the vice of covetousness.

---

[1] Two lines with small red capital *D* and small cursive *d* in the margin beside.   [2] MS. *synners* with a contraction mark over the *y*.

88 Alexander to the Brahmins. The pillars he raises.

Marginal notes:
The more one has the more one desires.
The Greeks worship wicked men, being themselves wicked, offering up beasts to their idols.
Thus do they, who shall die, honour themselves.

* Leaf 37.
Alexander to Dindimus.
The Brahmins live as they do because they do not mingle with other men, but are shut off from them.
They suffer even as those who lie in prison. He holds them as wretched fools, and could he but do it would march towards them with an army to make them leave their miserable life and become warriors.

For ay þe mare þat a man̄ hase þare-offe, þe mare he couetes. Wikkede men̄ are wyrchippede amangez ȝow. For comonly a man̄ luffes hym þat es lyke tiƚƚ hym selfen̄. Ȝe say þat godd' takes nane hede tiƚƚ dedly thynges. And neuer-þe-lesse ȝe bygge 4 temples, and makes autres in þam̄, and settis vp mawmettes abownn̄ þam̄, and grete delyte hase when̄ bestes ere offerde, & in þam, and at ȝour name es noysede, þis was done to þi fader, to thyn̄ Eldfader, & tiƚƚ aƚƚ thi progenytours. And þe 8 same also es highte on-to þe. Wit swilke wirchipes þay ere rewarded', þat knawes noȝte þam̄ selfe dedly.' When Alexander hadd' redd' þis lettre onane he sente anoþer agayne and that was of this tenour þe whilk þat folowes.¹

² * ' Alexander, þe son̄ of godd' Amon̄ & of þe quene Olympias, 12 kyng of kyngeȝ & lorde of lordeȝ, vn-to Dyndymus kynge of þe Bragmayns we sende. For als mekiƚƚ als ȝour duellynge es in þat partye of þe werlde fra þe begynynge, whare na strangers 16 may com̄ to ȝow, bot if it be riȝte fewe, ne ȝe may noȝte passe forthe of ȝour cuntree, but als swa say ȝe, are parred' in, and na ferrere may passe ; þarefore ȝe magnyfye ȝour manere of lyffynge and supposeȝ þat ȝe are blyssed' be-cause þat ȝe er so spered' in, 20 þat if ȝe walde neuer so gladly passe furthe for to lere þe customes þat oþer men̄ vseȝ, ȝe may noȝte ; and nyƚƚ-ȝe wiƚƚ-ȝe, ȝow by-houeȝ nedis suffere þat caytefftee þat ȝe lyffe in. Wharefore it semeȝ bi ȝour techynge, that þay þat liggeȝ in presonn̄, 24 are als mekiƚƚ at comend' als ȝe, þe whilke vn-to þaire lyues ende suffres sorowe and nede. And as me thynke, þe gudnesse þat ȝe ruse ȝow offe, may wele be lykkened' to þe paynes of þaim þat ere in presonn̄. And so þat that oure lawe demes to be done t[i]ll wikked' 28 men̄, ȝe suffere kyndely. And þare-fore hym þat we halde wyse, ȝe halde an Ebbere fule³. Sothely me thynk ȝour lyffynge es noȝte blyssed' bot wrechid' and as it ware a chastyng to ȝowe. I swere ȝow by oure goddeȝ of myghte, þat, & I myghte come 32 to ȝow with an oste, I sulde gare ȝow leue ȝour wrechid' lyfe, and by-come men̄ of armes, als many of ȝow als ware able.' When Alexander had' sent this lettre tiƚƚ Dyndimus he gart

---

¹ The second vowel of *folowes* is often written so small as to render it uncertain whether it is an *o* or *e*.
² Four lines with red capital *A*.
³ *fou* written in MS. before *fule* and scratched out. This word *fon* or *fou* was complete and not a half-written word, as the MS. shows.

The wonders of India.   89

rayse vp a pelare of Marble a wonder grete, & an heghe, and gart writt þare-apon this title wit lettres of grewe, of latyne, and of þe langage of Inde. 'I Alexander, Philipp son of
4 Macedoyne, after þe discomfytour & þe dedd of Darius & Porus come on werre vn-to this place.'

¹ Fra þeine kyng Alexander & his Oste remowed & come intill a felde, þat was called Actea & þare þay luged. Abowte
8 þat felde was a thikke wodd of treesse berand fruyte; of þe whilke wilde men þat duelt in þe Same wodd vsede for till hafe þaire fude, whase bodyes ware grete as geauntez, and þaire clethynge ware made of skynnes of dyuerse bestez. And when
12 þay saw Alexander Oste luge þare, onane þare come oute of þe wodd, a grete multitude of þam wit lange roddes in þaire handz & bi-gan for to feghte wit þe oste. And þan Alexander commanded þat all [þe] oste schulde sette vp a schowte at anes. And also
16 sone als þe wylde* men herde þat² noyse, þay were wondere fered be-cause þay had neuer be-fore herde swilke a noyse. And than þay be-gan to flee hedir & thedir in þe wodd. And Alexander & his men persued þam and slewe of þam vi^c xxx iiij. And þay slew
20 of Alexander knyghtes xxvij. In þat felde Alexander & his oste leuged iij dayes and vetailed þam of þat fruyte þat growed in þe wodd.

³ Fra þeine þay remowed and come till a grete ryuer, & luged
24 þam þare. And as it ware abowte none, þare come apon þam a wilde man, als mekill als a geaunte. And he was rughe of hare all ouer, and his hede was lyke till a swyne, And his voyce also. And when Alexander saw hym, he bad his knyghtis tak
28 hym & bryng hym bi-for hym. And when þay come abowte hym, he was na thynge fered, ne fledd noȝte, bot stodd baldly bifore þam. And when Alexander saw that, he comanded þat þay sulde take a ȝonge damesell & nakken hir & sett hir bi-fore hym.
32 And þay did soo. And onane, he ranne apon hir romyandd as he hadd bene wodd. Bot þe knyghtes wit grete deficcultee refte hyr fra hym. And ay he romyed & made grete mane. And efte þay broghte hym till Alexander and sett hym bi-fore hym.
36 And Alexander wonderd gretly of his figure. And þan he

Alexander raised up a pillar and wrote his victories on it in Greek, Latin, and in the language of India.

They come to a forest full of wild men eating fruit and clothed in the skins of beasts. They fight Alexander with rods in their hands.

* Leaf 37 bk.

The Greeks put them to flight by shouting, and slay many of them.

They come to a great river and stay there. There they meet a wondrous wild man with a swine's head and voice.

They tempt him with a naked damsel and

---

¹ Four lines with red capital F.
² þat at the bottom of leaf 37 and þe at the top of leaf 37 bk.
³ Five lines with large red F, small f beside.

then burn him alive. They come to a wondrous woodland with trees that spring up in the day-time and at sunset sink back into the earth, with fruit of sweet smell but of bitter taste. A knight takes of this, but is smitten dead by an evil spirit, and a voice proclaims the same to any that come nigh. In that * Leaf 38. place are tame birds, and who touches them is scorched by fire. They come to a mountain, climb for 8 days, and at the top they fight dragons, etc. Going down they come into a dark valley with wondrous trees and streams, and a mountain with thick air.	gerte bynd hym till a tree & make a fyre abowte hym & brynne hym. And so þay didd. ¹ Fra þeine þay remowed & come till anoþer felde in þe whilke þare ware growand treesse, of a wonderfull heghte, and þay bigan for to sprynge vp at þe son rysynge ; 4 And bi þe son settynge þay wyted a-way in-to þe erthe agayne. At þe firste houre of þe day þay bi-gan to sprynge oute of þe erthe, & so þay wex ay to myddaye, and þan þay bi-gan to decresse. And by þe son settynge þay ware in þe erthe agayne, 8 And was na thyng of þam sene bi-fore on þe morne. Þir treesse bare a fruyte wonder swete of reflayre bot þay [ware] bitter of taste. When Alexander saw þat fruyte he bade a knyghte bryng hym þareoffe. And he went & tuk þare-offe, and onane 12 a wikked spirit smate hym, and he-lyfe he was dede. And þan þay herd a voyce in þe ayer þat said on þis wyse : ' What man so neghes þir treesse he sall dye onane.' Þare was also in þat felde fewles wonder meke & tame. Bot what man so layde 16 hande on any of þam, onane þare come fire oute of þam, & brynt hym riȝte greuosly. *² Than þay remowed fra þeine, And come till a Mountayne, þat was so hye, þat þay ware viij dayes in gangyng ar þay 20 myȝte wyne to þe heghte þare-offe. And when þay come to þe heghte of it, þare come agaynes þam a grete multitude of dragones, Serpentes, and lyones þe whilke turmentid Alexander & his men reghte gretely. And at þe laste, þay askaped þaire 24 daungere, and went doune of þe mountayne and come in-till a vaylay þat was so myrke þat vnnethes myghte ane of þam See anoþer. In þat depe valay ware treesse growand of whilke þe fruyte & þe lefes ware wonder sauory in þe tastynge, and reuells 28 of water faire & clere. Aghte dayes contenuelly þay saw na son. And at þe viij days end þay come to þe fote of a mountayne whare all þe Oste thurgh a wikked thikk ayer ware so gretley disessed þat þay ware in poynte to hafe bene choked 32 þare-offe. And when þay come a-bown on þe mountayne, þay fande þe ayer mare sotell, and þe lighte of þe day mare clere. And þus þay ware wendand vpwarde, on þis Mountayne Elleuen, xj, days wit grete trauaile. And when þay come to þe 36

¹ Four lines with red capital *F* and small *f* beside.
² Four lines with red capital *T* and a dragon within, and the head of a dragon above with sting out.

The mountains that border the skies. The battle with the Basilisk. 91

hegheste of þis Mountayne, þay saw on þe toþer syde faire weder
& bryghte. And þan þay went down of þis Mountayne, and
come in till a grete playne of whilke þe erthe was wonder rede.
4 And in þis playne þare ware growande treesse wit-owtten
nowmer; and þay passed noȝte a cubit in heghte, & þaire fruyte
& þaire lefes ware passandly swete as þay had bene fyges. And
þay fande þare reuells riȝte many, of clere water as cristalle.
8 And it was als nureschand to manes body, as it hadd bene
mylke wit-outen eny oþer mete. Thurgh þat ilk playne þay
went fourty .xl. days and þan þay com till wonder heghe
Mountaynes; and it semed as þe toppes had towched þe firma-
12 ment. And þir Mountaynes ware als brant vp-riȝte as þay had
bene walles. So þat þare was na clymbyng vpon þam. And at
þe laste þay fande twa passageȝ be-twix. þase Mountaynes, of
whilke, þe tane streched to-warde þe west, and þe toþer towarde
16 þe Este. Than Alexander demed þat that dyuyson be-twix þase
Mountaynes was made thurgh Noye flode. And þan þay went
by þat passage þat streched to warde þe Este Seuen days.
And on þe heghten .viij. day þay fande a Basilisc þat men
20 calleȝ a Cocatrys, a grete & ane horrible. And bicause of his
grete elde he was foull stynkand. *Þis ilke Basilisc was so
venymous, þat noȝte all anely thurgh his stynke, bot also
thurgh his sighte allane, whaym so he luked on, he sulde dy
24 onane; þan þe Macedoynes and þe persyenes, as þay passede
thurgh þe strayt way dyed thikk-falde thurgh þe sighte of þat [1]
Basilisc. And when Alexander knyghtis saw that perill, þay
durste passe na forther bot said amangeȝ þam: 'Þe vertue of
28 oure goddes,' quoth þay, 'es bifore vs, þat schewes vs þat we
schulde ga na forthir.' Bot Alexander went bi hym ane vppon
an heghe cragge, where he myghte see on ferrome fra hym.
And þan he saw this pestellencius beste þe Basilisc lygg
32 slepande in myddes of þe passage. Þe kynde of hym was þat,
als so sone als he felid a man or a beste com nere hym,
for to open his eghne & stare appon þam, and als many
als he luked on, solde sudaynly falle doun & dye. When
36 Alexander had sene hym, Be lyfe he went dounne of þe [2]
cragge, and gart sett a merke þat na man sulde passe. And

They climb
this mountain
for eleven days
and then they
come through
clear weather
into a land of
red earth grow-
ing dwarf trees
with wonder-
fully sweet
fruit. And
here they
find crystal
streams whose
waters nourish
as though they
were milk.
They march
through that
plain forty
days, and then
they come to
mountains
whose tops
reach the skies
and in which
were two
passages, one
towards the
west and the
other towards
* Leaf 38 bk.
the east, which
Alexander
thinks were
made by the
Flood. They go
east seven
days.
On the
eighth day
they find a
Basilisk that
slays through
look alone.
He kills many.
Alexander sur-
veys him from
afar off.

---

[1] þat inserted above the line by scribe.
[2] g first turned into c, then finally erased between þe and cragge.

The wondrous mountain and the palace of the sun.

Alexander approaches him shielded by a mirror, so that the Basilisk slays himself with his own glances.

þan he gart a pavysse be made seuen cubites of lenghte & foure on brede; and on þe vtter syde þare-offe he gart sett a grete Mirroure, And a large. And at þe nethir ende of þe pavisse he gart nayle a burde þe lenthe of a cubit for to couere wit his legges, and his fete, so þat na party of hym my3te be sene. And þan Alexander tuk þis pavisse in his handis, and went towarde this Basilisc, and warned his men þat nan of þam sulde passe his termes. And when he come nere þe basilisc, þe basilisc opynde his eghne. And wit a grete ire he bi-helde þe Mirroure and saw hym-selfe þare-in. And of þe refleccion of þe bemes of his sighte strykande appon hym-selfe

The Basilisk being slain they burn him, and praise Alexander.

Sudanly he was dede. And when Alexander knewe wele þat he was dede, he called till his knyghtis; And bad þam come see hym þat slewe þaire felawes. And when þay come till hym, þay saw þe Basilisc dede. And þan þay comended & prayssed gretly his hardynesse and his hye witt, And went & brynede þe Basilisc at þe commandement of Alexander.

At last they found their way barred, and must come back to the plain. Then they went westward fifteen days and then to the left. They come to a mountain of adamant hung

¹ Fra þeine þay went till þey come to þe ferreste of þat waye; and ferrere my3te þay no3te wynn. For þare ware so hye Mountaynes agaynes þam and cragges like walles þat þay my3te passe no forþer. And þan þay turned agayne, and come to þe forsaide playne; and went by þat way þat streched towarde þe weste fyvftene .xv. days. And þan þay lefte þat way, And turnede on þe lefte hande. And so þay went foure score
xx
iiij days, and at þe laste þay come till a Mountayne of adamande; and at þe fute þare-offe þare hange chynes of golde. Þis Mountayne hadd made * of saphyres twa thowsande gree3 & a halfe, by þe whilke men ascendid to þe summit of þe Mountayne. And þare Alexander & his Oste luged þam.

* Leaf 39.

around with chains of gold and with sapphire steps.

Alexander goes up the mountain with twelve princes, and finds a wondrous palace of precious

² And on þe morne Alexander Offerd sacrafice till his goddes, And þan he tuk with hym xij twelue prynce3 of þe wyrchipfulleste þat he hade, and went vp bi þe forsaid gree3 till he come aboun on þe Mountayne. And þare he fande a palace wonder faire and curiously wroghte; and it hade twelue 3ates and thre score & ten wyndows. And þe lyntalls bathe of þe durs and of þe wyndows ware of fyn golde, wele burnescht, and þat Palace was called þe howse of þe son. Þare was also

---

¹ Four lines with red capital *F* and small *f* beside.   ² Four lines with red capital *A*.

Then Alexander meets the warden of the holy trees. 93

a temple all of golde & of precious stanes, And bi-fore þe
dores þare-offe þare was a vyne of golde, berande grapes of
charbuncles, of Rubyes, Dyamandeȝ, and many oþer maneres of
4 precyous stanes. Þan kyng Alexander & his princeȝ went in-to
þe palace; and fande þare a man liggand' in a bedd' of golde, and
couerd' wit a riche clathe of golde. And he was riȝte a mekill
man and a faire, And his berde & his heued' ware als whitt
8 als any wolle; and hym semed' lyke a Bischoppe. Als son als
Alexander & his prynceȝ saw þis alde man þay knelid' dounne
on þaire kneesse and saluste hym. And he answerd' & saide:
'Welcom Alexander,' quoþ he, 'I telle the þou sall see, þat neuer
12 flescly man bi-fore this tyme sawe; And þou sall here þat neuer
erthly man herde are.' And Alexander answerd' & sayd': 'Maste
blyssed' alde man,' quoth he, 'how hase þou knawyng of me?'
'For sothe,' quoth he, 'bi-fore Noy flode couerde all þe erthe,
16 knewe I bathe the, & thi dedis. I wate wele þou desyres for
to See þe haly treeȝ of þe Son And þe Mone þe whilke telleȝ
thyngeȝ þat ere to come.' 'Ȝaa for sothe,' quoþ Alexander,
'þer es na-thynge þat I desyre mare, þan for to see þam.'
20 And he was riȝt gladd'. Þan saide þe alde man till hym:
'And ȝe be clene of flescly dede wit women, þan es it leefull
to ȝow to see þam and to entir in-to þat haly place þat es
a sette of godd'. And if ȝe be noȝte clene, it es noȝte leefull
24 to ȝow.' 'Ȝis, sir, sothely,' quoþ Alexander, 'we ere clene.'
Þan raise þe alde man vp of þe bedd' þat he lay in, and
said' vn-to þam: 'Putteȝ offe ȝour ryngeȝ,' quoþ he, 'and ȝoure
clathes, & ȝour schone, and folowes me.' And þay dyd'[1] so.
28 And þan Alexander tuk wit hym tholomeus and Antiochus,
& folowed' þe alde man, and went thurgh þe wodd' þat
was aboun on þe Mountayne closed' with mannes handeȝ.
Þe * treesse of þat wodd' ware an hundreth .c. fote lange &
32 hye, and þay ware lyke lorers or Olyue treesse; And out
of þam þare ran rykyles & fynne bawme. And as þay went
thurgh þat wodd' þay saw a tree wondere hye, in þe whilke
þare satt a mekill fewle. Þat tree hadd' noþer þare-on lefes ne
36 fruyte. Þe fewle þat satt þare-on hadd' on his hedd a creste
lyk till a pacokke, & his beeke also crested'. Abowte his nekke,
he hadd' fethirs lyke golde. Þe hynder of hym was lyk purpure;

metal and stones.
He goes into the palace.
He finds an aged man there of Bishop-like appearance.
He kneels and salutes him.
The aged man speaks and tells him he shall see and hear what never earthly man did before. He shall have his desire and know the future.
He can only see the holy trees of the sun and the moon if clean of fleshly deeds.
He must put off everything to see them.
Alexander, Ptolemy, and Antiochus follow the
* Leaf 39 bk.
old man through the wood on the mountain, through wondrous trees that shed incense and balm.

---
[1] The scribe first wrote de and then changed the e into a y, making it into dyd.

Alexander speaks with the Holy Trees.

They see the Phoenix. They come to the holy trees of the sun and the moon. The old man tells him to look up and think and the Spirit of the Trees shall answer his thought. These trees were high. The leaves of the sun tree golden red, of the moon tree shining white. Alexander would sacrifice to these trees but may not. The sun tree speaks in Indian or Greek, the moon tree begins in Greek and ends in the language of India. He gets his answer. He shall win the world but never see home again.

* Leaf 40.

Twenty months

and þe tayle was ownnded͛ ouerthwert, wit a colour reede as rose & wit blewe. And his fethers ware riȝte faire schynand͛. Wheñ Alexander saw þis fewle he was gretely meruailled͛ of þe faired͛ of hym; þañ saide þe Alde mañ : 'Alexander,' quoþ 4 he, 'þis ilke fewle þat þou here seese es a fenix.' And þañ þay went forþer thurgħ þe forsaid͛ wodd͛, And come to thiese haly treeȝ of þe soñ & þe mone þat growed͛ in myddeȝ of þe wodde. And þañ þe alde mañ saide tiħ Alexander : 'Luke vp,' 8 quoþ he, ' to ȝone haly treeȝ, and thynke in thi hert what preuatee so þe liste, and þou saħ hafe a trewe ansuere. Bot luke þat þou speke na worde in opyñ. And þare-by saħ þou witt þat it es a gude spiritt, þat knawes thi thoghte.' Thir 12 twa treeȝ were wonder hye. And þe tree of þe Soñ had͛ leues lyk fyne golde, reed & faire schynande. And þe tree of þe mone had lefes whitt als syluer & faire schynande. And þañ walde Alexander hafe Offrede Sacrafyce to þir treeȝ. Bot 16 þe alde mañ walde noȝte suffre hym͂, bot said͛: 'It es noȝte leuefuħ,' quoþ he, ' in þis haly place, nowþer to offre encense, ne to slaa na besteȝ, Bot to knele douñ to þe boles of þir treeȝ & kysse þam͂ & pray þe soñ & þe mone to giffe trew ansuers.' 20 And þan Alexander spirred͛ þe alde mañ, in what langage þe treeȝ sulde giffe þaire answers. And þe alde mañ ansuerd͛ & said͛: ' The tree of þe Son,' quoþ he, ' answers owþer aħ in þe langage of Inde or eħs of grewe. And þe tree of þe Mone 24 begynneȝ wit þe langage of grewe & endeȝ wit þe langage of Inde.'

And as þay stode þus spekande, Sudaynly þare come a bryghte beme fra þe weste þat schane ouer aħ þe wodde. And þañ Alexander kneled͛ douñ, and kyssede þe treeȝ an 28 thoght þus in his hert: 'Saħ I conquere aħ þe werlde, and efterwardeȝ wit þe victorye wende hame to Macedoyne tiħ my moder Olympias, and my sisters ? And * þañ þe tree of þe soñ ansuerd͛ softly in þe langage of Inde, And said þir verseȝ : 32

'Tú dominátorum orbis dominus simul et pater extas,
Set patrum rignum[1] per tempora nulla videbis ; '

þat es at say, 'þou ert bathe lorde & fader of aħe þe werlde,
Bot þe Rewme of thy Fadyrs saħ þou neuer see wit thyñ eghne.' 36
Þañ bygañ Alexander to thynke how lange he sulde lyffe,

[1] *Sic* in MS.

Having heard the answers he weeps and goes back.

and whate dedď he sulde dye. And þe tree of þe Mone *shall he live and his friend shall poison him.*
ansuerď by þir twa verseȝ:
'Anno completo viues & mensib*us* octo,
4 De quo confidis tibi mortis pocula dabit.'
Þat es at saye, 'A twluemonthe & aughte monethes saⱶ þou lyffe.
And þaƞ he þat þou traisteȝ oƞ, saⱶ giffe þee a drynke of dedď.'
Þaƞ bi-gaƞ Alex*ander* to thynke in his hert oƞ þis wyse,
8 'Tell me nòw, hály trèe,
Wha he ès þat sall sláa mèe.'
And þaƞ þe tree of þe soƞ ansuerď by þir twa verseȝ:
'Si tibi pandat*ur* vir qui tua facta resoluet,
12 Ill*um* confrynges & sic mea carmina fallent.'
Þat es at say: 'And I schew the þe manes name, þat saⱶ vndo *Did he but know the man's name, he would try to undo the prophecies. The old man bids him not incommode the trees.*
thi dedis, þou wiⱶ slaa hyɱ, and so saⱶ my *p*rophycye fayle.'
And þaƞ þe forsaide ald maƞ sayď tiⱶ Alexander: 'Disese
16 na mare þir trees,' *quo*þ he, '*wi*t thyne askynges. Bot to*ur*ne
we agayne, as we come hedir.' And þaƞ Alexander & his twa
prynceȝ *wi*t hy*m* to*ur*neď agayne *wi*t þe alde maƞ. And ay as
he went, he wepeď bitterly, bi-cause of his schorte tyme; and
20 his prynceȝ also weped riȝte sare. Bot he commandeď þaɱ þat
þay schulde noȝte teⱶe to na maƞ of his Oste þat that þay hadď *He goes away weeping. He commands his friends to tell no man. The old man bids him turn back and travel to the west.*
herde & sene. And wheƞ þay ware comeƞ to þe forsaide Palace
þe alde [man] saiď vn-tiⱶ Alex*ander*: 'Torne bakke agayne,'
24 *quoth* he, 'for it es noȝte leefuⱶ to na maƞ to passe forthire.
If þe liste wende towarď þe weste, þou saⱶ noȝte traueⱶe fuⱶ
lange are þou come to þe place, whare þe liste to bee.' And
wheƞ þe alde maƞ had saiď þir wordeȝ, he went in-to þe palace
28 and Alexander and his twa prynceȝ went douƞ by þe forsaide
greeȝ & come to þe Oste.
¹ Apon þe morne Alex*ander* & his Oste remoweď þeine & went *Alexander journeys fifteen days and then raises up two marble pillars, between them a table of*
agaynewarď fyftene days, And come agayne to þe forsaiď
32 playne & þare þay luged þaɱ. And þare at þe entree of þa
twa forsaiď ways, Alex*ander* gart rayse vp twa pelers of Marble,
and by-twixe þaɱ he haude a table of golde, on þe whilke was
wretyn in þe langage of grewe, hebrew, of latyne, and of Inde,
36 one this wyse: 'I, Alexander, Phillipp̄ soƞ of Macedoyne,

---

¹ Four lines with red capital *A*.

96   *King Alexander and Queen Candace.*

<small>gold with letters in Greek,
* Leaf 40 bk.
Hebrew, Latin, and Indian, telling of his great deeds and guiding aftercomers.
Thence they go westwards towards Macedonia and come to the country of Prasiac.
The men of the country bring him presents.
There is in that country a city of precious stones ruled over by a widow queen and her sons.
Alexander writes to Queen Candace sending presents, asking her to come that they may offer sacrifice together.
Queen Candace writes to Alexander on his conquests, but proclaims that they may not</small>

sett thir pelers here, after þe dedd' of Darius kyng of Perse and of Porus kynge of Inde. What mañ so will passe forþer late hyɱ * tourne one þe lefte hand. For wha so tournez one þe rizte hande he sall fynde many obstaclez & greuancez þat 4 sall perauenture lett his agayne-commynge.'

[1] Fra þeine þay remowed' thurgh þat playne and lefte þase strayte wayes, takand' þe way westeward' þe gayneste towarde Macedoyne. And at þe laste þay come till a cuntree þat highte 8 Prasiac, And þare þay luged' þaɱ. And wheñ meñ of þat cuntree herd' of þe commynge of Alexander, wit grete wirchipe þay broghte hym grete presantez of swilk thyngez as þay hadd' in þaire lande, þat es at say, skynnes of fischez lyke vn-to þe 12 skynnes of pardes, or of lyouns also, and lawmpray skynnes of sex cubites lange. In þat cuntree was a noble citee all of precyous stanes made wit-owtteñ lyme or sande, sett apoñ an hill. Of þe whilke citee, a wirchipfull lady and a faire hadd' 16 þe lordechipe. Þis lady was wedowe and scho hadd' three sones. The firste of þaɱ highte Candeolus, þe secand' Marcipius, And þe thirde hight Carator. To þis lady Alexander sent a lettre of þis tenour: 20

[2] 'Alexander þe soñ of godd' Amoñ & of þe quene Olympias, kyng of kynges & lorde of lordes vn-to queue Candace of Meroñ ioy & gretyng. We sende zow ane ymage of godd' Amoñ all of fyne golde; And þarefore comez till vs þat we may wende 24 togeder to þe Mountayne for to make sacrafyce þare to godd' Amon.' Wheñ þe Qwene Candace hadd' redd' þis lettre, Scho sent hir embassatours till kyng Alexander wit grete presantez and with a lettre of this tenour: 28

[3] 'Candace, quene of Meroñ, vn-till Alexander, kyng of kyngez, ioy. Wele we knawe þat ze hafe by reuelacioñ of godd' Amoñ þat ze schulde conquere Perse, Inde and Egipte, and subiecte vn-to zow all oþer nacions. And all þat ze hafe 32 done, nozte allanly was graunted' bot also of all oþer goddez. Till vs þat hase faire saules & bryghte it nedez noghte to make sacrafyce to godd' Amoñ in þe Mountaynes. Neuer-þe-lesse bicause we will nozte offende zowere maiestatee, we sende till 36

---

[1] Four lines with red capital *F* and small *f* in margin beside.
[2] Four lines with red capital *A* and *a* beside.
[3] Four lines with red capital *C* and *c* in the margin.

King Alexander and Queen Candace. The story of Candeolus. 97

Amoṅ ȝoure godd' a Coroṅ of golde and precyouse stanes, And sacrifice to Amon.
teṅ chynes¹ of golde sett fuł of precious stanes. And vn-to Nevertheless.
ȝow we sende a hundrethe Besauuteȝ of golde; And twa
4 hundreth papeiayes closed' in cageȝ * of golde, c childer of * Leaf 41. she
Ethipes, cc apes, cccc Olyphantis, xxxiiii vnycornes, iij panters sends him presents—
skynneȝ, of pardeȝ & lyounes cccc, and we beseke ȝowre hye a crown of
maieste þat ȝe wiłł notyfye vn-tiłł vs bi ȝour wirchipfułł lettres, gold, a hundred
8 wheder ȝe haue conquered' ałłe þe werlde and made it subiecte bezants, slave-
vn-to ȝow or noȝte.' Amangeȝ her embassatours þat scho sent children,
tiłł Alexander þare was a wonder crafty & a suteł payntoure. and various strange
And hym scho charged' þat he schulde besely by-halde Alexander beasts. These gifts
12 & purtray his fygure in a parchemyṅ skynṅ and brynge it to hir. she sends
And so he did. Alexander ressayued' þe forsaid' gyftes reuerently by a painter who is to
and sent hir noble gyftes agayne wit hir embassatours. And portray Alexander
wheṅ þay come hame þe payntour tuke hir þe fegure of Alexander on a parch-
16 purtrayed' as I saide be-fore. And wheṅ þe quene saw it, Scho ment skin. And so it
was riȝte gladde, for scho desyred' gretly for to see his fygure. was done.

² After þis ane of þe quene sonnes þat hight Candeolus went Candeolus
furthe of þe Citee wit his wyfe and a fewe of his menȝee for to goes out of the city
20 take þe sporte. And onane þe kyng of þe Bebrikes, knawyng with his wife and a
þe fairehed' of Candeolus wyfe, come appoṅ þaṁ with a grete few for sport. A
multitude of meṅ, and slew many of Candeolus menȝee and hostile
refte hym his wyfe & went his way. And þaṅ Candeolus and king knowing the
24 his meṅ þat ware lefte on lyfe went tiłł Alexander Oste for to wife's
be-seke hym of helpe agaynes þe kynge of Bebrikes. And þe beauty comes and
waches of þe oste tuke Candeolus & broghte hym bi-fore reaves her away. Can-
Tholomeus, þat was þe secund' persoṅ after Alexander. And deolus
28 Tholomeus spirred' hym what he was, & what he did' þare. comes for help and
'I am,' quoþ he, 'quene Candace soṅ and þis day als I went is brought to Ptolemy.
wit my wyfe & a preuee menȝee for to take þe sporte, þe kynge He pro-
of þe Bebrikes come apoṅ vs wit a grete multitude of meṅ and claims who he is and
32 hase slayne many of my menȝee & refte me my wyfe. And his errand.
þare-fore I am comeṅ heder for to beseke my lord', þe Emperour,
of helpe & socoure.' When Tholomeus had herd' þis onane Ptolemy
he garte take kepe of Candeolus & went tiłł Alexander tentis sends to Alexander
36 and wakkned' Alexander & talde hym & talde ilk a dele þat and wakens
Candeolus had talde hym. And wheṅ Alexander hadd' herde him.

¹ *Chenes* first written; but when the scribe had written *e* he wrote *y* over it and joined it to the next letter. ² Four lines with red capital *A*.

98 Alexander's stratagem with Candeolus.

Marginal notes (left):
Alexander bids Ptolemy put on a crown as though he were Alexander and let him send for Antiochus, and Alexander will come as Antiochus and ask counsel of Alexander as though he were Antiochus. Ptolemy does as Alexander bids him. Alexander then counsels that the king should be commanded to deliver up Candeolus' wife that night or otherwise destroy his city. Candeolus thanks Alexander as though he were Antiochus. Alexander does as he counsels and with a great force calls on the king to deliver back Candeolus' wife or else they will burn

* Leaf 41 bk.

his tale he badd' hym gange agayne till his tent and do a coroun on his hede and putt apon hym þe kynge3 clothynge, * and sett hym in the kynge3 trone & say vn-to Candeolus þat he was kyng Alexander. 'And bidd an of thi men,' quoþ he, 'feche vn-to þe Antyochus, And late hym bryng me to þe insteedd' of Antyochus, and when I come bi-for thee telle me bi-fore Candeolus[1] all þat he talde the. And aske me consell, als I ware Antyochus, what es beste to do in þat mater.' Tholomeus went and didd' all als Alexander badd' hym. And he asched' Alexander in stedd' of Antyochus be-fore Candeolus what was beste to do. And Alexander ansuerd' & sayde on herand' Candeolus: 'Wirchipfull Emperour,' quoþ he, 'if it be plesynge to 3our maiestee I will go wit Candeolus þis same nyghte to þe kynge of þe Bebrikes, and comande hym one 3our byhalue þat he 3elde Candeolus his wyfe agayne. And if he will no3te do soo, I sall late hym witt þat 3e sall sende a grete powere to his Citee & bryne it vp stikke & stourre.' When Candeolus hadd' herde hym say þus, he knelyd' vn-till hym & said': 'A a, wirchipfull Antyochus,' quoþ he, 'wele walde it seme þe for to be a kyng for þe hye witt and þe manhede þat es in the.' Than kyng Alexander tuke wit hym a grete powere and went apon þe same nyghte wit Candeolus vn-to þe Citee, whare þe kyng of þe Bebrikes lay. And whan þay come to þe citee, þe waytes cryed' apon þam, and askede what þay ware. And Alexander ansuerd' & sayd': 'Candeolus,' quoþ he, 'es here wit ane Oste of men, and þe cause of his commynge es to be restorede agayne of his wyfe þe whilke 3our kynge raueste away fro hym þis same day. And my lord' kyng Alexander commande3 3ow þat 3e delyuer hir anone, or sewrely we sall brynne this citee & 3our selfe are we passe hethyn.' And when þe men of þe citee herde this, þay ware ferde ynoghe [2] and onane went to þe kynge3 palace & brakke vp þe 3ates, & tuke Candeolus wyfe & delyuerd' hir till hir lorde. Þan Candeolus kneled' doun till Alexander & saide vn-till hym: 'A a, my dere frende,' quoþ he, 'wirchipfull Antyochus, Blyssed mot þou be for þis grete gudnes þat þou hase schewed' mee. And I beseke the nowe þat

(line numbers in right margin: 4, 8, 12, 16, 20, 24, 28, 32, 36)

---

[1] The scribe has written *Antyochus* instead of *Candeolus*, then scratched it out, and written *Candeolus* again.

[2] The scribe has first written *ynghe* and inserted the *o* above.

Alexander and Queen Candace. 99

þou will vouche-saffe for to wende with me vn-to my moder quene
Candace, þat scho may rewarde þe for þis þat þou hase done for
me.' And when Alexander herde this he was riʒte gladde. For
4 he had gretely desyrede for to see quene Candace & hir citee also.
And þan he sayd': 'Goo we,' quoþ he, 'to þe emperour and asche
hym leue.' And þay did' soo ; and when he had leue, he went
wit Candeolus. And as þay went to-gedir þay come till [1] heghe
8 mountaynes þat reched vp to þe clowdes and apon þam þare growed'
trees of a wonderfull heghte lyke * vn-to [2] cedres þat bare appills
of Inde riʒte grete, Of þe whilk Alexander wonnderde hym
gretly. Þay saw also þare vynes growe wit wondere grete
12 bobbis of grapes; for a man myʒte vnnetheʒ bere an of þam.
Þare ware also trees þat bare nutteʒ als grete als gourddeʒ.
And þare ware also many apes. Fra þeine þay went & come
to þe citee of quene Candace.
16 And when Candace herd tell þat hir son Candeolus and
his wyfe ware comande and ware safe & sounde, And at
a messangere of kyng Alexander come wit þam, scho was
wonder gladde; and onane scho arayed' hir ryally as a
20 quene suld be, and sett apon hir hedde a croun full ryche
all of golde sett full of precyouse stanes, and went furthe
wit hir lordes to þe ʒates of hir palace, for to mete hir son
Candeolus and Alexander messanger. This quene was a won-
24 dere faire lady & a semely; And when Alexander saw hir, hym
thoghte als he hade sene his moder Olympias. Hir palace was
wonder ryalle & precyouse and all þe ruffe þare-of schane wit
golde & precyouse stanes. Than quene Candace tuke Alexander
28 bi þe hande, And ledd' hym vp till hir chambir, whare þare
ware beddes arayed' wit þe fyneste clathes of golde þat myghte
be getyn; And þat chambir was of golde & precyous stanes,
þe whilke are called Onychyns & þe burdeʒ & þe bynkes of
32 euour & Smaragdeʒ & Amatistes. Þe Pelers of þe Palace ware
all of Marble, And þar ware grauen in þam cartes of werre,
þat semed' to mannes sighte as þay hadd' bene rynnand'; And
Olyphauntes tredand' men vnder þaire fete. Vnder nethe þat
36 Palace rane a water wonder swete, & clere as any cristalle.

the city.
The citizens
revolt and
return Can-
deolus' wife.
Candeolus
thanks Alex-
ander again as
Antiochus, and
invites him to
come to his
mother's city.
At this Alex-
* Leaf 42.
ander is glad,
for he had
greatly desired
to see Queen
Candace and
her city. They
ask leave of the
Emperor
as it were.
He goes with
Candeolus.
They come to
mountains
that reach
up to the sky,
with wondrous
tall trees and
vines with
great bunches
of grapes and
nut-like
gourds, and
many apes
were there.
They come to
Candace, who
comes arrayed
to meet them
as a queen.
She is of
great beauty;
and her palace
is rich.
She takes him
to her privy
chamber with
its wonderful
works of art.

---

[1] The scribe first wrote 'an heghe', but
then scratched out the an.
[2] On leaf 41 we have the words lyke to
þe cedres. On leaf 42 it continues lyke
vn-to cedres.

7—2

The next day she goes alone with Alexander to her withdrawing room, which lies beyond her bedroom. Her withdrawing room is moved on wheels by Alexander utters his wonder. * Leaf 42 bk. Queen Candace addresses him by name. Alexander's fear. She shows him his portrait. Alexander fears again. She rails at him that he, the conqueror of the world, is fallen into a woman's hands. Alexander is angered. She rails at him further.	Þat day Alexander ete wit quene Candace & hir childire. [1] Apoñ þe morne quene Candace tuk Alexander by þe right hande & ledd' hym in-till hir bedd'-chambir, and nane wit þaɱ, Bot þay twa allañ. Þis chambir was couerde all ouer wit-in wit golde & precious stanes. And it schane wit-in, as it had bene þe sonne. And oute of þis chambir scho ledd' hym in-till a wit-drawyng chambir made of cypresse. Þis chambir was sett apoñ foure wheles by crafte of clergy; And twenty xx^{ti} Olyphauntis drewe it whedir as scho wolde hafe it. And wheñ Alexander & þe quene ware entrede in-to þat chambir, onane it stirredd' & by-gan for to remowe. And þañ Alexander was astonayde & meruaylled' hyɱ gretly & said vn-to þe quene : ' For sothe,' quoþ he, ' & þir meruaills ware in oure cuntree þay ware riȝte commendable & mekill worthy * to be praysede.' The quene answerde : ' Þou saise sothe, Alexander,' quoþ scho, ' þay ware mare commendable amangeȝ þe Grekeȝ, þañ amangeȝ vs.' And also sone als Alexander herde hys name be neuenede, he was gretly trubblede, and his vesage bi-gañ to waxe pale, and his chere to change. And than the quene said efte vn-to hym: 'Alexander,' quoþ she, ' for to schewe þe mare verrayly þat þou ert Alexander, coɱ with me.' And þañ scho tuk hyɱ by þe hande & leedde hym in-till anoþer chambir, and schewed' hym þare his awenñ Fygure purtrayed' in a parchemyñ skyne. And wheñ Alexander saw þat, he wex pale & wanne & biganne to tremblee. And þañ þe quene said vn-till hym : ' Alexander,' quoþ scho, ' where-fore ert þou ferde, & why chaungeȝ þou chere. Thou þat hase distroyed' all þe werlde; conquerour of Perse, of Inde, of Mede, and many oþer rewmes & landeȝ, Now arte þou witowtteñ scheddynge of blode falleñ in þe dawngere & in þe handeȝ of quene Candace vnauysyli. And þare-by may þou wele knawe þat a manes hert sulde on na wyse be enhanced' in pride. For if all it bee þat ofte tymmes grete prosperitee fall to mañ, Sodaynly falleȝ adversitee till hym wheñ he leste wenes.' Wheñ Alexander herde þis he bigañ to grayste wit þe teethe and to torne his hede hedir & thedir, And quene Candace saide vn-till hyɱ : ' Whare to angers þou þe,' quoþ scho, ' & trubleȝ thi selfe? What may now thi grete Imperiall glory, thi witt & thi mighte serue

Line numbers: 4, 8, 12, 16, 20, 24, 28, 32, 36

[1] Four lines with red capital *A*.

the offe?' Alexander ansuerde & said: 'Forsothe', quoþ
Alexander, 'resonably I am angry at my selfe bi-cause I hafe
na swerde here.' Quoþ þe quene: 'I suppose þou hadd a
4 swerde, nowe, what walde do þare-wit?' 'Sothely,' quoþ he,
'bi-cause I hafe wilfully betrayed my-selfe vn-to þe. First
I solde sla þe and pan, I dowte it noȝt, I sulde be slayne for þe.'
'Now for sothe,' quoþ scho, 'þis was wisely & manfully sayde.
8 Neuer-þe-less be nathynge heuy. For as þou delyuerde my
son wyfe Candeolus oute of þe daungere of þe kyng of Bebrikes
Swaa salt I delyuer the oute of þe daungere of thyn enemys
þat þou hase here. For I say þe in certayne, and it ware
12 knawen þat þou ware here vn-to my menȝee, onane þay walde
slaa þe by-cause þou slewe Porus þe kynge of Inde. For my
son wyfe Carator was his doughter.' And when scho had
said þis, Scho tuk Alexander bi þe hande & ledd hym forthe
16 in-till hir forchambire and said vntill hir sones: 'My dere
sonnes,' quoþ scho, 'I pray ȝow late vs make þis knyghte of
Alexander gude chere, and schew hym all þe humanytee þat
we can. For Alexander has schewed vs grete frendchipe
20 and grete gudnesse.' And þan hir ȝongeste ansuerde & said:
'Moder,' * quoþ he, 'sothe it es þat he es a messangere of
Alexanders, & a knyghte of his, and þat he delyuerde my broþer
wyfe of þe handeȝ of þe kynge of þe Bebrikes and broghte hym
24 & hir hame vn-till vs bathe safe & sownde. Neuer-þe-lesse my
wyfe constreyneȝ me for to do Antyochus to dede bi-cause of þe
dede of hir Fadir Porus, whilke Alexander slewe, So þat
Alexander may hafe sorow for his knyghte. Quoþ quene
28 Candace þan: 'Lefe son, what wirchip may we get þare-offe
if we slaa this knyghte þus traytourusly.' And þan Candeolus
sayde wit a grete Ire, 'Þis knyghte,' quoþ he, 'saued me & my
wyfe & broghte vs hedir safe & sonde; And als saffe sall I hafe
32 hym, agayne till his lorde, or I sall be dede þarefore.' And
Carator ansuerde & saide: 'Broþer,' quoþ he, 'what says þou?
will þou þat aythere of vs here slaa oþer?' 'In gud faythe
broþer,' quoþ he, 'it es noȝte my will, ne my liste. Neuer-
36 þe-lesse if it be thi liste, I am redy, rather þan þis knyghte be
dedde.' And when þe quene saw þat hir sonnes walde ayther
of þam slaa oþer, scho was wonder sary, and tuk Alexander on
syde, and saide vn-till hym preualy: 'A, a, kyng Alexander,'

Alexander is angry at himself.
Had he but a sword he would slay her and die for it.
She commends him, therefore she bids him not fear, for since he helped her son she will deliver him from another son who is Porus' son-in-law.
She introduces Alexander as one of his own knights, Antiochus.

* Leaf 43
Her younger son would slay him for his wife's sake, to grieve Alexander.

Candeolus offers to defend Alexander with his own life.

Candace appeals to Alexander to save her sons from

102   *Alexander's stratagem and parting. The cave of the Gods.*

combat by his wit, so that either slay not other.
Alexander promises to do so.
Alexander offers to betray Alexander to Carator.

quoþ scho, 'whi wilt þou noȝte schewe thi witt, and helpe thurgh thi wisdom þat my sonnes slaa noȝt ayther of þam oþer?' And Alexander answerde and said: 'Late me goo speke wit þam,' quoþ he. And scho lete hym goo. And he went to þam and sayde vn-to Carator: 'For sothe, Carator,' quoþ he, 'I late þe wite þat if þou slaa me, þou salt wynne bot lyttill wirchipe þareoffe. For I say þe, kyng Alexander hase many worthyer knyghtis wit hym þan I am; And þare-fore he will hafe littill sorowe for my dede. Trowes þou þat and Alexander hadd lufed me wele þat he walde hafe sent me hyder to be killed amangeȝ ȝowe. Bot if þou will þat I beken the Alexander þe slaere of þi wyfe fader & bryng hym bi-for the, Swere me þat what so I asche þe, þou salt graunte mee it, And I sure þe bi þe faythe of my body, I salt bryng Alexander in-to

Carator assents.

þis palace be-fore þe.' And when Carator herde this, he was riȝte glade, and trowed þat that Alexander said. And so ware þe twa breþer pesede, And highte Alexander þat his askynge sulde be fulfilled als ferforthe als þaire powere reched, if so ware

Queen Candace parts from Alexander with many gifts.

þat he helde couenant. Þan quene Candace leedd Alexander on syde & sayd vn-till hym in preuatee: 'Wele ware me,' quoþ scho, 'myghte I ilke day hafe þe present be-fore myn eghne as I hafe myn awenn childere. For thurgh the sulde I ouercome all myn Enemys.' And þan [scho] gaffe Alexander a coroun of golde sett full of precyous dyamandeȝ, and a mantill Imperiall

* Leaf 43 bk.

of a clathe of golde * wit sternes wofen þare-in, and sett full of precyouse stanes. And þan scho kyssed hym & oþer preuee thyngeȝ didd till hym, And badde hym goo in hir blyssynge.

Alexander and Candeolus come to a cave.
Alexander, sacrificing, goes in.
He sees a great god sitting with eyes like stars.
The god greets him.

¹ Than kyng Alexander and Candeolus went furthe all that daye, And come till a grete spelunc, and þare þay herberde þam. And Candeolus saide till Alexander : 'In this spelunc,' quoþ hee, ' þat you here seeȝ all goddeȝ ere wount for to ete and halde þaire consaill.' And þan onane Alexander made sacrafyceȝ till his goddeȝ and enterde in-to þe caue by hym ane. And þare he sawe a myrke clowde, & in þat myrknesse, he sawe as it ware bryghte sternes, and amangeȝ þase sternes he saw a grete godd sitt, And his eghne lyke twa lanternes. And when Alexander saw hym he was so fered þat he was as it hadd bene

4

8

12

16

20

24

28

32

36

---

¹ Red capital *T* in four lines space and small *t* in margin.

The prophecies. Strange beasts.

in a transynge. And þan þe godd said vn-to hym: 'Haile, Alexander,' quoþ he. And Alexander ansuerde & said: 'Lorde,' quoþ he, 'what art þou?' 'I am,' quoþ he, 'Sensonchosis þat gouernez þe kyngdom of þe werlde and þat hase made men sugettes vn-to the. And þou hase bigged þiselfe many ryaʒe citeez. Bot temple walde þou nane make in þe wirchippe of me.' And Alexander ansuerd & said: 'Lorde,' quoþ he, '& þou will graunt me þat I sall wit prosperitee come in-to Macedoyne I sall ordeyne the a temple þare sall noʒte be swilke anoþer in all þe werlde.' And he ansuerd agayne & saide: 'For sothe,' quoþ hee, 'Macedoyne sall þou neuer see wit thyn eghne. Neuer-þe-lesse walke Innermare & luke what þou seez.' Alexander þan went forthirmare & saw anoþer myrke clowde and saw a godd sitt in a trone lyke a kynge, and Alexander said vn-till hym: 'Lorde,' quoþ he, 'what art þou?' 'I am,' quoþ he, 'þe begynnynge of all goddez and Serapis es my name. I sawe the in þe lande of liby & nowe I see þe here.' 'Serapis,' quoþ Alexander, 'I beseke þe telle me wha it es þat sall sla me.' Quod Serapis: 'I talde þe bi-fore, þat and þe cause of a manes dede ware knawen vn-till hym, he solde dy for sorowe. Þou hase bygged a gloricus citee agaynes þe whilke many emperours sall fighte. Þare-in sall thi graue be made and þare-in sall þou be beried.' And þan Alexander come oute of þe caue, and tuke his leue at Candeolus and went till his Oste.

¹ One þe morne he remowed his Oste And come till a valay þat was full of grete ² serpentes þe whilk hade in þaire heuedis Grete smaragdez. Thir serpentez *lyffede all wit gyngere and pepir þat growede in þe valaye. And ilke a ʒere þay feghte to-gedir and many of þam slaez oþer. Off þe forsaid Smaragdes tuk Alexander sum wit hym of þe grettester þat he couthe gett.

³ Fra þeine þay remowed & come in-till a place in þe whilke þare ware bestez þat hade one ilke a fote twa clees as swyne hase, and þase clees ware three fote brade wit þe whilke þay smate Alexander knyghtes. Þay had also heuedes lyke swyne & tayles lyke lyouns. Þare ware also amangez þam grypes þe

---

¹ Three lines with red capital *O* and small *o* in the margin.
² MS. '*serpe*' crossed out and '*serpentes*' written.
³ Three lines with red capital *F* and small *f* in the margin beside.

whilke smate kynghtes in þe vesageȝ reghte felly. Þay ware so strange þat ane of þam̅ wolde bere away an armed̄ knyghte & his horse also. Þaɪ̄ kynge Alexander rade hedir & þedir amangeȝ his meɪ̄ and comforthed̄ þam̅ and badd̄ þam̅ feghte manly agaynes þam̅ wit speres and wit arowes. And so þay did̄. Bot þare was slayne of Alexander knyghtes ccviii.

[1] And fra þeine þay remowed̄ and come till a grete ryuer þe whilke was twenty furlange on brede fra þe ta banke to þe toþer. And on þase bankes þare growed̄ redis wonder grete and hye. Of þase redes garte Alexander mak bates & anoynte þam̅ wit terre & talgh of besteȝ, And badd̄ his knyghtis row ouer þe water in þase bates. And þay did̄ soo. And wheɪ̄ þe [pople][2] of þe cunntree herde tell of þe commynge of Alexander & his Oste, þay sent hym gyftes of swylk thyngeȝ als was in þaire cuntree, þat es at say Grete spoungeȝ bathe whitte & purpure & schelles of þe see so grete þat an of þam̅ walde halde twa pekkes or three. Þay sent hym also wormes þat þay drew owte of þat ryuer grettere þaɪ̄ a manes thee, and þay ware swetter of taste þaɪ̄ any fysche. Þay gaffe hym Cukstoles all rede þat ware of a wonderfull gretnesse. In þat ryuer ware womans þat ware wonder faire & þay hade oɪ̄ þam̅ mekill here þat rechedd̄ douɪ̄ to thaire fete. Þir womeɪ̄, when þay saw any straunge meɪ̄ swymme in þat riuer, owþer þay drownned̄ þam̅ in þe water, or ells þay walde lede þam̅ to þe redeȝ þat growed̄ oɪ̄ þe water bankes and garre þam̅ lye by þam̅ ay till any lyfe was in þam̅. Þe Macedoynes persued þam̅ & tuke twa of þam̅ and broghte þam̅ till Alexander,* and þay ware als white as any snawe, and þay ware ten fote lange and þaire teethe ware lyke dogge teethe.

[3] Efter this Alexander went and closed̄ in a maner of folkes þat are called̄ Gog & Magog, with-in þe hilleȝ of Caspy. Þis folkeȝ were of þe ten kyndeȝ of Israel, and þay ware leedd̄ owte of þaire aweɪ̄ɪ̄ land̄ bi a kyng of Perse be-cause of þaire synneȝ and halden in thralledom̅. And þay asched̄ Alexander leue for to wende furth of þat cuntree. And Alexander gert spirre þe cause of þaire thraldom̅, and he was encensed̄ þat be-cause þay

---

[1] Three lines with red capital *A* and small *a* in margin beside.
[2] MS. reads, *And when þe of þe cunntree* (? *þe[i] of*, &c.).
[3] Three lines with red capital *E* and small *c* in the margin beside.

hadd' forsakeñ þaire godde3 lawe, þat es at say, godd' of Isrł,
and wirchiped' Calues & oþer Mawmettes, þare-fore þay ware
ledd' oute of þaire awenñ lande & haldeñ in thralldoɱ, and þat
4 prophetes had prophiced' be-fore þat þay sulde neuer come oute
of thraldoɱ bi-fore agayne þe day of dome. And þañ Alexander
ansuerde & said þat he sulde sperre þaɱ Iñ mare seurely. And
þañ he garte close aƚƚ þe entree3 wit stane & lyme & sand; Bot
8 aƚƚ þat he garte make on þe day was fordone oñ þe nyghte. And
wheñ Alexander saw þat mannes laboure myghte no3te staude in
stede, he bi-soghte godd' of Isrł þat if it ware his liste þat þay
habade þare, þat he walde close þaɱ in. And þe nexte nyghte
12 aftir ilk a cragge feƚƚe tiƚƚ oþer, and so þare may nathynge
passe in nor owte. And þare-by it seme3 þat it es no3te godde3
wiƚƚ þat þay come oute. Neuer-þe-lesse abowte þe Ende of þe
werlde þay saƚƚ breke oute and do mekiƚƚ schathe & slaa many
16 meñ.

¹ Fra þeine þay remowed' & come to þe grete See Occeane. In
þat See þay sawe ane Ile a littiƚƚ fra þe lande. And in þat Ile
þay herde meñ speke grewe. And þañ Alexander commanded'
20 þat suɱ of his knyghts sulde do off þaire clathes and swyme
ouer to þe ile. And þay did' soo. And als sone als þay come
in þe See þare come gret crabbes vp oute of þe water & pullede
þaɱ downne to þe grounde & drownned' þaɱ.

24 ² Thanne remowed' þay fra thethyñ and went ay endlande
þe See syde to-warde þe solstice of wynter trauellande xł days;
and at þe laste þay come to a reede See, and þare þay lugede
þaɱ. Þare was faste by a Mountayne wonder hye, One
28 þe whilke Alexander went vp. And wheñ he was abowñ oñ
þe heghte þare-offe, hym thoghte þat he was nerre þe Firmament
þan þe erthe; þañ he ymagned' in his hert swilk a gynñ how
he myghte make * grippes bere hym vp in-to þe ayere. And
32 onane he come doune of þe Mountayne and garte come bi-fore
hyɱ his Maistre wrightes and comandid' þaɱ þat þay sulde
make hym a chayer and trelesse it wit barre3 of Ireñ one ilk
a syde so þat he my3te sauely sitt þare-in. And þañ he gart
36 brynge foure gripes and tye þaɱ faste wit Ireñ cheynes vn-to þe
chayere, and in þe ouermare party of þe chayere he gart putt

But he learns that they had forsaken the True God for idols, and therefore they are banished and imprisoned till Doomsday.
Alexander says he shall bar them in more surely.
God answers his prayers, and rocks fall down and shut them in until Doomsday, when they shall come forth to do great harm.
They come to the sea and an isle near the shore.
They hear men speak Greek there.
Alexander's messengers to the isle are killed by crabs.
They travel along the
* Leaf 45.
seashore to the Red Sea.
Alexander goes up a mountain.
His master workers make him

¹ Four lines with red capital F and small f in the margin beside.   ² Three lines with red capital T and small capital T in margin.

106 *Alexander ascends into the air and descends into the sea.*

<small>a chair whereby he is borne by griffons up into the air.</small>

mete for þe grippes. And þaⁿ he wente and sett hym̅ in þe chayere. And onane þe grippes bare hym vp in þe ayer so hye þat Alex*ander* thoghte all þe erthe na mare þaⁿ a flure þ*are* meⁿ thressche₃ corne, and þe See lyke a dragoⁿ abowte 4 þe erthe. Þaⁿ sodaynly a specyall vertu of godd' vmbilapped

<small>He comes down about ten days' march from his army.</small>

þe grippes þat gart þam̅ discende doune to þe erthe in a felde : ten .x. day io*ur*nee fra þe Oste, and he hadd' na hurt ne na schathe in þe chayere. Bot w*i*t grete disesse at þe laste he 8 come till his Oste.

<small>Then he lusteth to know the depths of the sea. The master glaziers make him a glazen cage with iron bars and it is lowered down into the sea, and there he beholds many wonders and strange beasts until he is drawn up again by his knights.</small>

¹ After þis Alex*ander* ymagened in his hert þat he walde knaw þe preuates þat are in þe see. And onane he gart come bifore hym̅ all þe Maist*er* glasyers þat ware in þe Oste, And comandede 12 þam̅ to make hym a grete tounne of pɔssandly clere glasse þat he myghte thurgh it clerely see all man*er* of thynge þat ware w*i*towtteⁿ it. And wheⁿ it was made he gart trelesse it al abowte w*i*towtteⁿ w*i*t barres of yreⁿ and feste þ*are*-to lang cheynes of 16 yreⁿ, and gart a certane of þe strangeste & maste tristy knyghtes þat langed'vn-till hym halde þir cheynes. And þaⁿ he went in-to þe tounne & gart pykke wele þe entree whare he went in, and þaⁿ late it douⁿ into þe See. And þare he sawe dyu*er*se 20 schappes of fisches of dyu*er*se colo*ur*s; and sum̅ he sawe hafe þe schappe of dyu*er*se beste₃ here one þe lande, gangande on fete as beste₃ dose here & etande fruyte of treesse þat growe₃ on þe See grunde. Þir beste₃ come till hym. Bot onane as þay 24 saw hym thorow þe glasse þay fledde fra hym. He sawe þ*are* also many oþ*er* meruaylous thynge₃, þe whilke he walde tell na maⁿ bi-cause meⁿ walde noghte hafe trowed' þam̅ if he had talde þam̅, and at a certayne houre þase þat he hadd' assyngned 28 be-fore, his knyghtes drewe hym vp oute of þe See.

<small>They march on and have to fight *Leaf 45 bk. strange horned beasts. They come to the wilderness of</small>

² Fra þeine þay Remowed' Folowande þe bankes of þe Rede See, and luged þam̅ in a place, whare þare ware wylde Beste₃ that hade oⁿ þaire heuedis hornes lyke vn-to *sawes, and þay 32 ware als scharpe als swerde₃. And with thire hornes þay slewe & hurte many knyghtis of Alexanders & cloue þaire cheldes in sonder. Neu*er*-þe-lesse Alex*ander* knyghtis slew of þam̅ ccccli.

³ And fra þeine þay remowed' and come in-till wilderness 36

---

¹ Four lines with red capital *A* and small *a* in the margin beside.
² Three lines with red capital *F* and small *f* in margin besides.
³ Three lines with red capital *A* and small *a* in the margin beside.

The strange beasts. The death of Bucephalus. 107

bitwex þe reed' See and Araby, whare grete multitude of Pepir   pepper
growed'; And þare ware many grete nedders wit hornnes on   trees and horned
þaire hedes lyke tuppe hornes, wit þe whilke þay smate Alex-   adders.
4 ander knyghtis riȝt felly. Off þase nedderes slew þe Macedoynes
a grete party.

¹ Þeine þay removed' and luged' in a place whare many   They meet
Rynocephales ware, þe whilke hade heuedes & manes lyke   and have to fight
8 horseȝ. And þay hade grete bodys, and wonder grete teethe   Rhinoceri that spit
and lange, and oute of þaire mouthes þay schotte flawmeȝ   forth fire.
of fyre. And wheñ þay saw þe Oste luge þare þay come
& assaylled' þam͞. And Alexander rañ hyder and thedir   They fight them
12 amangeȝ þe oste and comforthed' his knyghtes and bad þam͞   fiercely.
feghte manly wit þase monstres. And so þay didd'. Neuer-þe-
lesse þare ware a grete multitude of his knyghtis slayne of þase
besteȝ. Bot of þe Rynocephales þare was slayne an hugge
16 multitude.

² Þañ þay removed' fra þeine and come in-till a champayne   Alexander's
cuntree and luged' þam͞ þare, And lay þare a certane days,   steed Bucephalus dies.
Bi-cause of his horse Buktyphalas þat fell seke þare; of þe   He makes
20 whilke sekenesse he dyed'. And wheñ Alexander saw hym dedd'   a rich tomb and builds
he made grete dole for hym and weped' for hym riȝt sare. For   a city round him.
he hadd' borne hym in many a Batelle, and broghte [hym] oute of
many perells. And þare-fore wheñ he was dede Alexander
24 gart doo aboute hym grete exequyes and gart make hym a full
riche toumbe & a hye and did' hym þare-in and made a grete
citee þare, þe whilke in mynde of his horse he gart call Buktyphalas.

28 ³ Fra þeine þay removed and come till a ryuere ⁴ þat was called'   They come to the
Cytan or Deciracy whare meñ of þe cuntree broghte hym͞   palace of Xerxès.
ṽ Olyphantes and ṽ cartes of werre. And fra þeine þay
removed' & come till kynge ȝerses palace. And in þat Palace
32 þay fande beddeȝ of clene golde many a thowsande. Þare ware   The birds that foretell the life
also grete fewles white als doufes, þe whilke had knawyng   or death of a man.
be-fore of a seke mañ wheder he schulde lyffe or dye. For
if þay by-helde þe seke mañ in þe vesage, he schulde mende &
36 fare wele. And if þay tourned' þam awaywarde witowtteñ

---

¹ Three lines.
² Three lines.
³ MS. has a small *f* written in margin, but no space for the large capital to be put.

⁴ The scribe first wrote *rever*, then altered it to *ryver*, then scratched it all out and wrote *ryvere* after it.

108   *The letters of Alexander. His throne.*

* Leaf 46. doute he schulde dye,* and if þay to*ur*ned hy*m* þe bakke w*i*t owtte*n̄* dowte he sulde dye.

They come to Babylon and capture it.
¹F*R*a þeine þay removed' and come to þe grete Citee of Babiloyne and wanne it oo werre and slew þe kynge þ*are*-offe 4 & þe Captayne also. And þare he duelled' vn-ti*ll* his lyffes end',

Thence Alexander writes to his mother and to Aristotle.
and þat was Bot vij seue*n̄* Monethes. In þat mene tyme Alex*ander* sent a *lettr*e ti*ll* Olympias his Moder and ti*ll* his Mayst*er* Arestotle, latand'þa*m̄* witte of þe Bate*ll*s and þe dyssese 8 þat þay suffred' bathe wynt*er*s and Somers in Inde and oþ*er* cuntreeȝ, and also of þe Bate*ll*s þat þay had' hadd'w*i*t dyu*er*se Monstres. And þa*n̄* Arestotle wrate anoþ*er lettr*e ti*ll* Alex*ander* agayne þe whilke was of this teno*ur* : 12

Aristotle writes to Alexander again praising him greatly for his victories.
² 'Un-ti*ll* Alexandere þe grete kynge of kyngeȝ Arestotle sendeȝ ioy and seruyce. Whe*n̄* I hade redde ȝo*ur* wyrchipfu*ll lettr*es I was gretly astonayd'. For whilke cause I desyre with a*ll* my*n̄* hert for to fynde lonynge þat I myghte ȝelde vn-to þe. 16 I take witnes*s*e at oure goddeȝ þat for þe passande hardenesse of þi hert & þe grete auento*ur*s þat þou hase put þe in, þou erte wele worthy for to be loued' & p*r*aysede. For þou hase sene & assayed' thyngeȝ þat neu*er* ma*n̄* or þis durste assaye. Whare-for 20 thankynge & lonynge I ȝelde to þe makere of a*ll* þis wyde werlde þat swylke victoryes hase grantede vn-to þe. For þou hase ou*er*comme*n̄* a*ll* & nane hase ou*er*come*n̄* þe. Fu*ll* blyssede are a*ll* thy prynceȝ þat hase bene obeyande vnto þe, and helped' þe 24 in a*ll* thi disesseȝ.'

Alexander has a wondrous throne made.
³ Afftir þis Alex*ander* gart make in Babyloyne a wonder curio*u*s trone ⁴ of golde, þ*are* was noȝte swilke anoþ*er in* þe werlde. For þe grekeȝ broghte so meki*ll* golde oute of p*er*se & 28 oute of Inde, þat it ware wonder for to telle. Þis ilke toure was twlue cubyteȝ hye and by twelue greceȝ ⁵ me*n̄* ascended'

The throne of Alexander with its images, its ruby, and its inscriptions.
þ*are*-too, and þase greeȝ ware a*ll* of golde. Þis trone was wonderfully wroghte and sett apo*n̄* twelue ymageȝ of golde, þe 32 whilke trone þe forsaid'ymageȝ helde vp w*i*t þaire hende. And on þase twelue ymageȝ ware wretyn̄ þe names of þe twelue prynceȝ of Macedoyne. Þe seet of þe trone was of a Smaragde,

---

¹ Three lines with big capital *F* followed by small capital.
² Four lines with red capital *U* and small *u* in the margin.
³ Four lines with red capital *A* and small *a* in the margin beside.
⁴ *toure* scratched out and *trone* written in.
⁵ The first part of this word reads *gr* + blot + *ceȝ*.

The crown of Alexander. The Philosopher. 109

& þe sydeʒ þare off ware of Topaʒes & in ilkaɴ of þe greeʒ ware
sett dyuerse maneres of precyouse stanes. In þe summyt of þis
trone þare was sett a ruby þat schane on þe nyghte as it hade
4 bene þe Mone. In þis trone also was þare sett oɴ ilke a syde
dyuerse ymageʒ on þe whilke ware wretyɴ bathe in latyne & in
grew* verseʒ þat contened' all þe nammes of þe rewmes & cuntreeʒ   * Leaf 46 bk.
þat Alexandere had conquered' and ware sugetes vn-till hym.
8 ¹ After þis ⁴ Alexander gert make a coroɴ of golde sett full   The crown
of all maner of precyouse stanes, and gert wryte apoɴ it a tytle   of Alex-ander and
in grew & in latyɴ : ' Ortus & occasus, Aquilo michi seruit   the inscrip-tions there-
& Auster.' Þat es at saye : ' Est & weste, Northe & southe dose   on.
12 seruyce vn-to me.' In the mene tyme whils Alexander was in   The strange child born
babyloyne, a womaɴ was delyuer of a knaue childe þe whilke fra   in Babylon
þe heuede to þe nauyll hadd' schappe of maɴ, & was borne dedd'.   half alive and
And fra þe nauyll downwardeʒ it had lyknesse of dyuerse   half dead,
16 besteʒ and was qwykke. Þis Monstre was takeɴ & broghte till   half man and half
Alexander; and als soɴ als he saw it he meruaylled' gretly   animal, and the mean-
þare-off, and gart come bi-fore hyɱ a philosopher þat couthe of   ing it has.
wiche-crafte, & aschede hym what it sygnyfyed'. And wheɴ þe   The death of Alex-
20 philosopher saw it, he syghede, & saye wepand' sayde vn-to   ander and the coming
hym : ' Sothely wirchipfull emperour,' quoþ he, ' þe tyme commeʒ   of his suc-cessor.
nere that þou sall passe oute of this werlde.' ' Telle me,' quoþ   In what
Alexander, ' whareby þou knawes þat.' And þe philosophre   they shall not be like
24 ansuerde & sayde : ' My lorde,' quoþ he, ' þe halfe of þis Monstre   him.
þat hase þe schappe of maɴ & es dedd', betakens þat þou sall
passe out of þis werlde in haste. And þe toþer party þat hase
þe lyknes of dyuerse besteʒ & es on lyfe, betakynges þe kynges
28 þat sall come after þe. Bot þare sall nane of þaɴ be lyke
vn-to þe, na mare þaɴ a beste es lyke vn-till a maɴ.' Wheɴ   The sorrow of Alex-
Alexander herde þis he was wonder heuy, and sare wepand'   ander.
he sayde on þis wyse : ' O Allmyghty Iubiter,' quoþ he, ' what
32 meneʒ it þat my dayes sall be so schortte ? Me thynke þat it
had bene semely þat I had leffed' langere for till haf endid'
thyngeʒ þat are in my thoghte. Bot for als mekill als it es
noʒte plesande vn-to þe, I beseke the þat þou resayffe me wheɴ
36 I sall passe hetheɴ als thyɴ aweɴ seruante.'
² In this mene tyme þare was in Macedoyne a lorde þat highte   Antipator wishes for

¹ Three lines with red capital *A* and   ² Four lines with red capital *I* and
small *a* in the margin beside.   small *i* in margin beside.

The betrayal and poisoning of Alexander.

the death of Alexander, who is warned of him by Olympias.

Antipater, þe whilke of langetyme be-fore hadd’ casten for þe dedde of Alexander; And wit many oþer þat he hadd’ confedred’ vn-till hym he conspyred’ for to brynge it tyll ende, bot he myghte neuer come aboute þer-with. For Olympias, Alexander moder, wrate vn-till hym ofte-sythes and warned’ hym þat he scholde be warre wit Antipater & his childre, and herefore was Antypater wonder sary. So apon a tyme he vmbythoghte hym þat he myghte neuer come aboute wit his purpose for to slaa Alexander, bot if it ware thurgh enpuysonynge. *And so apon a daye he went till a Sotell leche, and boghte of hym a maner of drynke made of puyson that was so felle & so ranke þat þare myghte no vesselle halde it Bot a vessell made of Iren; and þare-in he putt it. And þan he gaffe it his son Cassandre, and bad’ hym bere it till his broþer Iobas and byd’ hym, quoþ he, gyffe it to kyng Alexander in his drynke, when he see3 his tyme. This ilk Iobas was a faire 3ong man & was duellyng with Alexander, and gretly by-luffede & cheriste of hym. Bot so it be-felle apon a tyme þat Alexander smate Iobas on þe heued wit a warderere for na trespasse. Whare-fore Iobas was gretly angred’ and greued’ at Alexander and consented’till his dede, and tuke þe puyson of his broþer þat was ordeyned’ for Alexander dede þat luffed’ hym so mekill.

Leaf 47.

He buys poison and gives it to his son to have it given to Alexander by a protégé whom he has struck.

4

8

12

16

20

¹ And apon a daye Alexander gart ordeyne a grete reuelle in Babyloyne and called’ þare too all his prynce3 on ilke a syde. And as he satt at þe mete Imange his prynce3 he was wonder mery & gladde & iocund’, and reheted’ his lorde3 & prayed’ þam þat þay schulde be mery. Þan Iobas þat serued’ þe kyng of his coupe tuke of þe puyson a porcyon, and putt it vnder þe nayle of his thowme, and broghte þe coppe to þe kynge full of wyne. And as he gaffe it to þe kynge, he lete þe puyson falle in þe wyne priualy. And als sone als þe kyng hadd’ dronken þe puyson, Sudaynly he gaffe a grete scryke, and lened’ hym downn towarde þe ri3te syde. For hym thoghte reghte als a man hadd’ smyten hym in-to þe lyuere wit a suerde. Neuer-þe-lesse he feyned’ & forbare a while & suffred’ a grete penance, and when he my3te na langere habyde, he rase vp fra þe burde and saide till his lorde3 & his knyghtes: 'Lordyngis,' quoþ he,

His protégé gives the king a drop of poison in his cup from his thumb. Alexander cries out with pain, but forbears awhile to leave the feast.

24

28

32

36

¹ Three lines with red capital *A* and small *a* in the margin beside.

The agony of Alexander. 111

'I pray ȝow sitt ȝe still & eteȝ & drynkeȝ & beeȝ mery.' Bot
þay ware gretly troubbled and rase vp fra þe burdeȝ and stode
witowtten for to see þe ende. And Alexander went in-till   He uses a
4 his chambir gretly tourmentid, and soghte a fethir for to putt   feather to spew it
in his throtte for to garre hym hafe a vomet of þe puyson   forth, but again the
þat he hadd resayffed. And Iobas, þat was cheffe of all this   feather is poisoned.
hye treson, gatt a fethir & enoynt it wit þe same puyson
8 & broghte it till Alexander; and he tuk it & putt it in his
throtte, and belyfe * þe puyson vexed hym ay mare & mare.   * Leaf 47 bk.
And þan Alexander bade ane gange & open þe palace ȝates   In his agony he
þat ware on Eufrates banke. And alle þat nyȝte he woke   goes to the Euphrates
12 in grete payneȝ & tourment. And aboute mydnyȝthte he rase   to drown himself.
oute of þe bedde þat he lay in and putt oute þe lyghte þat brynt
by-fore hym, and for he myghte noghte ga vprighteȝ, he creped
one hende & one fete doune to-warde Eufrateȝ for till hafe
16 drownned hym selfe, þat þe strenth of þe water myȝth hafe
borne hym away whare neuer man solde hafe fun hym.
And Rosan his wyfe folowed as faste as scho myghte. And   But his wife
when scho come to hym scho felle vpon hym & enbraced hym   Roxana follows and
20 in hir armes & said vn-till hym: 'Allas, my lorde Alexander,'   prevents him
quoþ scho, 'will þou now leue me & gaa slaa thi-selfe.' And   and tries to console
scho wepe þat it was dole to see; and Alexander ansuerde   him.
& sayde: 'I beseke þe Rosan,' quoþ he, 'þat ert so dere to me
24 & so swete, late nane wit of myn Endynge, if all it be þat we
may na langare hafe ioy togedir.' And þan Rosan ledd   She asks him first to provide for her.
Alexander agayne to his bedd, and layde her armes aboute his
nekke and kyssede hym many a tyme, and sare wepand said
28 vn-till hym: 'A, A, my swete lorde,' quoþ scho, 'if þine ende be
nowe commen, ordayne firste for vs or ȝe passe heþine.' And   He calls his notary.
onane he callede vn-till hym Iobas & bade hym feche vn-till
hym Semyon his notary. And when he was comen he garte
32 bere hym down in-to þe haulle, and he garte come by-fore hym
all his prynceȝ & bade his notary wryte his testament bi-fore
þam all on þis wyse.
¹ 'ARestotle oure dere Maister, we comande the & prayse the,   He commands Aristotle to give to
36 þat of oure awen tresour þou sende to þe presteȝ of Egipt þat
ministreȝ in þe temple, whare-in oure body sall be beryed

---

¹ Three lines with red capital A, and small a in the margin beside, small capital R following.

112 The will of Alexander. The earthquake.

<small>the Egyptian priest of his mausoleum. Ptolemy is the governor.</small>
<small>If Roxana bear a man child he shall be Emperor;</small>
<small>* Leaf 48.</small>
<small>if a girl they shall choose their own.</small>
<small>He apportions his domains.</small>

& entered, ȝ besandeȝ of golde. Also I wiłł that Tholomeus þat es kepare of oure body be ȝour Gouernour, And forgetis noghte my laste wiłł, Bot lateȝ my testament be alway bi-fore ȝour eghne so þat it be fulfilled & noghte forgetyn. My wiłł es 4 also þat if Rosan my wyfe be delyuer of a knafe childe þat he be ȝour Emperour and gyffeȝ hym what name so ȝow liste, and if scho be delyuer of a mayden childe, þan es it my wiłł þat the Macedoynes chese þam a kynge, and þat my wyfe be lady of * ałł 8 my mobles. Also I wiłł þat Tholomeus be kyng of Egipt, and þat he tak tiłł his wyfe Cleopatra, þat my Fader wedded sum-tyme here bi-fore, and þat he be lorde & prynce ouer ałł þe lordeȝ of þe Este euen vn-to Bactrian. Also I wiłł þat my 12 broþer Arrideus be kynge of þe Pelopones, also þat Cleopater be kyng of Perse, Mellagere kyng of Ethopy, And Anthiochus be kyng vn-to þe landeȝ of Gog & magoge, Aresteȝ kynge of Inde, Lissymacus lorde of Seleuce, Lythamon kyng of hungary, Caulus 16 kyng of Ermony, Illicus kyng of Dalmace. Symeon my Notary, wiłł I, be Kyng of Capadoce & Pamphily, Cassander & Iobas be lordeȝ vn-to þe Ryuer þat es called Sołł, Antipater þaire Fader

<small>The earthquake.</small>

be kyng of Cicile.' When this testament was in wrytynge 20 bi-fore Alexander Sodeynly þare come a thonnere & a leuennynge & ane erthedoun riȝte a hedous, so þat ałł babyloyne qwoke þare-wit. And than thorowte ałł Babyloyne þe noyse rase þat

<small>The Macedonians come armed and demand to see their Emperor.</small>

Alexander was dede. And þan ałł þe Macedoynes rasse hallely 24 and come armed to þe Palace, and cryed on þe prynceȝ & said vn-to þam : 'Sothely,' quoþ þay, 'but if ȝe onaue schewe vs oure Emperour we sałł slaa ȝow ilk ane.' And when kyng Alexander herde swilke noyse he askede whate it ment, and þe prynceȝ 28 ansuerde & sayde : 'Þe Macedoynes,' quoþ þay, 'are comen armede hedir before þe ȝates, & says sekerly bot if þay see ȝow þay sałł slaa vs ałłe are þay passe heþine.' And when Alexander herde

<small>He prays his knights bear him before them.</small>

þis, he badd his knyghtis þat þay scholde take hym vp, and bere 32 hym in-to þe consistorye. And þay did soo. And þan he garte open þe Palace ȝates þat þe Macedoynes myȝte come by-fore hym. And þan kyng Alexander be-gan to comend þam of þaire strenth & þaire grete doghtynes, and charged þam þat 36

<small>He praises them.</small>
<small>They speak with him and pray</small>

þay scholde be in pesse & reste ilkane wit oþer. Þan þe Macedoynes, sare wepande, sayde vn-tiłł Alexander : 'A, A, wirchipfułł,' quoþ þay, 'ordayne & tełłe vs are ȝe passe

Alexander and the Macedonians. 113

heyne whaṁ ȝe wiłł þat be oure emper*our* efter ȝow.' And
Alex*ander* ansuerď & sayde, ' A, A, my dere knyghtis,' quoþ he,
' wheñ I am dede whayṁ so ȝe wiłł chese, be ȝo*ur* emper*our*
4 eft*er* mee.' And þay ansuerde, ' Lord,' quoþ þay, ' we beseke
ȝowe þat ȝe wiłł graunt vs Perdic to be oure Emper*our*.'
'I vouche wele saffe,' quoþ Alex*ander*, ' þat Perdic be ȝo*ur*
Emper*our*. Gers hy*m* come be-fore mee.' ¹And wheñ he was
8 comeñ by-fore hy*m* he gaffe hy*m* þe kyngdome* of Macedoyne
w*i*t þe Emper*our*chipe. And he gaffe hy*m* also Rosañ for to be
his wyffe, and prayeď hy*m* þat he walde be gude & gentiłł tiłł
hir. And þan he kyssede ałł þe lordeȝ & þe knyghtis of
12 Macedoyne ilkane after oþ*er*, and sighed and wepeď wonder
sare. Þare was þañ so grete dole & wepynge, þat it was lyke
a thonere. For meñ Supposeȝ þat noȝte allanly meñ made
Sorow for þe dede of so worthy ane Emper*our*, Bot also þe soñ
16 and ałł þe oþ*er* planetis and element*es* ware troubled.

²A prynce of Macedoyne stode nere Alex*ander* bedď þat
highte Seleuc*us*, & w*i*t grete dole & wepynge he sayď: ' A, A,
þou wirchipfułł emper*our*,' quoþ he, ' what sałł we do wheñ þou
20 ert dede. Philippe þi fader gouerneď vs wele & ałłe oure
rewme, Bot þe gentilnes & þe largesse of the na tunge may tełł.'
And þañ Alex*ander* sett hy*m* vp in his bedď and gaffe hyṁ
selfe a grete flappe on þe cheke and by-gañ for to wepe riȝte
24 bitt*er*ly, and in þe langage of Macedoyne, he sayde on þis wyse :
'Fułł waa es me vnhappy wreche,' quoþ he, ' þat eu*er* I was
borne to mañ. For now Alex*ander* dyes and Macedoyne sałł
waxe ay lesse & lesse and emenische day bi day.' Thañ ałł þe
Macedoynes w*i*t an hye voyce and bitt*er* wepynge sayd vn-tiłł
hy*m* : ' Bett*er* it ware tiłł vs,' quoþ þay, ' for to dy w*i*t þe þañ
for to se þe dy in oure p*re*sence. For wele we wate þat, efter
þe dede of the, þe kyngdoṁ of Macedoyne es vndone for eu*er*e.
32 Allas oure wirchipfułł Alexander, why lefes þou vs here and
wendeȝ away be thyñ ane, withowteñ thi Macedoynes ? ' Thañ
kyng Alexander alway sighanď & wepanď said vn-to þam :
' A, A, my dere Macedoynes,' quoþ he, 'fra this tyṁ forwarde
36 sałł neu*er* ȝo*ur* name hafe lordchipe ou*er* þe Barbarenes.' And
þañ þe Macedoynes cryeď and sayde : ' O wirchipfułł lorde,' quoþ

him for Perdicas for their king.

He gives ⁎ Leaf 48 bk. Perdicas Macedonia and the Emperorship, and also Roxana as wife. He kisses all the Macedonian Lords.

Seleucus grieves by Alexander's bedside that they shall have no good leader.

Alexander bewails his fate that Macedonia shall dwindle with his death. All the Macedonians say it were better to die with him.

The grief of the Macedonians.

---

¹ Three lines with red capital *A*, and smaller *a* in the margin beside.   ² Four lines with red capital *A*, and small *a* in the margin beside.

8

114   The death and burial of Alexander.

þay, 'þou ledd' vs in-to Perse, Arraby, and Inde, and vn-to the
werldeȝ ende, and in-to what cuntree þat þe liste wende; why,
lorde, fleeȝ þou now fra vs? Lede vs wit the whedir so þou gase.'

Alexander sends rich gifts to the Temple of Apollo in Athens and makes order for the embalming of his body.

Þan kyng Alexander sent to þe templee of Appollo in 4
Athenes many riche iowels, and on þe same wyse till all oþer
temples. And þan he commanded þat when he ware dede, þay
schulde enoynte his body and embawme it wit riche oynementes,
þe whilke kepis menes bodys in graues wit-owtten corupcioun. 8
Þan he badde Tholomeus þat he scholde [take] a c̄ besantes of
golde, & þare-off gere make hym a tombe in Alexander. And

Leaf 49.
His death.

onane * as he had' commanded' hym þus, one-seeand' þam all, he
swelt. And þan his prynceȝ lifte vp his body, and did' apon his 12
clethyng of astate and putt a riche coron on his heued, and
sett hym in þe emperours chayer, þe whilke twelue prynceȝ

The funeral of Alexander.

drewe wit þaire brestes fra Babiloyne till Alexander. Tholomeus went alway bi-fore þe chayere wepande & sayande one þis 16
wyse: 'Full waa es me, My lord' Alexander, waa es me. For in
all thi lyfe slew þou neuer so many men as þou dose nowe after
þi dede.' All Alexanders knyghtis also weped' & made grete
dole & sayde on þis wyse: 'Waa es vs wreches! whatt schall wee 20
now do after þe dede of oure lorde Alexander? Whedir sall we
now gaa or whate partye may we now chese? Whare schall
we now get any helpe till oure lyfelade?' One þis wyse þay
went wepand' after Alexander, till þay come till þe citee of 24

His burial and wonderful tomb.

Alexander. And þare þay beryed' hym in a toumbe þat was
riȝte hye and wonder curyouslye wroghte. Þis tombe was all
of fyne golde sett full of precyous stanes, and on þat toumbe
þer was sett xxx ymages of golde wonder craftily made. 28

The description of Alexander.

[1] Alexander was a man bot of a comon stature, wit a lange
nekke, Faire eghne & glad, his chekes ruddy, and all þe remenant of his lymmes ware faire & semely & lyke vn-till a lorde.

The years of his life and his warlike deeds.

He ouercome all men & neuer was ouercomen. The lenthe 32
of his lyffe was xxxij ȝere, twa & thritty ȝere & seuen monethes.
Fra þe twentyd' ȝere of his birthe he gaffe hym to werre, and in
twelue ȝere he conquered' all þe werlde, and made subiect un-till
hym alkyn nacyonns. Seuen monethes he ristede hym. He was 36
borne on þe vij kl of January, and dyed' on þe vij kl of August.

---

[1] Large red capital *A*.

His names. 115

He byggid͛ also in his lyfe xij grete citeeȝ þat hider-to-wardeȝ bene enhabyt, and þis are þaire names. Firste Alex*ander* þat es called͛ yprysilicas, þe secu*n*d Alexander es called͛ Bepypor*um*, 4 þe thrid͛ Alexander es callede Sithia, þe ferthe Alexander es called͛ Bicontristi, þe fifte Alex*ander* es called͛ Þerauctoñ, þe sext Alex*ander* es called͛ Buctiphaloñ, þe seuent es called͛ vnder þe ryu*er* of Tygre, þe aghtend͛ New Babiloyne, þe nyend͛ Aptreadam̃, 8 þe tend͛ Messagetes, þe elleuend͛ Ypsyacoñ, þe twelfed͛ es called Egipt.

Explicit vita Alexandry magni co*n*questoris.

Here endeȝ þe lyf of gret Alexander co*n*querou*r* of all þe 12 worlde.

The twelve great cities that he built.

The manufacturer's authorised representative in the EU for product safety is Oxford University Press España S.A. of El Parque Empresarial San Fernando de Henares, Avenida de Castilla, 2 - 28830 Madrid (www.oup.es/en or product.safety@oup.com). OUP España S.A. also acts as importer into Spain of products made by the manufacturer.

Printed and bound by CPI Group (UK) Ltd, Croydon, CR0 4YY

23/03/2026

02076308-0006